WHAT OTHERS ARE SAYING:

The passion and intimacy that is revealed in J. M. Barlow's *Too Brief a Candle* is stunning. She captures the critical time-sensitive details and the raw emotions of a family wrought by an unspeakable tragedy while weaving them together for the reader. A difficult event, very well done.

—Elaine C. Pereira, MA OTR/L,
author of the award-winning
and best-selling memoir
I Will Never Forget.

Sometimes the heart that opens itself to love becomes so overwhelmed with the feelings to which it has made itself vulnerable that it breaks. J. M. Barlow's true story, *Too Brief a Candle*, tells how a young baby was ripped out of the lives of a young Christian mother and her precious Christian grandparents. It's a book filled with grief, anger, frustration, and, finally, justice.

—Kimberly Ledbetter,
missionary to Haiti

TOO BRIEF A
CANDLE

TOO BRIEF A
CANDLE

THE TRUE STORY OF CHILD ABUSE
AND DEATH IN A HOME DAYCARE

To Susan
Jm Barlow
Best Wishes!

J. M. BARLOW

TATE PUBLISHING
AND ENTERPRISES, LLC

Published by Tate Publishing & Enterprises, LLC
127 E. Trade Center Terrace | Mustang, Oklahoma 73064 USA
1.888.361.9473 | www.tatepublishing.com

Tate Publishing is committed to excellence in the publishing industry. The company reflects the philosophy established by the founders, based on Psalm 68:11,
"The Lord gave the word and great was the company of those who published it."

Book design copyright © 2015 by Tate Publishing, LLC. All rights reserved.
Cover design by Ivan Charlem Igot
Interior design by Jimmy Sevilleno

Published in the United States of America

ISBN: 978-1-63268-862-0
True Crime/Murder/General
14.11.28

TO MY MOM, Julia Laing. I hope you are still living when this book is published, but if not, you will know from heaven. You always said I would write a book, and I'm sorry it took so long. I love you very much.

TRUTH IS NOT only a matter of offense, in that it makes certain assertions. It is also a matter of defense in that it must be able to make a cogent and sensible response to the counterpoints that are raised.

—Ravi Zacharias

Acknowledgments

WHEN I FIRST decided to write a book about what happened to Maria Harris, and asked and received verbal permission from the Harris family to do so, I had no idea what a formidable task lay ahead. Without the efforts of many people, this work would not have gotten off the ground, let alone completed. My deep gratitude goes to the Harris family, Esther, Clyde, and especially Pat, who conversed with me many times both in person and on the phone as the case moved forward post-trial. Also, I thank them for the interviews about their family history information leading up to the trial.

During the writing itself, I bounced ideas off my friends Carole Steele and Diane Campbell, who were both instrumental in helping me focus on the details. They brought up scenarios that I might otherwise have missed, and I appreciate their input enormously. My thanks to my friend Bob Hilton for helping me gather some information that I sorely needed early on. Scott Nichols was instrumental in attending the hearing for the Williams Rule and taking superb notes for me. I can't thank you enough, Scott! You dotted every *i* and crossed every *t*! Curtis Krueger from the *Tampa Bay Times* was a wonderful encouragement to me at the trial and afterwards, even if we did not speak to each other on specific days. Just to see him there helped me in knowing I wasn't alone in documenting this case. A heartfelt thanks to my dear friend, Kim Ledbetter, who listened to my rollercoaster of emotional outbursts about this book, and became my shoulder to cry on every time things went wrong, which was often. To bestselling true crime writer, Ann Rule, who gave me some tidbits of advice via email regarding publishing (among other things) which led me to seek out a reputable publishing firm that I am very pleased with! A big thank you goes to my brother Douglas Laing, who helped me with formatting this manuscript. I could never have figured it out myself! And of course, to my wonderful husband, Bob, who didn't see me for the countless hours and hours I spent hidden away in our library/office as I typed and researched. You are my soul mate because no one else would put up with me. And lastly, to you, the reader, thank you for reading my first book; whether you agree with my conclusions or not, it was and always will be my prayer to seek the truth in all things.

INTRODUCTION

WHEN PATRICIA HARRIS left the day care with her one-year-old granddaughter, Maria, on August 21, 2008, she knew something just wasn't right. Maria was sleeping too soundly. She had not awakened at all when Pat had taken her from the arms of Stephanie Spurgeon, the thirty-seven-year-old woman who ran the in-home day care in Palm Harbor, and carried her to the car. Maria felt limp and heavy, like a bag of rice.

Pat strapped her in her car seat, which was directly behind the driver's seat. Maria did not help her grandmother at all; in fact, she did not stir from her deep sleep. Her eyes didn't open, and her head, covered with a mop of thick and shiny black hair, leaned slightly to one side in the car seat. An anxious feeling began to materialize in Patricia's chest. Maybe Maria just had played very hard her first day there, as Stephanie had said.

Pat headed home, a short twelve- to fifteen-minute drive. She wanted to get Maria home to her mother. All the while, she talked and cooed to her one-year-old granddaughter. "Wake up, baby girl! Maria! Are you all right?" No sound came from the backseat. Pat couldn't see little Maria in the rearview mirror because she was directly behind her. Pat felt her heart start to pound as she sped up a little faster.

"Maria! Honey, wake up!" Then she heard a gurgling noise and a soft cough, and she wondered if she should pull over right then and there and check on her granddaughter. But she was almost home, less than a mile to go now. Besides, there was nowhere to pull over on the busy, narrow, two-lane road. Pat had worked herself into a state of panic and tried without success to calm down. She prayed over and over under her breath, "Jesus, help Baby, help her be okay..."

At last, she turned down the street to her house where Maria's mother, Esther, also lived and who was home from school by now. Pat whipped into her driveway, crying uncontrollably now. She jumped out of the car and threw open the back door, reaching in to unstrap Maria. She noticed that Maria had vomited on her little top, and her head was sagging unnaturally downward onto her chest. Sobbing, she yelled for her daughter as she ran to the front door with her granddaughter limp in her arms. "Esther! Come quick! Something is wrong with Maria!"

PRELUDE

THE VACATION HAD been long overdue. Fifty-three-year-old Patricia Harris and her fifteen-year-old daughter, Esther, had made plans to get away together to Chambersburg, Pennsylvania in the summer of 2007. It was not a random destination. The family had lived there before Clyde Harris's career had moved them to Florida. Pat missed the deep green hills of the countryside and the small town atmosphere and longed to go back and visit some old friends. Esther too, wanted to get away from the blistering Florida heat and traffic and spend some time with her mother away from the mundane pressures of home. They had been planning this mother-daughter trip for some time. They were both excited to get back to visit their old home town—the place where Esther had spent her childhood years with her older brother, Christopher.

Esther's father, Clyde, or Buster, as Pat and his family called him, had to work, and so did Chris, so this was a perfect time for Pat and Esther to spend together up north. School was out, and Esther was so grateful to get away from the stress of being in high school. She loved being with her friends, but she struggled to maintain average grades and she had spent an inordinate amount of time doing homework this past school year. She had just completed the tenth grade and was looking forward to her sixteenth birthday.

So off they flew, and they had a wonderful time visiting old friends and places. Chambersburg was a quaint and charming community, located just west of Gettysburg. But like many historic and picturesque towns, it had grown over the years and had become imbedded with strip malls and fast-food restaurants, which made Patricia sad. As their vacation wound to a close, they decided to pay a visit to the local mall and see what had changed inside. While there, Pat thought she would get her hair done. That was just fine with Esther. She liked the mall, and she decided that she would just stroll around and wait for her mother. She wandered from store to store, looking at various items, but she wasn't really interested in buying anything. Suddenly, she found herself looking into the deep, dark eyes of a wiry young man. He smiled at her, his teeth very white, a dimple breaking the surface of his cheek. She smiled back, hesitantly thinking that he was rather cute. He struck up a conversation, obviously attracted to the young girl with black curly hair and perfect olive complexion.

Esther, having been heavyset for most of her young life, was somewhat on the shy side, and she was also wary of strangers, but she felt an attraction to this young man as well, so in the short space of less than an hour, she had given Javier Romero* her phone number and Florida address. Little did either of them know what that perchance meeting would set in motion and the tremendous heartbreak that would ensue and ripple throughout the Harris family and their home community in the months ahead.

---

*Any time an asterisk appears after a name in this book, the name has been changed for the privacy of the person being discussed.

All too soon, Patricia and Esther were back at home and into their routine again, well rested after an enjoyable trip. Pat was back working as a home health aide, caring for elderly people in their own homes who could not care for themselves. Sometimes, she would be gone for ten to twelve hours a day, doing custodial care for an aging adult—bathing, feeding, dressing, dispensing medication, cleaning his or her home, doing the laundry, changing the bedding, and being a friend. She usually would go above and beyond what her job required of her simply because her Christian heart led her to be compassionate and tender toward these people who were nearing the end stages of life. Sometimes they had no one else to depend on. Pat absolutely hated to miss a day of work.

Esther's responsibilities were in her own home when she was not at school. During the summer months, she was responsible for keeping the house clean and performing household chores such as laundry, vacuuming, and tidying up the bedrooms. She was very good at it, and she loved playing the domestic role. The Harrises have a lovely Florida-style home with a beautifully manicured yard and an enclosed swimming pool. It is light and airy and well kept. I am always amazed at how people can avoid the clutter that seems to accumulate like a magnet on my tables and countertops!

Esther wasn't sure if she would hear from handsome Javier again, but a few weeks later, she was surprised and pleased to hear from him! He had relocated to Florida, just to be near her. Needless to say, her parents were not happy. She was not even sixteen years old, and he was an adult. At the time, they didn't even know if he was in the country legally. He was enamored with Esther though, and it wasn't long before they thought that they were deeply in love. They dated for eight months, and Esther's sixteenth birthday came and went. Then they began to talk about marriage. He came over one day to meet her family. Javier took Esther out to dinner, and Pat went along. Patricia and Clyde were concerned because Esther was far too young to get married, so they wanted to slow things down between their daughter and Javier. His English was not very good, and he had trouble looking them in the eye when they spoke to him. It was decided that the couple should never be alone together anywhere for a while. Esther was not allowed to see him anywhere, except in her home when one or both of her parents were there. That was the hard and fast rule.

But one day shortly after that, Esther found herself home alone in the evening. As often happens in Florida, an intense storm suddenly developed, with fierce thunder and lightning. It was dark out, and her parents were not close to home. She was very frightened, so she took action, making a phone call.

"Hello? Javier?"

"Hi, Esther. What is the matter?"

"I'm scared of the storm. I just need to talk to you."

"I am coming. I be over."

"No! No, you can't!"

But he had already hung up the phone and was on his way. It was unclear at the time exactly where he was staying, possibly with some cousins or friends that he had met in the area. At one point, he even stayed for a while with a nice man from our church who otherwise lived alone. The man passed away unexpectedly, after having been at church the evening before. It was an apparent heart attack, but no autopsy was ever ordered. I remember everyone being very shook up about that. Javier had to move out of the man's home when that happened. But initially, he was staying somewhere else in the county.

When he arrived at Esther's home, both sixteen-year-old Esther and twenty-two-year-old Javier took advantage of the situation and became intimate, resulting in Esther becoming pregnant with Maria. Neither of them had apparently considered the consequences of their actions, and there were far more to them than a minor having relations with an adult who turned out to be an illegal immigrant from Mexico. This was not how Esther was raised, and she immediately regretted her behavior. She was further angered when, after informing him that she was pregnant, Javier suggested that she have an abortion. She was raised in a Christian home and would never even consider such an option.

Javier seemed pretty naïve for a twenty-two-year-old man. Did he understand the laws of the United States? His English may have been broken, but he likely understood more than he could speak. Esther's parents wondered if he started pushing marriage in order to get citizenship, after he realized that Esther was not going to have an abortion. He was not aware that Esther had finally told them that he was an illegal, because she had hoped that he would be able to become a legal citizen, and she thought he was attempting to do so. Esther denied that Javier only wanted to marry her in order to obtain citizenship and also said that he knew he could not take her back to Mexico. Actually, he thought he may not even be able to marry her because he didn't have the proper paperwork to marry her here or in Mexico. He was correct. Marrying Esther would not have automatically given him citizenship because he was in the country illegally.

Only her child could receive that birthright. Javier could be forced to leave the country at any time for any reason. Besides, Esther had reached a decision. In spite of Javier's continued pleas to her for marriage, she wanted to see how he behaved around Maria after she was born before she even considered marrying him. She wanted to see if he would make a good father. The two young people had also sought counseling with the Harrises' pastor who told them that people don't get married just because there is a pregnancy. At first, Esther's father didn't agree and felt that she should marry him because she had shamed the family. Javier wanted Esther to quit school since he had only gone through the tenth grade himself. He felt he had a good handle on managing money. She wisely continued with her schooling, however.

Javier had tried to be nice to Esther during her pregnancy, but she could sense he feared fatherhood. There were cultural differences too. In addition to his inability to communicate well in English and Esther's lack of ability in conversing in Spanish, he thought babies should sleep in the same bed with their mothers, and not in a crib. He also did not believe in settling down in one place. His brothers and cousins worked in Pennsylvania, Michigan, and Florida. They farmed; they worked assembly lines. When they got tired of the jobs or got laid off, they moved on. Javier had gotten fired from his last job and had been without work for three months. He wasn't lazy and usually found work fairly easily. He just didn't have his priorities straight.

Esther's decision turned out to be one that prevented much harm and hurt feelings in the long run because shortly after Maria's birth, within a month in fact, Javier left the state of Florida and returned to Pennsylvania to be with his brother. He did have phone contact with Esther during his absence, but these conversations were arguments about when and if he would return. Javier did return with some friends when Maria was about nine months old, but he didn't come back to Palm Harbor. Instead, he went to a small town in central Florida. There, he borrowed a car and came to see Maria. He spent less than two hours with her, bought her some clothes, and then left again, saying that he needed to return the car.

Esther, although disappointed in his behavior, was not altogether surprised. She told me that he seemed afraid of being a father and wasn't sure if he could handle it. She actually felt a sense of relief that he was out of the picture at least physically, and that she could raise Maria the way that she wanted to. Patricia Harris was proud of her daughter for not rushing into a marriage that had foreseeable problems. She admired how Esther had carefully thought the situation through and had not let her emotions get in the way in spite of her young age. Now, Clyde was especially glad that things had worked out the way they had, and he was able to soften his attitude and renew his relationship with his daughter. He was already forming a deep bond with his granddaughter and wouldn't let her out of his sight when he was home from work.

Before Maria's birth, Javier had been hot and cold toward Esther, which had helped her to reach her decision in the first place. She didn't know for sure if he loved her, and she was beginning to wonder if she ever really loved him. She had been feeling very protective toward her unborn child and did not want the complications of a missing or unstable father figure in Maria's life.

After Javier left this time, Esther contacted him to let him know she wanted his rights as Maria's father taken away. He agreed, allowing Maria to be strictly Esther's child, and if something should happen to Esther, then Maria would stay with her grandparents, Pat and Clyde. She didn't know Javier and his family. In fact, Javier's own mother who lived in Mexico didn't even know she had a granddaughter. Javier said he would sign papers surrendering his rights, so Pat and Esther took little Maria up to Pennsylvania to meet him and he signed them. They wanted him to see his daughter again. It was July of 2008. Maria was eleven months old. No one knew that it would be the last time he would ever see her.

But Javier was in the country illegally. Esther suspected this when she had met him. So she called an attorney and was told that Javier had no rights to Maria anyway because he never had asked for a paternity test to declare himself as her father. This meant that he could never claim her as his own if something were to happen to Esther. The papers that they had him sign were meaningless.

Because Esther was sixteen and Javier was twenty-two when she became pregnant, not only was Javier an illegal immigrant, her parents thought that he was also guilty of statutory rape. Clyde was livid. He wanted Javier arrested and thrown in jail. But Pat protested, saying that Maria would have grown up resenting him for doing this to her father. "Don't put him in a position of an easy way out by putting him in jail." She wanted him to prove that he would not be a father by his own volition. None of the Harrises knew that Florida law would not have ruled the relationship and resulting pregnancy as statutory rape since the law states that as long as both parties are within the age range of sixteen to twenty-three years old, and the intimacy was consensual, then it is not considered statutory rape.[1] But since Javier took off anyway, had Maria lived, she would have known her father was a loser and didn't want her in his life. Clyde would not have caused that. So in the end, it all had worked out for Esther and her family and little Maria until August 21, 2008.

CHAPTER 1

MAY 12, 2009

THERE IS A pretrial hearing scheduled at 8:30 a.m. at the Pinellas County Courthouse on Sixty-Sixth Street in Largo, Florida. Its only purpose is to set a date for a trial. I arrive at the courthouse a few minutes early, and already the temperature has reached a muggy eighty degrees under a bright and cloudless sky. Palm trees sway and whisper their long green-brown fronds in the hot breeze. They are thirsty. It hasn't rained in days, and there is no rain in the forecast. I know that we will not see a cold front again until October, at the earliest. Such are the seasons of warm and warmer in west central Florida.

A man who is a familiar sight to those who frequent the courthouse stands out front, not even bothering to find a shady spot. He is sweating, shouting, and yelling protests. He holds up homemade signs. Today he is yelling about the unfairness of the justice system to children. His mantra changes from time to time. Everyone ignores him.

The Pinellas County Criminal Justice Center is the only criminal courthouse in the densely populated county of 917,000 spread over only 274 square miles. The building itself is covered in a combination of stucco, brick and mortar, and all shades of ugly tan, with strange huge balls and ice cream cone shapes scattered uniformly across the plaza. *Hmm*, I consider, *it must be government art.*

The defendant herself stands a few feet away in the lobby, smiling and talking with other people, oblivious to my presence. I, an outsider, but who is inextricably woven into the whole scenario, will be documenting the story of the short life of little Maria Ruth Harris, first with the sanction of her mother and grandparents, and later, after I finish, oddly against their wishes. Stephanie Spurgeon, the defendant, is more solid and less fragile than I imagine her to be, seemingly taller than her diminutive height of five feet.

I slip into the courtroom, trying not to be noticed in spite of the fact that I am wearing what my husband refers to as my "bumblebee outfit," consisting of a bright yellow sweater with a black, white, and yellow shell underneath and black slacks.

In a lackluster manner, this hearing begins and the judge assigns another hearing for July 13 to set a trial date. This was expected. Patricia Harris is not supposed to be here today because her aunt is near death in West Virginia, having suffered a massive heart attack. Pat, the consummate caregiver for the elderly, was supposed to make the trip there to care for her ailing aunt. I note, however, that Pat Harris is there with her family, and that the Harrises seem to be in good spirits as this decision has given their attorney more time to prepare for his arguments. Little does anyone realize at this moment how much time that would stretch out to be.

CHAPTER 2

PERSPECTIVE IS EVERYTHING, and since there was an audience on both sides of the literal aisle—supporters for both the defense and the state—I wanted to put this trial in words in the present tense, as I experienced each moment and emotion in the courtroom. I was in attendance for every minute of the proceedings except the first three hours of jury selection, and I witnessed whatever took place, except when spectators and jury were not permitted in the courtroom. So what follows here is pretty much a play-by-play of what unfolded as I saw and heard it happen. I have also included some history of the Harris family and some of my own thoughts on the trial as it progressed. Only very irrelevant information is not included, such as facts and opinions that are repeated several times. I know that the supporters for the defendant would say differently, but I am confident that what I describe would be quite consistent with the trial transcripts. I have chosen not to use them as I wanted to integrate my own perspective of these testimonies, but I also know that I am able to take rapid and accurate notes—a skill I acquired in college long before the age of laptops and iPads. Memory recall is sketchy at best without notes to support what one remembers after several days pass, and a couple of dozen witnesses are called. It would be appropriate not to trust what anyone remembers on the basis of hearing alone in a courtroom, especially several months later, as I write these words.

THE TRIAL

February 7, 2012
1:00 p.m.

As I pull up at the Pinellas County courthouse around noon, it is drizzling and chilly, which happens often in west central Florida in early February. I realize that almost three years have passed since the first time I had arrived here on that much warmer day for that hearing in 2009. It has been a long and arduous wait for the Harris family, and with the Lord's help, they have abided patiently. However, it has not been without incidents, and these things will be noted throughout the course of this book.

I notice a Bay News 9 camera and a reporter under an umbrella. The reporter is speaking into her mike as I walk up the path to the four-story building. I overhear her talking about shaken baby syndrome and that the jury selection is still underway. I realize that the case has suddenly again not only become newsworthy but was taking on a life of its own.

I go inside the building and clear security. There are four floors with an escalator running up the center of each. Criminal cases are heard on the fourth floor. I check at the information desk to see if I am allowed as a nonjury candidate to be in the selection room. (Normally this is not an issue, but since the case was of interest to the media, and I did not know if the jury would be sequestered for the trial, I need to find out, and also determine where the jury selection was taking place.) It is not a problem, I am told, provided there is room. The video feed was picked up from courtroom 1, and they note that the judge is breaking for lunch. This could work out well, I think, as I take a seat outside the courtroom on a window ledge in a totally empty hallway. I hope to get in when the doors open and sit in the back, unnoticed, to see how the *voir dire* (jury selection) is coming along. Only forty-five minutes remain until the attorneys and jury candidates need to be back in the courtroom.

This jury pool is composed of approximately one hundred people, assuming everyone who is called to duty has shown up and accounting for some that have already been excused for circumstances beyond their control. The remainder of the group will be called into the courtroom to be screened by both the state (prosecution) and defense attorneys.

The attorneys for the defense, Bjorn Brunvand and Ron Kurpiers, are both bald, but only in that respect are they similar. Mr. Brunvand is tall, quiet, and stately; a respectable presence, probably in his late fifties or early sixties. It is obvious he is the lead attorney in this case, though Kurpiers will do most of the questioning and talking. In fact, Brunvand is the head of his own law firm, the Law Offices of Bjorn Brunvand, a fairly well-known firm in this county. Brunvand has a long and impressive career as a defense attorney and a formidable credentialed background. He was born in Norway and has a degree in political science from the University of South Florida. His law degree is from Stetson University College of Law. After his graduation, he worked as an assistant public defender in the Sixth Judicial Circuit from 1989 to 1992 where he gained experience trying a large number of jury trials. He also graduated from the National Criminal Defense College in Georgia in 1991 and began his private practice in the Tampa Bay area in 1992. He has since represented a wide spectrum of people and firms in the state and federal court system. He has tried a gamut of cases from Medicare fraud to child pornography to murder, as well as organized crime. Brunvand is a Florida board certified criminal attorney and is board certified nationally as a criminal trial lawyer. He was the former president of the Pinellas County Criminal Defense Lawyers Association and the Pinellas County Trial Lawyers Association, and he is still active in both groups. He also maintains a website, Acquitter. com, to advertise his firm and provide general advice in legal defense matters.[1]

Ron Kurpiers appears somewhat rough around the edges, if one is unaware of his background before he took this case. He is large, strong, and intimidating. His background, though diverse from Brunvand, is also lengthy and impressive. He obtained his Bachelor of Arts degree from Marquette University and went on to get his law degree at Valparaiso University School of Law in 1987. He turned down an offer to work in training as a special agent for the FBI and instead chose to work as an assistant state's attorney in Lake County, Illinois. From 1989 to 1995, Kurpiers was employed by the United States Attorney's Office for the Northern District of Indiana as an Assistant United States Attorney. He tried many high-profile cases for the Drug Enforcement Administration (DEA), Bureau of Alcohol, Tobacco, Firearms and Explosives (ATF), Internal Revenue Service (IRS), Federal Bureau of Investigation (FBI), and the Department of Justice (DOJ). In 1993, Kurpiers was awarded the Gil Amoroso Memorial Award as the nation's top prosecutor by the International Outlaw Motorcycle Gang Investigators Association for his efforts to dismantle a multistate outlaw motorcycle gang. From 1995 to 2002, Kurpiers served as the Arena Football League's first general counsel and deputy commissioner. His next stop was Tampa, Florida, where he opened his own law practice. He is a member of the Federal Bar Association, the Hillsborough County Bar, the Pinellas County Bar, the National Association of Criminal Defense Lawyers, the Illinois Bar, the Chicago Bar and the New York Bar Association.[2]

He cuts an imposing figure and wears his feelings openly on his face. During bench approaches, if he wins his arguments before the judge, he cannot avoid smirking as he struts back to his position next to the defendant. It is obvious he fully enjoys his role defending Stephanie Spurgeon and basks in the limelight. I would place him in his early fifties.

State attorneys by design usually do not provide their education and credentials as public information, since they are employed by the state. They do not need to advertise their services, and this is the case for the attorneys in the *State v. Spurgeon* trial. The state's attorney, Brian Daniels, is a slim and trim, handsome man in his early sixties who knows his way around a courtroom. His quiet nature is deceiving as he has many years of courtroom experience under his belt. However, when he does ask questions or tells his partner to ask questions, they are pertinent and to the point. This trial would be his last, and he will be retiring after over twenty-five years of practicing law.

Holly Grissinger is the standout attorney on either side. She is very attractive and polished in manner. With meticulously styled blond hair, wearing a no-nonsense but stylish suit, she looks like she could be the CEO of a Wall Street firm. Grissinger exudes energy and commands an air of respect when she questions the jury pool. Her intelligence and tenacity are quite evident. She is a graduate of Stetson University Law School, like Brunvand, and she also teaches some seminars and courses as an adjunct professor at Saint Petersburg College. I look forward to seeing her question witnesses in the trial, but what is most interesting is the contrast between the two teams. It would make for a good novel as the disparity is remarkable. There is the strong-willed and eager defense team who will vigorously protect the defendant almost like bodyguards, pitted against the quiet but keenly focused state team that is prepared to prove Stephanie Spurgeon guilty beyond reasonable doubt.

What I didn't know at the time, but found out soon after, was that Grissinger and Kurpiers had faced off in 2010 in a similar case where a baby died in the care of its foster mother and there were no witnesses.[3] The injuries were even similar. In that case, Kurpiers won by demonstrating that no one had seen any abuse inflicted by the defendant. In that case, though, the child had been sick for the previous few days. The state was unable to prove to the jury that the defendant was guilty. In Grissinger's mind, however, the woman did murder her foster child. The similarities are chilling, but the differences are stark enough to draw a line in the sand and put forth the question: If a caregiver abuses a child, eventually causing death, and there are no witnesses, can guilt be proven beyond a reasonable doubt? This victory must have given Kurpiers a boost of confidence heading into this new battle with Grissinger.

Another glaring contention that would be continuously debated in the *State vs. Spurgeon* trial was the term *shaken baby syndrome* (SBS) and whether it was the cause of Maria Harris's death. There is now heated controversy as to whether this condition actually exists or not, and if so, if it can be the cause of death of a young child or infant. Shaken baby syndrome is a condition where apparently, a baby's brain rapidly goes back and forth against the solid bone structure of its skull due to being shaken by an adult or a strong teen. It has been shown to result in internal bleeds and retinal hemorrhages, but usually in conjunction with a blunt force trauma to the head. This ongoing debate is pervasive on the Internet, and it is constantly being updated with compelling articles for and against the existence of SBS both with and without the addition of blunt force trauma to the head. (For a more in-depth discussion, see Appendix A.)

In the case of Maria Harris, it will be emphasized by the state's witnesses, who saw her after her injuries either while she was alive or postmortem, that she had been abused and this abuse was blunt force trauma to the head, not just SBS. But SBS is introduced early on by one witness, a pediatric neurologist, who believes it was the cause of death. *Abusive head trauma*, which can encompass more than just shaking, and *blunt force trauma to the head*, which implies that the head comes into contact with an immovable but not necessarily rock-hard object, are terms which will be brought up frequently in this trial. Another phrase that will often be reinforced by the state is *rapid acceleration/deceleration*, which describes how the brain moves back and forth within the subdural tissue surrounding it, often resulting in classic types of injuries. It is a rapid and often repetitive motion of a backward, then forward throwing or slamming of a child into an immovable object, accelerating the movement by pulling the child back so that there is more space to push/throw/slam the child forward. The sudden stopping, or deceleration part, is the blunt force trauma.

By the end of the trial, the state wants it to be evident that more than shaking or something other than shaking caused the death of Maria Harris—something violent and nonaccidental. The reader will note that each of these state witnesses was in agreement as to abuse, but none could say exactly how it happened.

It will also be noted that the defense witnesses will each argue a slightly different scenario as to what could have caused Maria's injury and subsequent death, but none of them had the opportunity to examine her or even see her. Some defense witnesses were even from out of state and one had not been board certified since the 1970s. But in fairness to the statement "innocent until proven guilty," I will proceed with the trial and make comments when necessary as to where I believe either legal team is headed with their questioning.

The jury selection continues. Eventually, the defense and the prosecution hope to agree on twelve jurors and two alternates in order to start proceedings. (As this is being written, another jury selection has just concluded for the case against George

Zimmerman, the man accused of murdering Trayvon Martin, which will no doubt become a very historic and well-documented case. I found it interesting that in that particular murder trial, there was only a need for six jurors total, with four alternates. It only takes one juror to make or break a verdict, which could have some major implications in that case, especially since that jury is made up entirely of women.)

Brian Daniels is hoping that the opening arguments will begin this afternoon, but it seems that there are many juror candidates remaining to be screened based on the number I saw seated on the benches on the closed circuit screen. It is likely that the arguments will not begin until tomorrow.

As this trial proceeds, I hope once again that I do not have difficulty getting into the courtroom because of the media attention. Many people will travel for miles and often wait for hours just to get into a courtroom and hear a case just for entertainment—up close and personal. It was in May of 2011 that the Casey Anthony trial was held less than one hundred miles away in Orange County in a packed courtroom. Of course, one major difference there was that Anthony's trial was broadcast live and received national attention, and this one will have neither. The jury selection for that particular trial took place in this very same building, here in Pinellas County. The state of Florida hoped to get a nonbiased jury by selecting people from a county located over ninety miles away from Orange County, where the crime occurred. But with all the attention the case received, it is hard to imagine that a jury was selected where the individuals knew little or nothing about it. That jury was sequestered for the entirety of the trial. The jury for the *State v. Spurgeon* trial would not be. Juries are the hardest groups to predict because, like well-trained actors, they sit stone faced throughout most of a trial, and their minds are impenetrable fortresses. Time and again, they return with a totally surprising rendered verdict that is unexpected and often disappointing, shocking, etc.

Talking heads like Nancy Grace put the Anthony case in the national limelight. Because she typically sides with the prosecution, Nancy Grace claimed Casey Anthony was guilty from the start. She has a huge fan base. There is a history here. But it ended with an acquittal for the defendant. Will that verdict come into play in this case? Will it lead to an acquittal based on that prior case where there was also no witness—at least not one who was willing to come forward? Or will that case put anger in the hearts of the jury and cause them to justify a conviction here? Either way, will it be fair? Anthony was acquitted because of reasonable doubt. But did she get away with murder? Only God knows what is in the heart of someone who is a defendant pleading not guilty.

In a utopian situation, could Stephanie Spurgeon stand in front of the courtroom and say with complete honesty, "As God is my witness, I did no harm to Maria Harris," whether intentionally or accidentally? We will never know because we do not employ this system of testimony. It is presumptuous for anyone else besides Stephanie and her attorneys who are defending her to claim her innocence because no other adult was there in the home besides Spurgeon when Maria Harris lapsed into unconsciousness, according to all testimony you will read here. In fact, Spurgeon will not speak at her own trial. Defendants are not required to prove that they are not guilty in America. Proving guilt beyond a reasonable doubt is the job of the prosecution. And as this trial progresses, we will see if they were able to accomplish this task. And the job of Spurgeon's attorneys is to keep her from going to prison by giving her the best defense possible. They will attempt to do this by continuing to plant seeds of doubt in the minds of the jurors.

The Harrises have been waiting a long time for this day. It has been nearly three and a half years since little Maria died at All Children's Hospital in St. Petersburg on August 28, 2008. They have tried to go on with their lives, but a deep sorrow overshadows each of them in spite of their strong faith in God. They miss their sweet baby girl who, though she was so unexpected, was such an absolute joy of a child. Not a day goes by when Pat, Clyde, or Esther does not think about her and mark the time gone, trying to imagine what she would be like now as a four-and-a-half-year-old dimpled preschooler with big brown eyes and shiny black hair.

Camera crews just tried the door to the courtroom across from where I sit in the hall, and it is locked. They were a reporter and two cameramen from Bay News 9; thankfully, at least, the case has received only local media attention on site. There is a half hour to go.

1:20 p.m.
Inside the courtroom for the second half of jury selection

The presiding judge for this trial is Cynthia L. Newton. She is tall, thin, and attractive, probably in her early to midforties, with long blonde hair, and a somber demeanor. She is not up for reelection in the county until 2016. But even if she were on this year's ballot, it is doubtful that she would be concerned about any negative publicity stemming from this trail affecting her future as a judge. After the trial is long underway, and the gallery becomes familiar with her style, it will become apparent that she has far too much integrity to let any potential reelection figure into how she rules in her courtroom.

Both prosecution and defense attorneys are in the courtroom. Spurgeon is flanked by her two attorneys, and all involved face the back of the courtroom where the jury pool is seated. Of course, the Harrises are witnesses so they cannot be present for this or any part of the trial until the verdict. There are plenty of seats around me, and from what I can tell, only a scattering of viewers and press are here. There are approximately seventy people seated in the jury pool area.

The judge asks all the potential jurors if they saw, heard, or read of any news coverage regarding this case this morning or during their lunch breaks because it has attracted media attention. When no one responds positively, she tells them firmly not to follow the case at all while they are being considered to be on the jury.

There are several people who had stated in the morning session that they are sole supporters for their dependents and that they are unable to fairly discern what evidence may be presented in the trial. As is typical in a case that could continue for several days and possibly longer than a week, there are many people who seem to be trying to get out of serving on this jury and answer no to their ability to be willing to "listen to the facts and circumstances" and feel they would have distractions.

There are students, working single parents, and just a general cluster of folks who are very concerned with the possibility of being away from work for a week or so. At one point, Stephanie adamantly tells her attorney, "No!" when a potential juror states that she works for an agency that helps children and that she could not be fair and impartial. A doctor says he cannot refer his patients elsewhere. After forty minutes of the state's attorneys questioning the people with issues concerning serving on this jury, both sides approach the bench and discuss who would be leaving and who would remain in the pool.

At this point, Spurgeon is staring directly at me, possibly wondering who I am, certainly not someone she recognizes from the press. She is seated about fifteen yards in front of me and can see that I am rapidly writing in a notebook, glancing up from time to time. She may remember me as the woman who is writing a book about the case (more on that later). The Harrises are isolated on the premises and will be updated by the state's attorneys. They have the victim's advocate with them, Bobbie Hodson, who has been a godsend in helping them through all the various hearings and proceedings.

2:00 p.m.

Some potential jurors are now being excused. The remaining mix is fairly and evenly split between men and women. And then a crucial question from the state: "Who has children living in their homes?" Eleven people say that they do and volunteer information not requested, such as the age and gender of the children living with them. Others have grown children at home, and these are obviously not ones that would concern the defense.

Next, there is an explanation of burden in a criminal case and proving guilt beyond a reasonable doubt. "Can everyone be fair and impartial to each and every witness? Doctors? Law enforcement?" All answer that yes, they can. As the reader will see later in the trial, it isn't necessarily the impartiality toward the witnesses that will be an issue, but the techniques of questioning those witnesses and the underlying emotions that ensue.

More questions are asked of the remaining pool as a group: "Will religious beliefs keep you from making a decision?" ("No.") "How many (of the remaining group) has had medical training?" Six answer in the affirmative, and one by one, they elaborate on their medical backgrounds.

Many in this pool have already served on a jury. All of these had reached a verdict. Had any of them been a witness to a crime? Could that incident effect their decision in this case? One woman said, yes, she had witnessed a "violent episode" and maybe it would affect her judgment.

A breakdown of the remaining people in the room reveals that there are five educators, one who worked with Child and Family

Services, one who did child care licensing, one social worker, two coast guard members, one who adopted an abused child, and several others in less controversial roles.

Another person works at a police department, and upon this person saying that he/she would give more credibility to those who exhibit professionalism than those who do not, Stephanie clearly exhibits body language that indicates that she wants this person eliminated from the pool. The attorneys approach again, and the judge calls for a fifteen-minute recess. I sit and muse on the remaining pool, thinking that maybe the teachers could be the key, but how, and for which side?

Oftentimes, it is during the breaks between court proceedings that valuable information can be gleaned from sitting quietly and just listening as the various friends and family and other interested parties of either side discuss the case. In all honesty, I cannot call it eavesdropping because the conversations are not in whispers, and I would be hard-pressed to *not* hear what is being voiced around me. Earlier, in the hall, someone who was either a friend or relative of Spurgeon said to another woman as I walked by, "Did you figure out who she is yet?" Not to be presumptuous, but there are very few observers here who are women that do not know each other. So the "she" being wondered about was most likely yours truly, which was unsettling, to say the least.

As the jury pool and observers sit and wait for the short break to be over, I hear various comments muttered around me. "It's not what you say. It's what you don't say," I hear from behind me. And from an elderly gentleman on my left, quite clearly, "I hope and pray she didn't do it. I pray every day. But who knows? Maybe she did it." And then a loud, "*Shhh!*" from a lady next to him. Quiet descends.

I glance out the window while we wait and see a couple of my favorite birds pivoting and soaring near the tops of light posts. Turkey buzzards. Yes, I know it sounds a little disgusting, but I've always admired these shiny black vultures. They have hunched shoulders and nearly naked heads and bright beady little eyes. When they are on the ground by the side of the road, just waiting to be nature's cleanup crew by going after roadkill, they parade around like little old men. They are snarky, serious, and brooding. I want to give each of them a name, a poetic name. Terrence and Hortense. Justice and Patience. Deliverance.

When the attorneys and judge reappear, it is now the defense's turn to question the jury pool. The proceedings take on a more casual tone as Ron Kurpiers attempts to catch people off guard with his questions. One person questioned has a background in theater. He is asked if he can separate lawyer theatrics from the evidence in the case. He says he can. Then it seems that Kurpiers is backing himself into a box by asking questions that he doesn't already know the answer to from the jury pool. "Anyone else have any thoughts on that?" He is looking for someone who cannot tell the difference between a performance by an attorney and evidence presented. No one responds. So then he looks at his list of names, picks one apparently at random, and addresses that person. "What are your thoughts on that?" This line of questioning does not seem to go where he wants it to, so he asks the penultimate question that causes a rapid objection from the state:

"How many of you have heard the phrase, "shaken baby syndrome" anywhere?" The state then approaches the bench with its objection, and Kurpiers sits drinking his water and rapidly writing. It seems that the defense is trying to shoot holes in the case before it is even presented—before the jury is established from the pool.

The SBS mantra will be floated as a trial balloon by the defense throughout the trial, but as almost all the state's witnesses will point out, it was not the cause of death. It is a typical ploy by defense attorneys to focus on something that is not pertinent to a case in order to get the jury thinking in another direction than the one being tried in court. There will be many incidences in this trial where the defense decides to point at other potential causes of Maria's death. It will seem as if they are going on the offense instead of defending Stephanie Spurgeon. In fact, after sitting through this trial from beginning to end, I could find nothing brought up by the defense that specifically defended Spurgeon outside of the statement that no one saw her commit the crime. There was no alibi, no statement from the defendant herself, no witnesses who could report how she ran her day care that day and in fact, no record of what she did at all throughout that tragic day at her day care involving her care of Maria and the other children. This left many unanswered questions in my mind, such as, Where are the phone records from Spurgeon's phone calls that were made and received that day? This would never be addressed by either side and may have provided crucial pieces of information. But the defense does not have to prove anything, especially what they believe to be the cause of death. But to bolster their case, they will bring in several witnesses who will refute the validity of SBS, which was not the cause of death on the death certificate. What is interesting is how the whole foundation of the defense's case is based on what could have happened to Maria instead, because they will repeatedly attempt to show that shaking a baby cannot cause death. Many other potential causes will be presented. These could come back to haunt them when they seek to admit what they believe to be new evidence after the verdict is rendered and it is pointing to yet another possible cause.

When one potential juror is asked his opinion of this type of case, he says, "It doesn't look good when someone chooses not to testify—take the Fifth, like the governor." (Florida's Governor Rick Scott had taken the Fifth during an investigation into Medicare fraud involving companies he owned a few years earlier, prior to his election.)

A pall settles over the room because it could be the question in the back of anyone's mind, why an innocent person would not be figuratively jumping up and down with impatience to shout her innocence. Given the opportunity to explain why one is not guilty, most innocent people would choose to do so. In spite of protection under the Fifth Amendment that one does not have to testify in his/her own trial due to self-incrimination, it still leaves an open question. The cards are stacked against defendants in the first place because they stand accused. In this case, Spurgeon was out on bond, but as soon as the murder charge came through, after Maria's death, she had to wear a GPS monitor. Of course, the jury was not aware of this, but the state had asked for this device in exchange for Spurgeon's bond release and they got it.

There is disappointment on the faces of Brian Daniels and Holly Grissinger when Judge Newton rules that she will allow questioning of the potential jurors concerning shaken baby syndrome. They shouldn't have been concerned. Ron Kurpiers starts the line of questioning with, "Do any of you have strong feelings about the validity of the syndrome?" Approximately ten to twelve people indicate that they do. A woman says that she believes it's a real syndrome, and she would be interested in knowing if anyone has an opinion contrary to hers. She could sway much of the pool.

Kurpiers asks her, "Can you give both sides equal valuation?"

She says that yes, she could, unless she actually sees it happening. My guess is that she will be eliminated from the pool by the defense. At this point, the state asks to approach the bench and a long discussion ensues.

When the attorneys come back to their desks, it is apparent that the defense has been asked by the judge to conclude this line of questioning.

Kurpiers asks a question designed to get a consensus from the pool but it backfires. "Can we all agree that violently shaking a baby is not a good thing?"

One of the jurors speaks out, saying, "You never defined shaken baby syndrome." Kurpiers mentions specialized knowledge, feelings, and preconceived notions, but he does not answer this question.

Another woman says that she watches Nancy Grace and says she mostly agrees with the prosecutors. She will no doubt be scratched. It is hard to tell if she wanted to be or if she was simply admitting to something that she didn't realize would indicate her bias.

Another potential juror says that the burden of proof would be on the state to prove that the defendant shook the baby, but that he considers it to be a real syndrome.

And another would favor the prosecution. How do these opinions affect the rest of the jury pool? Some may not admit that they agree. Does this unfairly paint the state into a corner? Preemptive discussion of SBS will become a moot point later, when it is shown not to be Maria's definitive cause of death. Did the defense just bring it up here, so early, to get the jury pool thinking down the wrong road? It would seem so, but I cannot blame them for that it as this is their job. Distracting the jury from the real factors involved in this case is similar to the federal government distracting the people from a failed policy decision by focusing on something else and getting the media to take off with it.

But then, a woman states, "We are confused," referring to SBS and keeping this can of worms open.

The lawyers approach the bench once again. People around me are watching me scribble in my notebook and no doubt want to see what is written, since I'm the only one doing this. I sense the woman next to me leaning over slightly to peer at my notebook. But my own devised shorthand is so good that I can barely read it later!

When the attorneys return, the questioning shifts. They have probably been told to drop the previous line of questioning and move on.

"Were any of you ever actively involved in a day care center?" Some people answer, but there is no one who fits into this category. Then, a paramedic in the group says that he has responded to more than twenty cases of unconscious children and may not be able to put harm aside regarding the defendant. His name will definitely be struck from this pool.

The defense wraps up and prepares to make elections from the pool. But first, a juror states that he is biased due to SBS that was brought up. I begin to wonder if the defense has caused damage to its own case by introducing this syndrome in *voir dire* questioning. The people in the pool seem to be much more abhorrent than expected and are reacting very negatively. It is obvious now that the defense will be unable to eliminate all of the people who believe that SBS is a valid syndrome.

As the attorneys filter through the remaining potential jurors and the defense or state challenge each other, they reach a roadblock on a juror who has an adopted son who had been abused prior to adoption. The person is interrogated extensively by the defense, but the judge argues that he/she gave all the right answers and that the state has the burden of proof in the case. If this person remains on this jury, it is evident that it was a hurdle overcome by the state.

At 4:45 p.m., the bailiffs change shifts. Three men and four women are gradually eliminated. As is usual in a jury pool, many do not seem to be concerned with the gravity of the case and just want to be excused. But the longest part of the *voir dire* now continues as the remaining group of thirty-three people wait while the two legal teams and the judge narrow it down to the final twelve jurors and two alternates.

Finally, a jury is selected. It appears to be a fairly diverse pool of people. There are three educators in the group. There are only two men in the actual jury, and another is an alternate. I am surprised to see ten women seated for the jury. This could bode well for the state as women are perceived to be more protective as well as sympathetic toward children. For the purposes of protecting the identities of the jury, I will not disclose if any of the people mentioned during questioning were eliminated or if they actually ended up serving on this jury. The jury is given specific instructions by the judge not to pay any attention to the case in the media or to discuss it with anyone, and the trial is set to begin in the morning.

CHAPTER 3

FEBRUARY 8, 2012

I ARRIVE ABOUT a half hour early for the trial and slip into Judge Newton's courtroom. The observers' seating area is surprisingly empty. There are a few pretrial motions being brought before the judge that are handled quickly and without any incident. Shortly after nine thirty, the attorneys enter and are seated.

I then realize that Clyde Harris has been placed on the witness list since he is not in the courtroom. He was really hoping that he would not be on the list since he had been working during the day of the incident and had not witnessed anything. I recall how Caylee Anthony's grandparents were allowed in the courtroom during the entire trial in which their daughter was the defendant, even though they testified themselves. It would seem in that case that hearing others' testimonies could certainly

affect what they would say themselves. Since each of them testified, it is an odd rule that they were allowed to be present in the
courtroom. But not Clyde Harris. He was, of course, a witness for
the prosecution, which was different. And Clyde did briefly see
Maria before leaving for work that fateful day, so as a result he
would have to testify. Keeping him out of the courtroom would
also prevent him from hearing other testimonies and telling his
family about it in case they were recalled to testify again later.

None of Spurgeon's own family including her husband,
from whom she is now divorced, would be called as a witness
by either the defense or the prosecution. Not knowing enough
about how these cases worked, I wondered later why her now
ex-husband was never called as he was possibly a person that
Pat saw when she arrived at the day care with Maria on August
21. The defense had their own strategy for trying this case,
and it would include keeping as much information about what
happened that day from their defendant's perspective, out of
the record. Perhaps the prosecution could not call him as a witness because he was still married to Stephanie at the time and
protected under spousal privilege. But what did he know about
what happened?

In the courtroom are about a dozen people on Spurgeon's side
of the gallery. There is plenty of room on my side. I see a camera crew enter, and they set up in front and to the right of me.
There will be a camera present in the courtroom for one station
or another throughout the trial. I found out later that they shared
the video clips so that only one cameraman needed to be present
at a time. Sometimes a reporter would come in from one of the
TV stations, but I didn't recognize any of them. I did recognize
the Pinellas County court journalist, Curtis Krueger, from what
was then the *St. Petersburg Times*, but has since been renamed the
Tampa Bay Times. Krueger would be present for good portions of
the trial, and he seemed to know when the critical moments were
and never failed to show up for those.

At Judge Newton's request, through a side door to my right, a bailiff escorts Stephanie Spurgeon into the courtroom. She had, of course, been free on bond, but wearing the court-ordered GPS monitor on her ankle. She looks composed but a little frightened, and her friends are murmuring amongst themselves quietly as they now see her as more than just their friend or relative. She is now officially "the defendant." Her thick auburn hair is pulled back neatly, unlike her incarceration photos where it hangs wild and wavy. She wears glasses, which were not evident in any photo I had seen of her. Perhaps they were readers, or maybe she wore them instead of contacts at the advice of her attorneys to make her appear more bookish.

I found it sad that on the blog sites there was so much bashing and ridicule of Pat and Esther because of their large sizes when here, the defendant Stephanie Spurgeon is looking every bit the 170 pounds listed on her arrest report, at a height of five feet. She is somber but interested in everything happening around her. Throughout the trial, she would be actively communicating with her attorneys, making suggestions and asking for clarification.

Everyone is now seated and the charge is read: murder in the first degree. The trial is officially under way.

The judge asks the state for its opening statement. It is read by attorney Brian Daniels and is summarized here. My comments are also interwoven.

On August 10, 2008, Maria Harris turned one year old. Four days later, she had an appointment with her doctor, Dr. McCormick, for a well-baby checkup. Then a week later, on August 21, she was to go to her new day care. Esther Harris had to attend school herself that day, so she arose very early at 4:00 a.m. She got Maria out of bed and played with her for a while. Maria walked and talked. Then at 5:00 a.m., Esther prepared a breakfast of oatmeal for Maria.

Pat Harris, Maria, and Esther got in the car and first went to Esther's bus stop where they had to wait for the bus. Maria wanted to get out of the car. Esther left on the bus. Pat left to go to the Spurgeon home. She carried Maria into the house and, after a period of time, handed her off to Stephanie Spurgeon. Pat stepped out the door between 6:45 a.m. and 7 a.m.

At 10:00 a.m., Pat called to check in. Maria got on the phone. She was whiny but seemed fine.

At noon, Esther called. Stephanie said that Maria was taking a nap. (This is critical because later it can be determined approximately how long Maria was not awake, since Pat picked her up at 2:45 p.m. It was not brought up, but for a one-year-old child, a nearly three-hour nap seems very long to this writer.)

At 2:45 p.m., Pat went to pick up Maria at the Spurgeon home. She talked with Stephanie. Maria was in bed. She was on her stomach, which was odd, since she always, without fail, slept on her back. Her pacifier was not in her mouth. She was at a widthwise angle in the Pack 'n Play bed and was unable to stretch out. She did not wake up during the time Pat and Stephanie were talking right there in the same room with her, after being "asleep" for at least two hours and forty-five minutes.

Stephanie told Pat that Maria did not wake up because she played hard and was tuckered out. Stephanie then picked her up, and she still didn't awaken. Pat didn't think anything of this at the time. (She also didn't know how long Maria had not been awake.) Pat took Maria to her car and placed her in her baby car seat directly behind the driver's seat. For the entire drive home, Pat talked to Maria. She received no answer. She grew very concerned and hurried home. The drive took fifteen minutes.

Pat yelled for Esther as she jumped out of the car in the driveway. Esther came out and Pat told her that Maria would not wake up. Esther called 911. Sunstar, the ambulance company, arrived and treated her, and transported her to Mease Countryside Hospital in Safety Harbor. During the drive, they put her on an IV. Her eyes were glazed over when a paramedic opened her lids to look at them. They checked her blood sugar and prepared her for the ten-minute ride to the hospital.

The emergency room physician ordered a brain scan and performed an examination. He called All Children's Hospital in St. Petersburg to arrange to have Maria transferred there, stat.

Dr. Luis Rodriguez, a board certified child neurologist at All Children's, performed an exam on Maria and evaluated her brain scan. A subdural hematoma was noted on the brain scan. This injury was serious enough to lead to unconsciousness shortly after occurring, and consciousness would not be regained. (It is important to point out here that there would be some degree of misunderstanding as to what *unconsciousness* or even *comatose* meant later in the trial. Defining these terms clearly as they were brought up could have eliminated doubt as to Maria's condition. For instance, it is not unheard of for unconscious or comatose people to cry or make noises and yet not awaken.)

At this point, the state proceeds to mention each of the witnesses that would testify in the trial on behalf of the state, their jobs, and what they concluded. The state wraps up its rather brief opening statement by saying that it would show that Stephanie Spurgeon is guilty beyond reasonable doubt.

When the Harris family testifies, each in turn at the beginning of the called witnesses for the state, it will be noted that what they say varies somewhat from what Brian Daniels presents in the opening statement. It does not change the scope of what happened, however, as these differences are minor. In particular, he states that Esther called to check on Maria at noon, and when Esther testifies, she will say that she called at 1:40 or 1:45 p.m. and that Spurgeon said Maria had been sleeping since noon. This still implies that Maria had been asleep for nearly three hours when Pat arrived to pick her up.

Also, Daniels states that Esther came out of the house to meet her mother who was carrying Maria from the car. Esther will say that that her mother banged on the door of the house, and she came running to open it. She wasn't dressed, since she had been changing clothes when she came home from school. These are small matters that the defense does not key in on, possibly because it does not want to draw attention to the length of Maria's "nap."

Ron Kurpiers quickly rises to speak for the defense in his opening argument, stating that the entire case and presentation of evidence will show that there is a death of a one-year-old child. He says that this will draw an emotional response, complicated and detailed medical testimony, and a challenge. The defense doesn't want to minimize the death, but with emotion comes the analysis of the facts.

He addresses the jury directly and contrasts emotion with facts but does not reference the defendant, Stephanie Spurgeon, at all in his analysis. This tactic draws attention away from her and aims instead at punching holes in the state's case.

"There is not one person that will walk into this courtroom that will say they saw, heard, or witnessed Stephanie Spurgeon harm Maria Harris." Although this argument is stated strongly here in the opening argument, it seems to disappear as the trial progresses, and the defense tries to lead the jury down many other alternative avenues. And although this author was admittedly biased in favor of the prosecution, the tone of Kurpiers' voice up to this point sounds weak, as if he is trying to convince himself of his client's innocence. But then, he suddenly stands straighter and fills the courtroom with his booming voice.

"There is [sic] no bruises, abrasions, cuts. There is [sic] no fingerprints of grasping [sic], spine injury, neck injury of this child! Not a single mark on this child as presented [sic] at Mease Hospital! How do we go with a child that has not a mark to this case?"

He then goes on to mention that Maria was supposed to be at the day care the day before, which will be brought up again during the testimony of Patricia Harris. I wondered why he brought this up here in the opening arguments, as it proved to be totally irrelevant later.

"Patricia Harris calls at 10:27 a.m., a 158-second call. The grandmother says she hears the child. There you go." If I were on the jury, I would have thought, "There you go, what?" What was the point of her hearing Maria when she called the day care to check on her? It would later be recorded that Maria did not go down for "a nap" until noon. The reason for the call was not brought up in this opening argument. As will be discussed later, Pat will admit that she not only called there, but that she actually spoke to Maria, supporting what Mr. Kurpiers says here, and making it a nonissue in the case.

When he mentions Pat going to pick up Maria at the Spurgeon home, he says that the child moans a little bit when picked up and "kind of makes some noises." This was at 2:50 p.m. I am presuming at this point that he is indicating that Maria was not unconscious but merely sleeping. This would not be elaborated on until later when state's witnesses would show that it is possible for a person to make sounds when unconscious.

Then Kurpiers goes on to lay out a general timeline of the events of the day, from 6:45 a.m. to 2:45 p.m. on August 21, 2008. He says that Stephanie Spurgeon has no other access beyond that span. The ride home in Pat's car takes fifteen to nineteen minutes. Maria coughs, "choking." Pat sees Maria has vomited when she gets out of the car. She grabs her and rushes into the house, yelling for Esther at around 3:10 p.m. Then there is the 911 call at 3:19 to 3:20 p.m. from Esther: "Help me! Something is wrong with my baby." A hang up. Dispatch of emergency personnel. At 3:26 p.m., "they find" Maria—who was not breathing, according to Esther—in Esther's arms. They started resuscitation and put her in the ambulance. Two sets of paramedics had arrived, those with Sunstar, the ambulance company, and county paramedics, (presumably from Pinellas County Fire Department, but Kurpiers does not elaborate). They leave for the hospital at 3:34 p.m.

Kurpiers says that en route, they check her vitals, etc., and attempt to stabilize her. He states that Maria cries periodically. Her blood/glucose level is 468. There is acetone and ketones in her urine. An hour after, at the hospital, her glucose level has dropped to 363 and eventually stabilized.

Apparently, he is attempting to make a case for Maria being a diabetic, but it will be shown later that she was not and also that elevated glucose levels can be a stress reaction, especially in young children. To back this point here, in an abstract published by the US National Library of Medicine:

> To determine whether elevations in blood glucose levels were related to neurologic outcomes following severe brain injuries in children, 54 patients 16 years of age or younger admitted to a regional trauma center with a Glasgow Coma Scale score of 8 or less over a 2-year period were retrospectively reviewed. The mean initial blood glucose level on hospital admission was significantly higher in the 16 patients with outcomes of death or vegetative state in comparison with that of the 38 patients with outcomes of good recovery, moderate disability, or severe disability (288 mg/100 mL vs. 194 mg/100 mL, t = -2.74, p = 0.01). Blood glucose levels correlated significantly with indicators of the severity of the brain injury, which were also related to outcome.[1]

Kurpiers further states that at 4:21 p.m., a CT scan was performed and showed a subdural hematoma and massive edema. The brain had swelled from lack of oxygen and blood. He introduces the medical terminology for this: *anoxic ischemic encephalopathy.* At 7:30 p.m. Maria is transferred to All Children's Hospital by Sunstar. (Sadly, all of the ambulances for All Children's are out on runs and are unavailable. Another option would have been to use the Bay-Flight helicopter system from upper to lower Pinellas County, but in the long run, it would not have helped.)

During her ambulance ride, Maria had multiple seizures which continued at All Children's. The next morning, an MRI was done "for comparison." I thought about this later when reviewing my notes that day because Maria had a CT scan at Mease and then an MRI at All Children's. They are two very diverse imaging techniques, and I thought that arguably a proper and true comparison could only be made if the same technique was used each time. Unfortunately, in a decision designed to save money, people admitted to the ER through what is now called The Baycare Health System can only receive X-rays and/ or CT scans, but not MRIs. The MRI performed the next day at All Children's confirmed the subdural hematoma, and retinal hemorrhaging from the CT scan was also noted. (It would have looked like a much different image than the CT scan, and indeed it is. An MRI is a magnetic resonance image, performed by combining strong magnetic fields, radio waves, and computer technology to create images of the body whereas a CT scan provides cross-sectional images of the body in slices. It is a stream of layered X-rays that bombard through the tissue, exposing the person to some degree of radiation. So in the long run, using CT scans to save money may end up costing much more down the road if the injured person has enough radiation exposure over time, and different or recurring injuries or illnesses to eventually cause cancer.)

Kurpiers continues, talking about the state's witnesses in the trial who are various medical professionals. He goes through the list, explaining what each will tell the jury when questioned. Kurpiers says there is a "wide disagreement among the doctors of what they are seeing, when it occurred, and how." He says that the defense is not required to present or prove any evidence, but that they would be introducing witnesses to testify, and he mentions each of them briefly and what they will testify to. These experts will also be discussed later on, but it is important to introduce one of them here for reasons that will become crystal clear later.

A biomechanical physicist with a PhD, Dr. James Ipser, does analyses of head injuries of adults and children, according to Kurpiers. He uses a head injury criteria index that shows the amount of force necessary for an adult individual to cause a subdural hematoma in another person without an external trauma. I am anxious, as a science geek myself, to hear what the esteemed physicist has to say and how the head injury chart was formulated, and by whom.

Kurpiers sums up his opening argument by stating, "Evidence will never show how it occurred or when it occurred. Doctors *will* show it can be caused by many things completely unrelated to trauma." (I make a mental note to see if he can make good on this proof with the doctors testifying for the defense.)

Brian Daniels then calls his first witness to the stand for the state. It is Maria's grandmother, Patricia Harris. Pat walks with her head held up high to the front of the courtroom and takes a seat behind the witness stand. She does not appear nervous, nor does she exude confidence, but only a deep sense of loss. Brian asks her about her relationship with Maria.

Pat describes a close bond because she was hands-on raising Maria in her own home. "Maria was a ray of sunshine, and she received a lot of attention from Mom, Grandma, and Pa. She was a happy baby, not hard to care for, but she hated the playpen and fought sleep. She cried when she was hungry and did not take naps. She always had to be rocked with her 'pacy' (pacifier), and always slept with it in her mouth."

Pat said that Maria slept on her back only, and never on her stomach. She was able to roll over. When asked about her health, she said that Maria had very good health—no injuries and no broken bones.

A summary of Patricia's description of events from the witness stand in answer to Daniel's questions is as follows:

When Esther went back to high school, Maria went with her to the day care at the school. It was one to two doors down at the same location as Esther's school, and it worked wonderfully. On breaks, Esther would go to take care of her daughter. She would sometimes call Pat and ask her to please talk to Maria and calm her down. If that didn't work, Pat would go to the day care and get her, or go and rock her to sleep at the day care. Maria was used to being held during her naps, and Pat was the one who did that. Maria sustained no injuries at the school day care. There were no head injuries; in fact, she had no injuries at all.

Here Pat is questioned about Maria's last visit to Dr. John McCormick. She tells the court that he was the doctor for the entire family, including Esther and then Maria. Pat says she went along on the doctor visit as she did on all the others. Maria only went to the doctor for well-baby check-ups. She also went once for a tear-duct "infection" (probably a blockage), and the doctor massaged it away.

On August 14, 2008, she did not have a complete physical. The doctor did note that she was on target and walking. She had started walking at eleven months old. (Later, Esther would contradict her mother's testimony by saying that Maria started walking at nine and one-half months old. This discrepancy would never be noted by the defense, and they could have used it to their advantage, as Maria had fallen and hit the back of her head on a wall *when she was learning to walk.* It still would have been quite a stretch because her mortal injury became apparent at either about ten weeks after the fall (if she started to walk at nine and one-half months) or around five weeks after (if she started walking at eleven months). Because the defense called several witnesses to testify that the injury could have occurred earlier than at the day care, they could have tied this fall and the two different walking dates into their argument and said that Patricia's recall was more credible. It is a moot point now and may have not swayed any juror anyway.)

Brian Daniels abruptly stops his line of questioning and asks Pat if she sees Stephanie Spurgeon in the courtroom. She says she does and describes her briefly, and then Brian states that the witness has identified the defendant. This routine method of identification allows him to proceed in questioning Pat about her contact with Spurgeon and her day care.

Pat says that an organization called The Coordinated Child Care Group had talked to Esther. Esther had been given several names, and the time was drawing near for her to return to school. Many day care facilities did not have space or did not return her phone calls. Approximately two weeks prior to school starting, she went to Spurgeon's home day care and decided that it would be the one for Maria.

Pat said that Stephanie told her that she always took the first day of school off to get ready with her own children, so she kept Maria home that day and took her the next day, August 21, which was a Thursday. Stephanie had seemed surprised by this change.

On August 21, Maria woke up early. Esther got dressed, and then fed Maria at about five in the morning. After that, she played with her on the floor and when Pa (Clyde) walked into the room, she was excited to go to him. She went to him with her hands up, and he picked her up and took her to look at a picture of the cat on the fridge. (Pat is breaking down in tears at this point). Daniels asks her if Maria had any motor problems that morning, and she said, "None. She was playing. She ate breakfast that morning."

Pat describes loading up the car with Esther and Maria at 6:10 a.m. She drove to Esther's bus stop where they waited for the bus, which was late. They played with Maria who wanted out of her car seat. Esther let her play with a little blue piano that was in the car. She banged on the piano. Then the bus came, and Esther left on the bus. There was no indication that Maria was not feeling good.

Pat told Maria that she was going on an "adventure." Maria hollered and banged on the piano. They arrived at the Spurgeon home at 6:45 a.m. When she pulled up, Pat could see no other adults there besides Stephanie. She says that there were no physical problems with Maria on the drive up to the Spurgeon home. They were supposed to be there by 7:00 a.m. Pat says that Stephanie had agreed to open early due to the requested 7:00 a.m. to 3:00 p.m. time slot. Maria needed to be picked up by 3:00 p.m. because a little girl was arriving at 3:30 p.m. on a bus.

Pat then says that a man ran out of the garage and got in a truck that was running as she was getting Maria out of the car. (This person, who I assume was Spurgeon's husband at the time, was never brought up again by either side. I thought it a bit strange that he *ran* out of the house. Even if an adult is late for work, he usually walks at a fast clip, but does not run.)

Pat had brought all the paperwork with her into Spurgeon's home. She was concerned about leaving Maria. (Maria had never been more than a few yards from anyone in the Harris family in her entire short life, so Pat's concern was quite credible.) Pat gave Stephanie everyone's phone number. She knew that Maria was a spoiled child and had woken up early. She stayed about fifteen minutes at the Spurgeon home to settle Maria in her new sur-roundings and just observe. She put Maria down because Maria wanted to "admire" Stephanie's cats.

Pat describes how Spurgeon distracted Maria with a cat. Spurgeon took her on her hip into the kitchen. Pat kissed Maria and told her she loved her and to have a good day. She said she went outside and watched through the window; she didn't want Maria to be upset. She wanted her to have other children to interact with and to develop social skills. Pat sat outside in her car until 7:20 a.m. and cried and prayed for Maria to have a good day and be safe. She didn't see Spurgeon's son or any other children. Stephanie's son would have been in middle school in 2008, which did not start until around 9:30 a.m. because of bus schedules. This would have been almost two hours later, but he was nowhere to be seen. Spurgeon had a daughter as well who was possibly in high school then. Public high schools began at 7:05 a.m.

It is important to note here that when Pat sat in her car and waited before she left, she was parked on the *side* of Spurgeon's house and could not be seen from the front. She told me this later. This fact is important as you will see later when another witness claims that there was no other car there when he dropped off his son.

Pat states she called the Spurgeon home at 10:15 a.m. when she was on her way to work. She was worried and concerned. Maria was used to a day care setting but not used to Spurgeon or other children that would be there. She told Spurgeon on the phone that she was sorry to bother her, that she knew she was busy, but she was having "grandma separation anxiety."

"Do you need me?" she asked Stephanie. Spurgeon told her that Maria was doing fine, playing with kids but still squeamish, clingy but doing well. Pat heard whining in the background. She asked to talk to Maria. Maria was whining but seemed okay. Pat said she was off the phone by 10:20 a.m. Spurgeon had told her before they hung up that she had tried to put Maria down for a nap, but that didn't go well at all.

That was the last time Pat talked to Maria and got a response. When she went back to the day care at 2:45 p.m. to pick her up, things had changed dramatically. She went into the house and talked to Spurgeon, who told her that Maria had had a good day! She played hard. She was a picky eater. She didn't like noodles and brown meat, but she liked macaroni and cheese. Pat states here that Maria had only just started eating "people foods." Spurgeon went on to tell Pat that Maria was so tired that she just zonked out. She said that after lunch, at 12:30 p.m., she put her in bed and *patted her on the back twice.* (I put this in italics because I thought it was a critical piece of information that neither side ever brings up in the course of the trial. Why would Spurgeon specifically tell Pat that she patted Maria on the back twice? It is irrelevant to the entire scenario if it truly happened in that way. Could it be, I speculate, that Spurgeon actually struck Maria at that point, twice, causing her head to hit a surface so hard that it knocked her unconscious? If she "patted" her on the back, it also meant that Maria was placed on her stomach. But she never slept on her stomach! Her pacifier was not mentioned. The time of 12:30 p.m. was important too, because as the reader will see, according to Esther, Spurgeon said that Maria went down for her nap at noon. Why would a defendant be so specific about the number of times she patted a child on the back? It sounded forced, but then again, people recall odd things.)

Pat says they talked for about seven to ten minutes before heading into the bedroom where Maria was asleep in the playpen (the Pack 'n Play). Stephanie repeated that she had a hard time getting her down in the morning. She told Pat that Maria "threw a fit," that she was "spoiled and strong-willed," and that she "got p——d off" that morning. She stomped and screamed and shook the playpen and threw everything out of the playpen.

Spurgeon's attitude seemed to have taken a dramatic turn. This became apparent in how she spoke about Maria to Pat after they had walked into the room where Maria appeared to be asleep. Did the sight of Maria in the playpen upset her in some way? Remember, Maria hated playpens. At this point, I am wondering why someone who is caring for a child for the first time would ever say such cruel things about the child to her grandmother, and use a cuss word to boot. There must have been some real frustration there. Even so, a professional does not act in this way toward a customer, particularly when it is a one-year-old child who is being discussed, to the relative of that customer. These words would reappear later in the trial and possibly impact the jury's decision.

Pat turns and addresses the jury, "I told her I knew she was spoiled." Daniels asks Pat if Maria would normally wake up upon hearing her voice, and Pat responds, "Yes. I knew she was tired. I just thought she was really sleepy and tired." Pat says that Spurgeon told her that she had attempted to rock her—"We had told her to do that"—but she said she didn't have time to rock her because she had four other children there.

"How was she laying in the bed?" Daniels asks.

Pat describes how it was odd, that Maria was laid *across* the bed (the Pack'n Play). She didn't fit this way at all. Her head was turned and her mouth was open. Her head was bulging through the mesh of the playpen and her toes were pushing against the other side. (Standard rectangular Pack'n Plays are about thirty-three inches long by twenty-eight inches wide by forty inches high. Twenty-eight inches is certainly not wide enough for a one-year-old child of average height to lie down in horizontally without pushing into either side or both.) Her "pacy" was in the corner of the bed, not in her mouth. She had never gone to sleep without her pacy. It was strange, but at the time Pat wasn't overly concerned.

Spurgeon told Pat again that Maria had gone to sleep at around 12:30 p.m. Pat explains that Maria did not wake up while they were in the room chatting. When Spurgeon took Maria out of the bed, she had one hand under her face and one hand under her belly. "Her head threw [*sic*] back a little bit."

"How did she carry her?" Brian asks.

"With her hand on her back facing toward her chest. She did not wake up." Pat responds. Pat goes on to say how they talked a little bit about whether to take one bottle or leave it there because Maria had nothing much to drink that day. Pat says that she usually drinks a lot.

Daniels glances at his notes. "How long did she walk around with Maria?"

"About three or more minutes." Then Pat describes how she took Maria and her diaper bag from Stephanie. Maria still did not wake up. She moaned a little bit but did not open her eyes. Pat carried her out the room and then out of the house. There were two girls coming off the bus. She said hello to them, and they exchanged words. Spurgeon came out there too, which meant she had apparently left four children in the house unattended.

In response to Daniels' questions and his gentle manner toward Pat, she continues on in her testimony, describing how she put Maria in her car. The car seat was right behind Pat's seat. She put Maria in and buckled her in. She had a hard time doing this because Maria did not work with her to get into her seat as she normally would.

During the drive home, Pat talked to Maria, even though she couldn't see her. She told her that they were "going home to see Mama."

Pat heard a faint little cry, a whispery cry, and then a gurgle. "Baby girl, are you all right?" There was no response. The actual drive time to get home would take twelve to fifteen minutes. Pat almost pulled over to see if Maria was okay, but she was so close to home. She pulled into the driveway, opened the back car door, and looked at Maria. Her head was slumped in her lap.

"Maria, what's wrong with you!?" Pat says she was completely limp and unresponsive. She breaks down on the witness stand, saying she got her out as gently as she could. "When I saw her there, she was never going to work with me. I ran to the door with her, yelling for Esther." She is crying hard now. The jury is captivated and totally silent. Tears run down the face of one juror, and another one dabs her eyes.

Pat takes a moment to compose herself, and then she says that she asked Esther to wake her up, and she told Esther that "something is terribly wrong." She remembers turning the fan on. She says that Esther tried to get her to respond. She called 911. Pat told her to hurry. "This baby's in trouble! She needs help..." Pat's voice trails off in tears of deep sadness and grief as she recalls that tragic time for all to see and hear. She says that "it took forever" for EMS to arrive. "It wasn't long, but it seemed like a lifetime."

She describes Esther pacing the sidewalk in front of the house, waiting. Pat called EMS again, but as she was calling, they arrived. She says they put Maria "on a bed on the porch." Another paramedic took Pat and Esther inside to answer questions while the first one worked on Maria. Then they transported her to the hospital via ambulance. The EMS driver told Pat to go the way she was familiar with. It had just started to rain.

Esther wanted to go in the ambulance with Maria, but she went with Pat. Pat says that "they did some kind of scans or something" and tried to get a response from her by having Esther talk to her. When they were putting a tube down her throat, she cried out. Pat said to the paramedic, "That's good, isn't it?"

"Yes, it is," he responded. Sometime later that day, she was transported to All Children's Hospital in St. Petersburg.

Brian asks a series of questions that are difficult for Pat to answer, but she responds quietly to each one. She knows that the cross examination will follow, and she is trying to keep calm.

"Was she on life support?"

"Yes, till death at All Children's Hospital."

"There was no brain activity?"

"The first night, but we didn't really correspond with the neurologist about Maria, about how gravely ill she was until the next day. He showed them on the computer..."

Bjorn Brunvand jumps up. "Objection! Hearsay!"

Pat is blocked from discussing what was seen on the scan of Maria's brain. She goes on to answer questions about Maria as a patient in All Children's Hospital. She was there until the twenty-eighth, when she passed away, exactly a week from when she left the Spurgeon home.

Brian asks gently, "Did you have a discussion to take her off life support?"

Pat responds in a quiet, shaky voice. "We had prayed to God not to have to make that decision." She pauses. "We did have her taken off life support."

"After Mease Hospital, were you interviewed by law enforcement?"

At this point, the defense asks to approach the bench. It is uncommon, though not unheard of, for a murder case not to call upon law enforcement to testify. During the entire trial, not one uniformed officer or detective testified. If I had been on the jury, this would have piqued my curiosity. But who do you ask? I did find out after the trial that the state thought it best to make their case without law enforcement testimony. However, if the defense thought the prosecution had erred in this decision, then they certainly would have called detectives to the stand. Both sides were silent on the matter, and we will apparently never know if it would have made any difference in the jury's verdict.

With respect to the direct questioning by Brian Daniels, Pat Harris's testimony is not only credible but appears to be damaging to the defense. It will take some effort on cross-examination by Bjorn Brunvand to keep from appearing to be the "bad-guy lawyer." The obvious love and protection Pat had felt toward Maria comes across as heartrending. The only part that would seem "wrong" was that she was a grandmother who spoiled her granddaughter. In fact, this very act of spoiling Maria so much could have caused her to cry and yell because she wasn't getting the treatment and comforting security that she was used to with her family when she was in Stephanie Spurgeon's day care. Such acting out can push the limits for those of us who have our own children, let alone having to remain calm and in control while watching someone else's.

CHAPTER 4

IF SPURGEON WOULD have taken a training course similar to the one mandated in the Kendra law that is now in place in South Carolina, this trial might not even be taking place. The Kendra bill was drafted and became law in South Carolina in 2010. It was named after a child, Kendra Gaddie[1], who, at six months of age, received trauma to her brain due to a slap from her caretaker in 2008. Similar to Maria, she had a subdural hematoma and retinal hemorrhaging.

The caretaker, Talisha Lavette, had admitted that she slapped Kendra and pleaded guilty to a charge of inflicting great bodily injury to a child. But Lavette did not call the family or EMS services until several hours after the occurrence. She originally received a ten-year sentence, but it was dropped to five years and probation. Kendra still lives and is still recovering as of this writing, but it appears that her brain injuries are permanent. Maria has passed away. Kendra's caretaker admitted to her guilt. Stephanie Spurgeon claims to be one hundred percent innocent.

The Kendra law mandates two hours of free training annually for child care operators and caregivers, and they must report the completion of the training to the Department of Social Services in South Carolina. The course teaches CPR and other child safety measures. This new law is considered an important part of regulating in-home day care centers, which were considered the least regulated day care facilities in South Carolina.

However, a year after Kendra's law went into effect, an investigation by HDNews 12 out of Augusta, Georgia, determined that out of fifty-one home day care providers in their viewing area, only fourteen had taken the course.[2] The problem seemed to be that there was no regulatory body at the time and no consequences for being in violation of Kendra's law. The state of South Carolina was working on statutory changes as of December 2011. There is a website available for people in South Carolina to check to see if their provider is in compliance with this training.

In the state of Georgia, all day care providers must take twenty hours of training before they can even register as providers. Some other states also have mandatory training requirements. In fact, Florida now has a Director Credential training course that was implemented in January 2010. In March of 2009, an annual ten-hour course was required for all day care workers between July 1 and June 30 of the following year. Since Maria had passed away in 2008, Spurgeon was not obligated to take either of these courses.

There is no public record of Spurgeon having taken any child training course, although this doesn't mean she did not do so. All licensing records are only for current day care providers in the state of Florida, so that information is unavailable as well.

Stephanie Spurgeon seems to have adhered to her claim of innocence from the start; however, what she initially told police is not public record. If a plea bargain had been considered, did she decide not to pursue one? Did her current attorneys push for a trial and not a plea bargain, or was this her decision? No one wants to go to prison, and if she really believes that her attorneys can prevent this from happening, she will avoid a plea bargain since it would entail at least some prison time if she accepted one. It is a big gamble, especially since Spurgeon, like most defendants, would choose not to testify. The current defense team had only taken the case after the original attorney; Gregory "Skip" Olney had been dropped, apparently fired by Spurgeon. The reasons for this change are unknown, but I have heard from several sources that it was because he wanted Spurgeon to accept a plea bargain and she would not do so. I have no proof as to whether this was actually true, but the Olney legal team was suddenly off the case.

By this time, Ron Kurpiers had already won the similar case against a St. Petersburg foster mom, Tenesia Brown, gaining her acquittal at trial. He would have had a lot of confidence in his ability to get Stephanie Spurgeon acquitted especially if he could use the tactic that SBS is arguably not a real syndrome. But the charges in this case are extremely severe as well. If Spurgeon is convicted of murder in the first degree, she will be sentenced to life without parole. She is banking on a not-guilty verdict by the jury due to reasonable doubt, a claim which will recur throughout this trial.

As the cross-examination of Patricia Harris commences by defense attorney Brunvand, there is a noticeable shift in her mannerisms and voice. She is afraid yet calm under the pressure, and she does not become defensive. Knowing her as I do, I am certain she has prayed a quick prayer.

First, she is asked about the distance to Spurgeon's house. She says that it is about four miles from where she lives. She explains that they took Lake St. George, a two-lane side road, because they always avoided US Highway 19. (Highway 19 is an infamous main artery running north and south through Pinellas County where many deadly accidents occur every week. It has improved in recent years as overpasses have replaced intersections where you could sit and literally read the paper at red lights. Accidents often occurred when drivers, impatient and not wanting to sit at the longest red lights in the country, would run them, either slamming into cross traffic or rear-ending a car ahead of them who assumed that they were doing the safe and legal thing by stopping at the red light.)

The drive from Pat's home to Stephanie's took about twelve to fifteen minutes that morning. Pat tells how she encountered three crossing areas—schools, with crossing guards. But she says that at 6:45 a.m., there were no crossing guards yet present. The ride back in the afternoon took a little longer. Pat knows this because they had taken a prior drive to visit Stephanie.

Brunvand shifts gears and asks Pat how old Esther was when Maria was born. "She was seventeen." He asks about Esther's treatment of Maria, her newborn. Pat relates how Esther did the best she could and was very protective of Maria, not wanting anything to happen to her.

Pat says that Maria had a doctor's appointment on August 14 for her one-year shots. This information would become a hook that the defense would grasp on to later in the trial in the attempt to create a diversion from what could have caused Maria's brain injury. The vaccinations were given an entire week before the fateful day at the day care, during which time Maria never once indicated she was not well. But the vaccines would be utilized by the defense to attempt to create reasonable doubt in the minds of the jury.

Brunvand asks her if Maria connected with the other children who were at the day care. Pat's response is "We had never had day care before. Maria was slow to interact with the other children." She even praises Spurgeon at this point, "We appreciated how Stephanie interacted with the children...She'd done a good job." (Pat does not count Maria's time at the day care at Esther's school the prior school year because Maria would have been between several weeks and ten months old, and would not have been able to interact with other children at that age. Then the summer months fell in between.)

Pat explains that the latest she can pick up Maria is at 3:00 p.m. Stephanie would open up her home at 7:00 a.m. but pick up was at 3:00 p.m. because she had to prepare for another girl who would be arriving at 3:30 p.m., "a handicapped-issued" child.

Detective Kelly Lyons, the lead detective in this case, was not called to testify. Pat had talked to her a long time, giving her as many details as she could, and Brunvand drew some of his information for the following testimony from that police report.

"Was she autistic?" Brunvand asks, referring to the handicapped child.

"She could have been autistic."

"Was it something at birth?"

"She was handicapped."

"On the morning of the twenty-first, it was your belief that Maria woke up around four o'clock?"

"No, 4:20 or 4:30 p.m. I don't recall if I told Detective Lyons that she woke up at four."

Brunvand asks if he could show Patricia a report, and Daniels objects, saying the question has been asked and answered. Judge Newton sustains the objection, and Brunvand asks for an approach to the bench. It is just my speculation that he is asking if his next direction in questioning would be permissible, because for some reason, establishing a more exact time that Maria awoke is important to the defense. Of course, it could be any number of things, but an attorney must be quick on his feet in rephrasing the question in such a way so as not to get another objection.

In this case, Brunvand walks back to his position in front of the witness, Patricia Harris, and says, "The bottom line is, you were not awake." Perhaps here, he is hoping to show that something could have happened to Maria that morning before Patricia sees her. But this line of questioning stops here and is never again pursued. I wonder if it is because Maria's behavior did not seem unusual in any way right up to when Pat left her at the Spurgeon home.

Pat explains that Maria was with her mother, Esther. Maria was in the baby bed. Then when Maria was eating breakfast, Pat saw her at 5:00 a.m. She goes on to indicate that usually Maria would wake up between 4:45 and 5 a.m. Esther needed to get ready for school and needed to get Maria ready as well.

She looks directly at Brunvand as she answers his questions about the morning routine that August morning in 2008. She relates how they were used to waking up early, around five to five thirty. "Whatever time my husband would go in and check on her, he wanted to play with her. Esther always got up with her baby in the mornings."

"And you would as well."

"Yes."

"At some time you would try to put Maria down for a nap."

"No schedule," Pat says. "Just Maria's schedule."

With this statement, and perhaps without even realizing it, Patricia is laying the groundwork that demonstrates an upbringing of a very young child who is used to having her way. Maria got up when she wanted to, napped when she needed to, demanded to be held and rocked to sleep, didn't like the playpen, and only ate certain foods. She was a spoiled child who was deeply loved, and nobody wanted her to cry. Someone from the Harris household was always there to take care of her, to keep her in sight, or to merely be a room or two away when Maria was at the high school day care the spring before, or in the church nursery on Sundays. Often, Esther or Pat would sit and rock her in the nursery during Sunday school or the church service. Even more often, she would be right with them in Sunday school or the service, held lovingly in Clyde's arms. She was always quiet when she was being held by one of them, shyly smiling at whomever looked at her.

"Around six, six thirty, seven," Pat states, "Maria was ready for a nap after she had eaten and played—ready for a nap. She would nap for no set time—as long as she needed—forty-five minutes, an hour, fifteen minutes."

Brunvand asks her how she knew Maria would need a nap.

"I knew the signs."

"What signs?" Brunvand asks, his voice rising slightly.

She would "rub her eyes, whining, didn't need this or that—needed a nap. She didn't always need a nap." Pat emphasizes that she would always rock Maria to sleep.

"I was not with Maria at the [Esther's high school] day care. She didn't nap much at school. They would put her in a little carrier and rock it with a foot. Maria required rocking."

Pat explains that in the summer of 2008, Pat or Esther rocked her. She never fell asleep on her own and never slept in her bed until nighttime. Pat would rock her at night; it was their bonding time. Esther had to get up early so she went to bed early. Maria would always be rocked and once she was asleep, Pat would place her in her crib. She reiterates that this only happened at night.

"If she slept, wonderful! If she didn't, then someone would have to get her up and rock her."

Pat talks about how she and Esther would help each other. Maria was never placed in her crib when she was awake, and told to "go asleep" [sic]. When she would nap during the day, she stayed in Pat's arms.

"I would always kiss and love on her. At church, she was rocked in the church pew."

Pat says that Maria was always already asleep when she was placed in her crib. She was always on her back, but one time she had rolled over on her side.

Brunvand asks her if Maria ever rolled onto her stomach.

"No, never on her stomach, on her *side*."

"Well...again, do you recall telling Detective Kelly Lyons—"

Pat sits up straighter and becomes visibly upset. "Sir! I was so beside myself that I don't really recall what I talked to her about—"

Brunvand interrupts. "You indicated that she hated playpens. How is it you know?"

"I knew for several reasons. If I or Esther were busy—going to go to the bathroom or to prep food—she needed to have a safe place to be while we did whatever we did. She screamed and cried. She couldn't see. She didn't like it. She wanted out. She was used to hands on her."

Brunvand abruptly dropped this line of questioning and changed course.

"You dropped Maria off around 6:45 a.m., spent maybe fifteen minutes there..."

Pat tells how she looked at her watch. Twice she says this. "It was a big thing for us—to go home to an empty house with her toys all there. I was praying and crying. She was in a strange house, strange people...I went to Target to buy things for Maria that she didn't need—grandma anxiety. I was worried. I would have never left her if I saw her carrying on through Stephanie's window.

"I called on my way to work. "Do you need me? I can call and cancel my client." It's all about Maria. I had to be at my client's house by ten thirty. I estimate it was ten fifteen. I was scared senseless."

She says she called Stephanie at about ten fifteen, and it was an eight- to ten-minute call.

Brunvand asks her if she would have any argument with it being a two-and-a-half-minute call.

"No. It was about Maria. Was she okay? I heard her. I talked with her."

Brunvand states, "She'd been playing."

"That's what Stephanie said, yes." Pat says that Stephanie told her that she'd had a hard time getting Maria to take a nap.

"Was that a problem?"

Pat says that a nap at ten fifteen or ten thirty was way past her usual morning naptime. She was very tired. "Maybe 'cause she had all these kids to play with...I don't know...maybe...I just don't know."

She said that Stephanie patted her twice on the back and she went to sleep. "That's what she said—she zonked out. I'm assuming that's what it was. There was [*sic*] no other naps. She tried one time and failed. The second time—it was my understanding—she put her down and she went to sleep."

"Were *you* present when Esther called?"

"No."

"Do you recall Stephanie Spurgeon telling you that Maria threw a fit when Maria was in the playpen? Consistent with what you knew about playpens."

"The first time, Stephanie said she threw everything out [of the playpen]. It didn't go very well." Pat manages to add, "I've *never* seen Maria throw anything out of her playpen."

I found this question interesting, because it gave Patricia a chance to emphasize how upset Maria would get when placed in a playpen. I wondered how it sounded from the jurors' perspective as it demonstrated that there was a physically and emotionally upset child perhaps screaming and already probably causing Spurgeon undue stress. She had a screaming child in a playpen, and several other toddlers to care for in the process. Perhaps there was at least one infant there to care for as well. That Brunvand uses the words "threw a fit" in the context of what his own defendant said doesn't put her in a good light. I didn't understand why he would want to do that.

Next, the car ride home is revisited. Pat explains that the car seat was facing forward on the driver's side. She tells how she and Esther and Maria went everywhere together. Esther would sit in the back with Maria.

Pat relates how she didn't call anyone since Maria appeared to be sleeping on her stomach. She carried her out to the car. Maria seemed to be in a deep sleep. Pat was not yet alarmed but a little concerned that Maria was out so soundly. She didn't help Pat at all when she was placed in the car seat. At that point, Pat just wanted to get Maria home because her mother, Esther, was anxious to see her.

She estimated the drive home to be about twenty minutes, five to eight minutes longer than the morning drive. She said she was very close to the road that led to her development when she heard the soft gurgling cough. "I heard a faint cough. Would you like me to show you?" Pat wanted to emphasize just how quiet that cough was.

Brunvand states to Pat that she told Detective Lyons that it was a "faint cough," repeating what Pat had just stated. (I wonder at this point in the trial if and when we would hear from Detective Kelly Lyons. As it turned out, we never would. She would never be called to testify. I still find that very odd in a murder trial. The prosecution or the defense can call a detective, but both sides chose not to. The reason for this decision is elusive at best since the testimony is regarding a police report, and it would have seemed much more effective to have Detective Lyons testify to her investigation.)

Brunvand paces a few steps, then turns to face Patricia. "You didn't stop the car. It didn't cause concern—"

"No, it *did* cause me concern, but there is no place to pull over on Alderman [Road], so making a judgment decision, I'll go home, since we were so close to home. I talked to her the whole way, but she did not answer. Once in our neighborhood, I wanted to get home—stop—I'm just right around the corner. I could not see her. I tried moving my mirror. I heard a cough, a gurgle, and a moan."

Pat continues to explain that when they pulled up in the driveway, she jumped out and opened the back driver's side door. Maria's head was down, and Pat couldn't see her face. She put her head back. "There was white foam all over her mouth and red chunky stuff on her upper shirt. I guess she threw up. I didn't hear her throw up."

"Based on what you saw."

"Yes."

"It appears she has a problem." Brunvand states the obvious.

Pat sighs. "Yes, at that point, there is a major, major problem." He leads her to continue by saying, "You unlatched the buckles on the car seat…"

"After I lifted her head"—Pat pauses, struggling to regain her composure—"she was just limp…" Pat begins to cry.

"Were you running in [sic] the house?"

As if not hearing his question, she continues describing Maria. "Like there's no bones there." The words come slowly and weakly, as she talks through her tears, reliving her horror. "Esther, please come quickly! Something's wrong with Baby! I need help! Wake this baby up!

"Esther takes the baby. She was crying and begging her to wake up. She said, 'Maria, please wake up!'"

Pat tells how Esther wanted to put a fan on Maria, that maybe she's hot and dehydrated. She says they didn't know what to do. They were patting her and rubbing her.

"Esther said, 'I need to call 911!'"

"Yes, you do, darling," Pat says.

"Esther called 911. Once. I was holding Maria. I hesitate to say that she called twice. I called also wanting to know where are you all [the paramedics], but I heard the siren in the distance, so I hung up. That's why the police showed up, they said later, because of the hang up." Pat has become so engrossed in her own testimony that she has, without realizing it, spoken to Brunvand as if he were one of the paramedics who had arrived on the scene!

Stephanie Spurgeon sits in obvious discomfort at the defense table, sliding her hands up and down her opposite upper arms and then placing them on each side of her head, looking anywhere but at Patricia Harris. It is quite evident that she does not want to hear this testimony.

Brunvand senses that he needs to deter Pat from her impassioned recollection. "What would Maria do if you put her in the playpen while being asleep [sic]?"

"She would wake up crying immediately."

Oddly, this is where Patricia Harris's cross examination ends. The defense did not follow through on the playpen scenario throughout the rest of the trial, so I don't know why Brunvand ended his questioning here, other than to distract the jury from the tragic scene at the Harris home. But it certainly was not long enough to divert them from what Pat had just described when she arrived at home with Maria. The tragic scene was certainly fresh in my mind after he said, "No further questions," and walked back to the defense table.

This case will go off on quite a few rabbit trails, and it will soon become apparent that focusing on Maria's one and only day in Stephanie Spurgeon's day care where she came out limp and unresponsive in the arms of her grandmother would not be the focus of the defense's approach. Why? There will not be a defense side to this story to refute what Patricia Harris stated on the witness stand. Instead, they will take it in a multitude of directions, all pointing away from Spurgeon, but with no explanation as to what that day was like. As the trial unfolded, I was constantly waiting to hear what the defense had to say about Maria's first and only day at that day care, but the walls of the Spurgeon home would refuse to speak, at least in the courtroom.

CHAPTER 5

THE DAYS ALL seem to blur together at All Children's Hospital. The Harrises, having been given accommodations at the Ronald MacDonald House for which they are forever grateful to the staff, are at Maria's comatose side. There has been no change, except that inside her small head, her brain cells continue to shut down. They are told that they must soon make a decision to end life support if they want to preserve her organs for donation.

Clyde Harris, trying to hold back his deep grief, announces this information to our church congregation on Sunday, where we all sit dumbfounded. How could this have happened to Maria Harris? She was just here last Wednesday, playing and laughing in the nursery. It didn't seem real. We were only in a daze. The Harrises were living a nightmare that they would not awaken from for four more years.

Esther had kept Maria's father, Javier, informed throughout the situation. But when she begged him to come down from Pennsylvania to say goodbye to his daughter, his only child, he wanted to bring his "girlfriend" with him. Esther ended the conversations at that point. However, Pat continued to try to get him to come down. She would talk to him late at night. "One day, you will regret this." But it was a lost cause, and she gave up, not wanting to waste her efforts on him any longer. She finally told Javier that if anything happened to Maria she would call him.

The Harris family gathered together in prayer around Maria's bedside on August 28, 2008. Suddenly it seemed like they had so little time to say goodbye. Her tiny body would have to be rushed out of the room to prepare to remove her heart, liver, spleen, and kidneys to be kept viable for transplant soon after the equipment keeping her alive was shut down. It was a very private and deeply sorrowful moment. Even though they knew she would be in the arms of Jesus very soon, and even though they knew they would one day see her again, they had already been missing her for a week now. They would be allowed to hold her lifeless body, very briefly...

Dr. McCormick takes the stand. He is a pleasant looking young man in his thirties, with dark brown hair and a slim build. He states that he has been licensed since 1998 and that he completed his residency in internal medicine and pediatrics in 2002.

He is questioned by Brian Daniels, who addresses him in a friendly but brisk tone. "Do you remember Maria?"

"Yes, very well, from her birth until her death." Even if this question had been rehearsed, it resonates jarringly throughout the courtroom. Some people in the gallery shuffle uncomfortably.

"Do you know Patricia and Esther?"

"Yes."

"Did you see Maria for a full year prior to her injury?"

"Yes."

The doctor answers many detailed questions about seeing Maria a week before her death for her well-child visit. (The fact that it was an entire week before her death is important, because, during that week, according to the Harris family and to those who saw her, myself included, she exhibited no signs of illness or unusual behavior. There was no warning sign at all that her vaccinations could have caused brain or retinal bleeding.)

Dr. McCormick explains that she had no prior injuries, no head injuries, and no problems with walking or talking; "a healthy kid, no neurological problems."

He recalls that she was "playful, inquisitive, and very happy. Completely normal, fine, on track," for her age. He says that Pat and Esther were both with Maria that day, and they had great interaction with Maria. She walked from Esther to Pat to him, and then she sat on his lap.

He says he gave her an MMR (measles, mumps, and rubella) and varicella vaccine. No Hepatitis A shot was given. Dr. McCormick emphasizes, "There were no problems with those immunizations as it relates to those injuries."

He struggled a bit when asked for the dates and numbers of vaccines and immunizations that Maria received when Ron Kurpiers begins his cross examination.

Dr. McCormick is asked the last time he looked at the records. "A month ago?"

"Four sets of shots?"

"Up to date."

There were what seemed to be an inordinate amount of vaccinations, but when one takes into consideration that an infant is not given the full doses one or two times as in the past, but instead the dosage is decreased and spread out over the first year of life, that it technically is safer and the cumulative dosing is the same. This information, though available, was not brought to light in the trial, leaving some speculation on online blogs about vaccinations causing Maria's death. Any of the few documented cases of death due to vaccinations that I have checked out show a much shorter time period between the vaccine and the death of the child who was almost always a very young infant. Usually, these rare events would occur immediately within minutes or hours of the vaccine as the child would go into anaphylactic shock. There were others that lasted a couple or three days, but I saw none that were a week later. The fact that Maria not only had a subdural hematoma and retinal hemorrhaging, but also that the bridging veins that connected her brain to the protective dural lining in the skull were torn would, in effect, rule out vaccines as a cause of death anyway. The debate about vaccines continues in many venues, but primarily now it is about whether they can cause autism and/or other disorders, not death in a toddler who had been previously vaccinated without problems.[1]

The defense would highlight the numerous dates that Maria saw her doctor and was vaccinated. His numbers were not out of the ordinary, and I believe that the defense knew it because they did not offer any expert testimony to counter the numbers and discredit them as too many.

Maria was given her first shot at eleven days after birth, ironically exactly a year before the tragic day at Spurgeon's house. Then as follows:

> 3 vaccines/shots on October 24, 2007
> 3 vaccines/shots on January 3, 2008
> 3 vaccines/shots on March 4, 2008
> 2 vaccines/shots on June 4, 2008
> And of course, the last ones, a week before her day at day care on August 14, 2008

Maria never had a CT scan; Dr. McCormick says there was no need for one, and she never had an MRI.

More importantly, during that first year of her life, she had no adverse effects to *any* of those vaccines, and if she didn't have reactions to the earlier ones, when she was tiny and much younger and more susceptible to adverse reactions, then it would seem quite improbable that the same type of vaccine, given later in her first year, would cause a problem. If it did, she certainly masked it well by being very active and friendly. Maria never even had a head cold or cough, which was pretty amazing for a young child, especially considering that she had spent time in the day care at the YWCA with other young children. My own children had numerous viruses, coughs, and flus which they generously passed on to me not long after they got them.

Christopher Chumbly, now a registered nurse, takes the stand next. He was a paramedic at the time of Maria's injury. He is not asked by Brian Daniels how long he had been a paramedic at that point. He appears to be quite young but could be anywhere from midtwenties to midthirties. He worked for Sunstar, the ambulance company here in Pinellas County. He was dispatched to the Harris home because of an unresponsive pediatric patient at 3:21 p.m. He arrived with his partner, who did not testify, at 3:26 p.m., and the Palm Harbor Fire Department arrived on the scene simultaneously. Someone from the fire department team brought Maria to the stretcher and assessed her. Chumbly explains that Maria was not acting normally—not afraid of loud noises, not alert, only responsive to painful stimuli, such as a sternal rub.

Brian asks him if her eyes were open. "No."

Chumbly explains the treatment regimen when Maria was moved into the ambulance. She was given oxygen, her blood sugar was checked, a heart monitor was hooked up, and she was given an IV insert for access. Maria's breathing was noted to be within adequate range, but then suddenly, she stopped breathing! Sternal rubs eventually brought her back around. The doctor and the emergency room at Mease Countryside Hospital in Safety Harbor were alerted.

Chumbly says that they didn't know her illness, so they were trying to treat her symptoms. They arrived at the hospital at 3:49 p.m. When the ambulance arrived, Maria was having more difficulty breathing—apnea. This was regulated with another sternal rub, and a pediatric bag was not necessary.

"Was it a code possibility?" Daniels asks.

"We always prepare for the worst," he humbly responds. "We applied patches for defibrillation just in case."

He goes on to say that when he looked under her eyelids, her eyes were glazed over and there was no tracking at all. They administered saline. There was no further contact with the family en route to the hospital.

This ends the state's questioning of this witness that was done to lay the groundwork on how quickly the ambulance and fire department worked together to get Maria stabilized and to the hospital. It also established her condition as unresponsive during the entire time she was with the paramedics.

Kurpiers begins his cross-examination by asking Chumbly several questions to dig into the specifics of the assessment of Maria's condition. He focuses on the blood sugar number in particular, which Chumbly says was 468, an extra-high number. He lets the number hang in the air for several seconds, before asking Chumbly about Maria's actual transport to the hospital.

Chumbly rode in the back of the ambulance with two fire department paramedics. He states that Maria did not cry during transport. Her only change in condition was the apnea. The siren was blaring, there was no crying, and there were three men in the back with her.

Kurpiers asks if she had an IV.

"Yes, in the right external jugular vein."

"Have you reviewed your records?"

"Yes."

"Do you have a copy today?"

"Yes."

Kurpiers hands him a record, and he says that it is not his own record but that of the fire department. It probably indicates that Maria did cry. In a case like this, it is very possible for three people in a stressed situation—an unresponsive child being rushed to the ER in the back of an ambulance, siren wailing, while they each are performing duties to stabilize and monitor her, that they each would remember different things. Did she cry? Very possibly. Can a child in an unresponsive state cry out? It is documented that this can happen. The defense would continue to focus on Maria's crying while she was supposed to be unconscious, and the prosecution would downplay the alleged crying episodes.

Clyde Harris enters the courtroom and takes the stand next. He is a large and solidly built man, with a full beard and a thick head of salt-and-pepper hair. His deep voice belies his struggle with asthma through the years. He is solemn, stoic, and uncomfortable at being the center of attention during his testimony about his only grandchild. Clyde was perhaps called to testify by the prosecution to hedge any cross-examination questions in advance, but he was asked very little and his testimony really did not come into play in any meaningful way. For him, this turned out to be a good thing. Clyde Harris is a very private man, and his testimony was short and focused solely on what he was asked without elaboration.

Brian Daniels asks him about his relationship with Maria. He responds quietly in a steady voice, saying that it was great. He had been teaching Maria how to swim. She was cuddly. He spoiled her as much as he could. He smiles. "Her grandmother and mother were very close to her." He mentioned the foods she disliked and that she liked her pacy and her hippo, and she loved water.

"What were her sleeping habits?" Daniels asks.

"As long as she was held, she would sleep. At nighttime, you could put her down when she fell asleep."

"How was her health?"

"Very good!"

"Did she have any physical injuries? Broken bones? Falls? Head injuries?"

"No."

According to Clyde, on the morning of August 21, 2008, Maria awoke around 4:30 to 5:00 a.m. He apparently was not aware that Esther had heard Maria earlier and had gotten her up to get her ready for the day and to play a little. But the time discrepancy was not important to the case.

What was important was Maria's reaction to "Pa" when she reached out to have him pick her up. She wanted to go see the cat picture on the refrigerator. Clyde asked for a kiss, and she laughed and gave him an "Eskimo kiss." Then he handed her to Pat. She had no physical problems. Her hand-eye coordination was good.

If anyone would be alerted to some unusual symptoms or behavior in a child, it would be those who spent a lot of time with that child. The Harrises were so protective and watchful of Maria that had she exhibited anything different in her behavior, one of them would have taken her to the doctor or the hospital. But she behaved perfectly normally, and no alarms went off in any of the Harrises' minds. With just a few minor variances, their memories of that day lined up well, and their testimonies seemed sincere and honest. It would now be a matter of how the jury would interpret them.

Ron Kurpiers on cross, approaches Clyde Harris but remains at a respectful distance.

"On August 21, 2008, when you awoke, was Maria already up?"

"A little after five, I went into the kitchen and she was up."

Kurpiers asks Clyde if Maria liked her playpen, and Clyde told him that he was not aware of whether she liked or disliked the playpen. This is not surprising since Clyde had probably never seen Maria in the playpen. When he was home, he could hold her or watch her play on the floor while Esther and Patricia did other things around the house. There was no need for her to be in the playpen during those times.

Surprisingly, these are the only questions that Clyde is asked, and I imagine that it is with much relief that he steps down from the witness box.

CHAPTER 6

FEBRUARY 2008

WHEN ESTHER HAD been feeling ill for a few days, Pat decided to take her to Dr. McCormick, who would later become Maria's doctor. She thought maybe Esther needed to change her medicine as she had been on an antibiotic. Maybe it was making her sick. She hadn't been eating and she certainly wasn't feeling well, and she had recently started vomiting all the time. But Pat laughed when her son Christopher said that Esther was acting like she was pregnant.

Pat thought about it though. She couldn't be! Pat was always around Esther. Pat asked Dr. McCormick for a pregnancy test just in case. Esther said no. But somehow one was taken, and at nine thirty that night another doctor, Dr. Goldstein called for Esther. "Can I help you," Pat asks him with curiosity. "She is in bed. She is going to school tomorrow." Then Pat told him that she had asked for the blood work, and she had been the one to bring Esther in. "Is everything all right?" Concern grew in Pat's heart for her daughter's health.

After a long pause, Dr. Goldstein responded, "I...I don't know. What was the test for?"

"Pregnancy," Pat whispered, barely audibly.

There was another long hesitation. Then Dr. Goldstein told Pat that the test was positive. Pat was shocked. She was also hurt. "No one wants their baby to be in this situation. It broke my heart. She was already thirteen weeks. I wasn't unhappy, but I was disappointed and in a lot of emotional distress, and her daddy wasn't here."

Buster (Clyde) was on a business trip in California, where he had to travel to frequently. He would be headed home soon. Pat wondered if she should she call him. *No*, she thought, *it wouldn't be right to tell him before he got on the plane.* She should wait until he was on the ground and heading back home. So that is what she did. Unlike Pat, Buster was not only shocked, but he was very angry. She thought he would never speak to Esther again. He was so hurt. This had been his little girl.

Prior to the pregnancy, Javier and Esther, unbeknownst to her parents, had seriously discussed getting married after she graduated. He even bought her a ring, which she still has. But now, things were different. When her father got home, he confronted her and called Javier to come over, and he confronted him too. Javier acted shocked as well, and he even thought it was a mistake. Christopher was home and demanded to know. "If Esther is pregnant then you better tell me now!" Everyone's emotions were running high. When left alone to discuss the situation between the two of them, Javier brought up the idea of an abortion for the first time. Esther was so upset that she slapped him across the face. For her, there was no backing out now. There was a life growing inside her—a baby.

Buster couldn't believe this had happened to his close-knit family. He told Javier, "You are older! You should know better! You are a Christian!"

Christopher had to remind his father not to put stress on Esther because of the baby. But Buster would not acknowledge his daughter again for a long time. She apologized to him. Esther was heartbroken because she was so close to her father, and she had betrayed his trust. For her parent's sake, she and Javier also apologized to the church. Javier didn't want to. He didn't think that it was anyone's business, but it was Esther's child to carry.

She did delay this apology though until she was obviously showing. She was showing so much that at first she thought she might be carrying twins. The doctors even thought so for a while. But as time passed, the ultrasounds continued to show one baby. The church received Esther's pregnancy admittedly with some reservation and shock, but most people were nonjudgmental and were nice to Esther and her parents. People at our church are very forgiving and realize that anyone can fall into sin. They appreciated Esther's desire to repent, and after Maria was born, it seemed everyone loved the sweet child.

As Maria's projected birth date approached, the church women gave Esther a beautiful baby shower, which was held at the home of one of our members. There was an abundance of blankets and adorable outfits, and many gifts a first-time mother could surely use. Some were even handmade! Esther and Pat were overwhelmed with appreciation and joy at the outpouring of love from their church family.

I hold my breath as Esther is called to the witness stand. I am worried that she will not be able to show in her voice or her emotions what she truly feels in her heart because she tends to hold everything inside. But I needn't have been concerned. Esther is in control and very responsive to the questions. She truly would demonstrate that she had been the mother of a dearly loved child.

She walks quickly to the witness stand, anxious to get the ordeal over with but not appearing nervous. Her jet-black shiny hair is cropped short. Although it is dark like her father's hair, it gathers curly around her head like her mother's. As she is seated, her large black eyes watch Daniels approach. She looks right at him. She rarely blinks. She does not smile.

Brian Daniels quietly starts his questioning with a blunt query. "How old was Maria when she died?"

"She was one year and two weeks at death."

"Where was her father?"

"He was living in Pennsylvania."

This information should have caused some people on some blog sites to not post the comments that they did, posting nonsense like Maria's father was responsible for her death, having dropped her on the floor. One poster actually said that Maria's father was in the ER telling doctors what happened. People may naively believe these posts, but in fact, Javier was out of the picture entirely and had not seen his daughter recently. He would not see her again. Ever. Why anyone would perpetuate such a lie is a mystery to me since it only does damage to the case for Stephanie Spurgeon, who needs truth on her side. But some people just like to spread rumors to confound other supporters and distract from the truth. In court, the truth about Maria's father's absence makes these bloggers look like fools.

Brian asks Esther about Dr. John McCormick, the family doctor, and she responds that they still go to him today. She says that Maria was at Dr. McCormick's office for every well-baby check-up, about every three months. She had no injuries. Esther said she was responsible about taking Maria to the doctor.

"How was her health in general?"

"Very good."

"How was her appetite?"

"Very picky. She loved applesauce, peaches, pears. She disliked yogurt. She liked veggies."

"How was her conduct around the family?"

"Very good. She liked everyone."

Esther goes on to answer questions about Maria's care soon after she was born. Two weeks after her birth, in fact, Esther was back in school at the YWCA where there was a day care for young mothers attending the high school there. Maria was at the day care while Esther attended classes. Esther would go and see her at the on-campus day care. Pat would also come from time to time or even talk to young Maria on the phone.

Daniels switches gears. "How was her eyesight?"

"Very good. She could pick things up easily, even the smallest little bugs."

Esther then describes how Maria was never laid down, but she was always rocked to sleep. She would also sleep in her arms.

"How long would she nap?"

"Twenty to forty-five minutes." (I underline this in my notes as I recall how long she "slept" at the Spurgeon home on August 21. I wonder at this point why Daniels does not ask Esther if Maria had ever taken a two-hour or longer nap in the last few months. Then he could have asked her if she would have thought that to be very unusual, since she had "slept" at the Spurgeon home from at least noon until Pat arrived, and even then, did not wake up—a time spanning almost three hours.)

Esther talks about the day of Maria's injury, responding to Brian Daniel's questions calmly because she knows what to expect. She maintains control over her emotions until later in her testimony.

As Pat described earlier, Esther also tells how she had set her alarm clock for 4:00 a.m. and woke up on August 21. At 4:20 a.m., Maria awoke. She stayed in her crib laughing, playing, and talking. Esther took her out of the crib at 4:30 a.m. Maria walked right into the living room. She had very good coordination. At 5:00 a.m. she ate breakfast: some oatmeal with peach Juicy-Juice.

At 6:15 a.m., they arrived at the bus stop with Pat driving, and Esther sitting in the back as usual next to Maria. They had to wait at the bus stop for about fifteen minutes. Esther played with Maria and talked to her. She was going to get her out of her car seat, but the bus came. Maria had been in a good mood.

Brian asked her if she called the Stephanie Spurgeon house later in the day.

"Yes, at 1:40 to 1:45. She told me that Maria had been sleeping since 12:00 p.m."

There it was again. When did Maria "go to sleep"? I don't think Spurgeon knew whether it was twelve or twelve thirty because she was probably too upset. So she gave one time to Patricia and another one to Esther. The contents of Maria's stomach were not known because her vomit was not analyzed. It is difficult to say if she ate lunch before going to sleep or ate something earlier that morning at the day care. She certainly had to have eaten something at the day care, because by 2:45 p.m., her breakfast from 5:00 a.m. would have been fully digested. If Spurgeon provided lunch at noon, perhaps Maria was already unconscious in the crib and not able to cause problems for her while she fed the other children. Or she could have fed Maria then and put her in the Pack 'n Play for the second attempted nap, only to have her begin screaming and yelling, causing Spurgeon to react in whatever way she did to cause Maria to become unconscious. Either way, Maria was "asleep" according to Spurgeon, since noon or twelve thirty, a long naptime to actually continue past when Pat arrived to pick her up at 2:45 p.m. By the time Pat arrived, Maria should have at least been nearing the end of her nap and woken up when she heard Pat, or especially when Pat placed her in the car seat. But as Pat said, she was told that Maria played hard and was really tired, so she took that at face value at the time.

Daniels asks Esther why she called the Spurgeon home.

"I wanted to check on Maria. Stephanie told me that she had a lot of fun with the kids. She played really hard."

"Was that unusual?"

Esther says it was unusual that she fell asleep in a Pack 'n Play because she was never laid down. And she always slept on her back. Esther hesitates and goes on to describe how she saw her mom arrive at home with Maria. She breaks down in tears, recalling Patricia beating on the door and shouting that something was wrong.

"I begged her to wake up, but she would never wake up."

"Did you call 911?" Daniels asks gently.

"Yes."

"Did she have problems breathing?"

"Yes."

Esther continues to answer Daniel's questions, and she is able to regain her composure. She also describes Maria feeling "like a bag of rice." Her eyes were closed, and it seemed like hours until the fire department and ambulance arrived, although it was only several minutes.

"Did she ever wake up?"

"No."

"Open her eyes?"

"No."

"Was she breathing before they got there?"

"She was, but later she stopped breathing."

Esther answers yes to Daniel's question about giving permission to All Children's Hospital to harvest her organs. This is a difficult decision for any parent to make, especially while the child is still technically alive, even though she may be medically brain-dead. And for Esther, at her young age, to be faced with making such a decision in the midst of this tragedy is devastating.

Kurpiers rises from his chair to cross-examine Esther, and she immediately becomes defensive. She sits a little taller and raises her head a little higher.

He asks when Maria was born, and how old Esther was at the time.

"On August 10, 2007. I was sixteen." She is not ashamed of this. (Pat had misstated earlier that Esther was seventeen when Maria was born. This discrepancy is not brought up by Kurpiers. Esther's birthday is in December.) Esther had dealt with the unexpected pregnancy and her parent's reaction back in the early part of 2007. She has put that behind her and her parents had accepted Maria with open arms. This case is about Maria, not about Esther. The defense could try and make it about Esther, but her history shows that she was not rebellious. She was a devoted and loving mother. The pregnancy was more a result of her naiveté, as she was so sheltered and close with her family. It took them all by surprise, although, for Esther, it should not have been so much as she knew the consequences of her intimacy with Javier. For any teenage girl, however, a positive pregnancy result can be a real shocker, with the mentality being, "It won't happen to me. I'll be more careful the next time."

Esther tells the court again that Maria's father resides in Pennsylvania. His name is not entered into the records. He is not relevant to the case. But she does describe how she and Patricia had travelled to Pennsylvania with Maria at the beginning of August of 2008 and spent four days there with a friend. Esther wanted Maria's father to see her and spend a little time with her even though the relationship between Javier and Esther was irreparably broken. She gives no details about this trip, and none are asked. Since it is now apparent to the defense that Javier had absolutely nothing to do with Maria's death, he is not mentioned again.

In a lighter moment for most of the courtroom, Kurpiers states that Esther took Maria to the YMCA while she attended school.

"No sir." She answers.

"No?"

"No, sir, it was the YWCA." A few hushed chuckles carry through the gallery. Kurpiers is not amused.

Maria was supposed to have started at Stephanie Spurgeon's day care on the twentieth of August, but Maria says that she didn't take her because "Ms. Spurgeon said she doesn't do the very first day of school—the twentieth—because she uses it for her own children [to get ready for their first day of school]."

"Did you or your mom call her the day before? If the records indicate that you called at 3:49 p.m.?"

"I don't remember," Esther replies quietly.

Nothing is said about what was relayed on the phone on the 3:49 p.m. call. By responding that she did not remember the call, Esther would also not remember what was said on the call. Spurgeon might have remembered, but of course she wouldn't testify. The response by Esther about it being a day that Spurgeon uses for preparing her own children for their first day of school was probably not what the defense was looking for. Were they hoping to show that Maria stayed home because she was ill? If so, the argument failed here. She was also seen by many people the evening of the twentieth at church and was obviously not sick.

Kurpiers asks Esther about Maria's sleeping habits, which have become intricately connected to that day in the day care already.

Esther tells the court that Maria would never be laid down to sleep. She was always rocked to sleep and held in her arms or her mom's arms.

"At night?"

"Of course."

Throughout her testimony, Esther responds to Kurpiers with many "Yes, sirs." They are not derogatory in tone, but they do indicate the distance that she has placed between herself and the defense attorney. Whether she knew it or not, this is an excellent way to respond to the "other side's" questioning because it can prevent the raising of voices or even bullying of the witness. Esther is very wise for her years, and the more I spoke with her, the more this became evident.

Kurpiers asks her about what happened on August 20, since Maria did not go to the day care.

She looks directly at him and curtly states that her mother took care of Maria while she went to school.

Then, some of the information that Kurpiers wanted to emphasize that was already in the records was reviewed. Perhaps he was looking for contradictions in Esther's testimony compared to her mother's. There was nothing that would alter the case.

Yes, she had to get up early to get to the bus. "It was not a problem for me."

She had called the Spurgeon home at around one thirty to check on Maria.

"The next time you saw Maria was approximately three o'clock?"

"I went back home [from school] and waited for my mom and Maria to come home." There was a problem. Her mom was beating on the door. She took Maria from her mom. She tried to open Maria's eyes and to hold her arms.

"Do you remember telling her you were trying to open her eyes? You were holding her arms?"

"Yes, sir."

"At any time, did you hand Maria back to your mother?"

"Yes, sir, so I could get dressed. I held her while I called 911. We were all trying to wake Maria up."

For anyone to try and recall events from a scene such as the one that took place in the Harris home three and a half years ago would be difficult to say the least. Esther and her mother were in panic mode, wondering what was wrong with little Maria and trying to do things to help her and also call for help. There must have been a lot of confusion about who had her at what point and who called 911 and when, since they both had done so. I don't believe that this chain of events changed the case in any way, since Maria was already unconscious when Pat arrived at home and had even stopped breathing at one point, according to the testimony of the paramedic. Going over these events would only seem to help the jury to picture this tragic scene more clearly.

Esther continues by describing how the paramedics who worked on Maria never came into the house. "I was holding Maria right there waiting for them—in the doorway.

"They physically took her from you?"

"Yes sir, and put her on the stretcher."

"She stopped breathing?"

"It was before the paramedics got there."

"How did you know?"

"Her stomach stopped going up and down...when I had her in my arms. It was maybe two minutes when I did not see her stomach moving up and down at all."

Kurpiers wants to distract the jury from this information because if they focus on Maria's stoppage of breathing before the paramedics arrived, it would indicate how grave the circumstances truly were. The two-minute time frame is not discussed at all. It could have been shorter, but it seemed like a long time for Esther because she was so frightened. So Kurpiers asks her if the situation was stressful. He would try and twist her response later in his closing arguments by saying that Esther was not stressed out, but it would not sound credible. Esther's responses to this and previous questions clearly indicate that the situation went far beyond stressful, and was in fact hysterical.

"I wouldn't call it *stressful*," Esther says, raising her voice. She has now become irritated, and I am hoping that she does not get angry at Kurpiers because that's what he wants. I hear a comment from behind and across the aisle from me in the gallery. Someone says about Esther that "she is just hostile."

It occurs to me that she is a mother who has lost her child in a most horrific way, but the protective mode has not left her voice and heart as she answers these difficult questions. Under this circumstance, most mothers would be somewhat hostile.

"I would call it a concerned mother who wants to know what's going on!" Esther tells how she was taken into the kitchen with her mother by one of the paramedics to get information. As this was happening, another paramedic was putting paddle stickers on Maria.

"What hospital did they take her to?"

"The closest one, which was Mease Countryside." The paramedics told Pat and Esther not to follow them because it was raining, and just to go at their own pace.

Then Kurpiers focuses on the falls that Maria had when she was learning to walk. Esther explains that Maria would normally fall on her butt. She had normal baby falls. Once she bumped her head on the wall. Esther called Dr. McCormick who told her what to look for. He said to just watch her.

"When did that fall happen?"

"When she was eight or nine months old."

"You had estimated six weeks prior?"

"I honestly don't remember."

"No further questions." Kurpiers wants to stop here to leave this particular incident hanging in the minds of the jury, to create reasonable doubt as to what could have caused her injuries. But six weeks is a long time to behave totally normally and then present with the type of injuries that Maria would have according to the expert witnesses who would be testifying soon. Even if the fall occurred when Maria was eleven months old, because according to what Patricia Harris stated earlier, that's when Maria began to walk, it still falls close to the six-week time reference made by Kurpiers.

But Brian Daniels has a couple of questions upon redirection to emphasize the timing of this fall. He asks the age that Maria started walking.

"Nine and one-half months old," Esther responds. (The difference between this time frame and Pat's eleven-month one could be that at nine and one-half months, Maria took her first step or two, and it wasn't until she was eleven months old that she started actually walking).

"Is that when she fell? When she started to walk?"

"Yes."

Daniels has just laid out to the jury that Maria, who had just turned a year old on August 10, eleven days before the day care date, had fallen approximately eleven weeks earlier according to Esther's testimony. If Kurpiers had wanted to pinpoint and memorialize the date of the fall because he considered it important to the case, he could ask for Dr. McCormick to return as a witness and indicate the date that Esther called his office to talk about the fall. But he did not do so. Maybe he already knew that Esther was correct in stating that the fall happened when Maria was nine and one-half months old. However, even if she was eleven months old, the fall would have happened over six weeks prior to August 21. And there was too much fresh and severe trauma present on the CT scan.

CHAPTER 7

DR. LUIS RODRIGUEZ is called to the stand by Holly
Grissinger. He is a pediatric neurosurgeon at All Children's
Hospital. Handsome and youthful, perhaps in his early to
midthirties, Dr. Rodriguez has an impressive curriculum vitae.
He graduated from the University of Michigan (my alma mater)
and did his residency there as well. He received a fellowship
in pediatric neurosurgery from the University of Utah. He has
published articles and given lectures, and he teaches residents
in neurosurgery training at All Children's Hospital. He is board
certified in pediatric neurology and neurology, having received
his fellowship by both oral and written exams and submitting a
caseload. Dr. Rodriguez's credentials are above and beyond that
of most pediatric neurosurgeons, and he is not bragging as he
states this information, but simply answers the questions regarding his education and designations as a matter of fact. He is also
a member of several neurological organizations.

Grissinger asks him if he sees children for all kinds of exams, and he says that he does. He doesn't evaluate a child presenting with nonaccidental trauma any differently than any other child. He gets a history from other doctors and paramedics, and assesses for life threatening conditions that may warrant surgery.

He explains that subdural hematomas (a bleeding occurring between the brain's protective dural layer and the brain) can be accidental, such as falling from a tree or a big height, or from a car accident.

"Is it normal to see external bruising [with a subdural hematoma]?"

"Yes."

Grissinger walks away from the podium, her voice crisp but conversational in tone. "Have you ever seen no external bruising with a subdural hematoma?"

"Yes."

"On August 21, 2008, you observed Maria Harris. What did you do when she first arrived?"

Dr. Rodriguez walks the court through his thorough neurological exam which included cranial and motor stimulus response exams, checking to see if Maria was awake or had loss of consciousness and looking over her imaging evaluations.

He ran through his normal list of possibilities with a case like Maria's. Would he need to operate? What type of procedure? Would she just need to be watched? In Maria's case, was she responsive?

Grissinger shows him his hospital records on Maria. He scans them quickly, verbally noting that she had been intubated and a machine was breathing for her, she had experienced seizures, her eyes deviated to the left side, and she was unresponsive for reasons unknown. She was not conscious at all during his exam.

He performed a cranial nerve exam and looked into her eyes for injury or elevated pressure. He observed that Maria had bilateral retinal hemorrhaging. He explained that this is an injury to the retina where vessels are broken and a bunch of red blotches are visible. He called in a pediatric ophthalmologist to do an exam.

Then the first piece of evidence is introduced: the CT scans of Maria's brain. The images are shown on a large screen at the front of the courtroom on the wall, just to the right of the jury. Dr. Rodriguez explains that the CT scan shows images that are "slices of X-ray from the base of the skull up. Like a loaf of bread." (There is a picture of a subdural hematoma CT in the photos section).

Dr. Rodriguez explains the images that are seen in the CT scan. He shows that there is a thickening in the front area of Maria's brain where the subdural hematoma splits the two hemispheres. This is called the false cerebrum. Blood is all along the false cerebrum. "This is a classic picture," he says. "When veins are torn, there is bleeding along the false cerebrum." He indicates other areas that are darker, like shadows on the photos. He tells the court that these areas denote brain injuries. They are hyperdense areas showing trauma and a lack of oxygen. No determination was made as to what caused them.

Next, there is a crucial observation that is key to the state's case against Stephanie Spurgeon. Dr. Rodriguez says that the time of this subdural hematoma makes it acute. (An acute subdural hematoma is a collection of blood that is clotting below the inner layer of the dura but outside the actual brain and its protective arachnoid membrane.) This means it happened within a short period of time of the CT scan. He knows this because, as he points out on one of the pictures, the bleeding looks bright like the skull. He also explains areas that are referred to as watershed areas. These are the pathways for blood flows through the brain—from big veins to the frontal lobes. Certain areas exist where these two overlap. If there is an issue with blood flow to the head, it will happen in the watershed areas.

Holly Grissinger asks about the physical response from a subdural hematoma.

"There is no chance a child could have walked around for a period of time after sustaining this subdural hematoma," Dr. Rodriguez responds.

"Not due to any underlying head conditions?"

"Due to nonaccidental trauma." He explains that it is the nature of where the blood is and how you get that to happen. "You only get this kind of head injury when those blood vessels are breaching from the brain into the false cerebrum, and it is from shaking." So here, Dr. Rodriguez, who has examined numerous pediatric victims of subdural hematomas, both acute and chronic, has introduced SBS into the mix. This is the first time it is mentioned by a witness. At this point in his examination, Maria was still living so he would not know that it would not be listed as her cause of death. But according to his observations, Maria's brain image on the CT scan exhibited the classic signs that her brain had been shaken back and forth within the skull to the point where the blood from torn vessels in her brain had seeped out into the false cerebrum below the surface of the dura, the protective layer underneath the skull.

Grissinger asks him if routine well-baby vaccinations could have caused the injury.

"No," he answers to both this and to whether diabetes could have caused it.

"It only could be caused by the tearing of bridging veins due to shaking back and forth leading to unconsciousness." He also notes that moaning and response to certain stimuli can still happen when a person is unconscious. This testimony is important to remember because these torn bridging veins are mentioned throughout the trial, and consistently the witnesses will agree that they can only be torn by physical trauma and not by an illness or metabolic condition.

Dr. Rodriguez discusses how young children have heads that are a much higher percentage of body height than adults. Their heads are bigger in relation to their bodies. "As we grow, we develop strength to hold up the head. In a child, the neck muscles and ligaments are not as well developed and much more apt to injure the head with rapid movement." This comment will become very important later on when the defense introduces witnesses who say that Maria could not have been shaken because there were no injuries evident in her neck. The medical examiner will also testify that he saw no neck injuries at autopsy and explain why he never uses the term *shaken baby syndrome* as a cause of death.

It is here that I also disagree with Dr. Rodriguez in part, even though I am not an expert at all. I agree with testimony that is yet to come about rapid acceleration/deceleration of the head when it hits a solid but soft object. This sudden stopping of the motion of the head would explain why there were no neck injuries noted. From my own uninformed position at the time, having not yet researched SBS, but having been involved in a car accident in my thirties where I sustained severe neck injuries, I know that they often do not show up on any scan or X-ray. Whiplash seldom if ever does. Whiplash is rapid acceleration/deceleration of a person's head when the car is hit from behind, throwing the head forward, then back, which mimics shaking fairly well but not a repetitive shaking. The neck injuries would not necessarily be visible in either case. But Maria's injuries, as testimony will show, stemmed from something beyond mere shaking.

Maria's head would possibly not have been shaken back and forth, but instead thrown forward into a mattress or other pliable surface where it abruptly stopped. Or, she could have first been shaken and then thrown, pushed, shoved, or slammed down. The brain, sheltered in its protective cover and layer of fluids, would have kept going, slamming into the dura and the skull, tearing the bridging veins, and resulting in the acute subdural hematoma. This would become my belief of what happened to Maria Harris, but I did not come up with this theory on my own. Other witnesses testifying for the state painted this picture from various points of view based on their fields of expertise. I simply took a virtual step back and thought about them in summary, coming up with the above scenario, which seems more plausible than any alternative that the defense will attempt to introduce.

Grissinger changes course before turning her witness over to the defense. "Would you expect a subdural hematoma to be accompanied by a skull fracture?"

"Not necessarily."

"Do you work in a vacuum?"

"No."

"Do you look at all doctor input, exams, and history?"

"Yes."

And the dramatic summation questions: "Do you believe that this was nonaccidental trauma?"

"Yes."

"Were the seizures related to the subdural hematoma?"

"Yes—the trauma."

So the first expert witness has just finished testifying for the state who would indicate that Maria's injuries were not the result of an accident. He would not be the last.

CHAPTER 8

RON KURPIERS APPEARS aggressive but not intimidating as he quickly gets to his feet and approaches Dr. Rodriguez. "In looking at your notes, you ordered a CT scan the next day."

"That was the CT scan from the outside hospital," Dr. Rodriguez replies, correcting Kurpiers, meaning the scan that he has in his notes from Countryside Mease Hospital.

"Why do you order a second one?"

"We continue to monitor the patient. Knowing injuries can progress, we repeat to be sure that nothing needs to be done."

"A subdural hematoma can rebleed, right?"

"No, not this kind—"

"Is it your testimony," Kurpiers interrupts, "that no subdural hematoma can rebleed?"

"Not this kind." Then Dr. Rodriguez explains that *acute* means "recent" and *chronic* means "two to four weeks ago."

"Have you ever seen a chronic subdural?" Kurpiers asks.

"Many times," the doctor responds.

"Have you ever seen one that becomes acute?"

"No."

Maria Harris's subdural hematoma was diagnosed as acute, meaning it had happened recently. It also meant that it wasn't a result of an illness, but instead of a sudden trauma. Dr. Rodriguez neglects to add this important difference between chronic and acute. Kurpiers asks a question that he probably wanted a different answer to, wanting to know if an older (chronic) subdural hematoma could start bleeding fresh and become acute. It is just a rephrasing of the earlier question that he asked, whether a subdural hematoma could rebleed. Dr. Rodriguez indicated that the type that Maria had could not rebleed. So now, it has been established by Dr. Rodriguez that chronic subdural hematomas cannot become "fresh" and rebleed, and acute subdural hematomas cannot rebleed. Then what types of subdural hematomas *do* rebleed? If Kurpiers notices a discrepancy here that was introduced with answers to his own questions, he does not pounce on it. I would have also asked a reverse question: "In order for a chronic subdural hematoma to be labeled as chronic, it needs to be weeks old. Wouldn't all subdural hematomas at one time be 'fresh' or acute, and then later become chronic with time going by?" But I already knew that this definition would also depend on the injury itself and how traumatic it was, or if it was caused by an illness.

Instead, Kurpiers' line of questioning continues with chronic subdural hematomas and how they are formed.

In response to these questions, Dr. Rodriguez describes in detail how blood collects in the subdural space between the brain and the skull lining. "The fluid gets thicker. People can walk around with subdural hematomas. There are often no symptoms."

"Then it can start bleeding, right?" Kurpiers tries to trap Dr. Rodriguez on the bleeding issue.

"No," he answers emphatically. "Bridging veins can tear and then an acute subdural hematoma can occur *on top* of the chronic." Dr. Rodriguez has basically reiterated that chronic subdural hematomas do not start bleeding again. They have just been there for a while. It seems to me to be a matter of semantics because the new acute subdural that is forming on top of the chronic would become chronic with time if it is not severe enough to kill the person. I remind myself at this point why I did not go to med school.

Kurpiers pointedly asks Dr. Rodriguez, "Do you remember talking to Detective Lyons?"

"No, it was four years ago."

Kurpiers goes to his desk and picks up some papers, which he hands to Dr. Rodriguez. "Does that refresh your memory?"

"No," the doctor says.

"That's not your written statement, is it?"

"No." (It must have been one of the evasive police reports that we would hear so little about).

"Is it possible that whatever caused the subdural hematoma in this kid occurred six to twelve hours earlier?" Kurpiers would frequently refer to Maria as "the kid" or "this kid" for the first few days of the trial. Then he switched to child, perhaps being told by Brunvand that "kid" was not a good word to use for the jury. Because I personally found it offensive, I will no longer put it in writing in Kurpiers' statements, but suffice it to say, he did use the terms several times a day for a while. (Later on, the medical examiner who testified as a witness for the state would also use the word "kid" when referring to Maria or a child in general).

"Yes," Dr. Rodriguez replies. "But I am not able to tell the exact time. I operate. I'm not a neurologist."

"You're not board certified in radiology. When you analyzed the CT scan, you were not board certified to read that." Kurpiers states this point. It is not a question.

Dr. Rodriguez goes into a discussion of epidural hematomas, a type of chronic hematoma, and how a person can have a lucid interval (where he is awake and aware), lose consciousness, come to, lose consciousness again, and then can die if nothing is done.

Kurpiers asks him if anyone with a *chronic* subdural hematoma can have a lucid interval.

"Many come in conscious because they may not have lost consciousness." (The injury was not acute.)

Next, a round of questioning ensues where Dr. Rodriguez describes the eyes as an extension of the brain, the optic nerve, and intercranial pressure. He says when there is this pressure, you expect to see a subdural hematoma and the swelling of the optic nerve, but not retinal hemorrhaging. (They are discussing chronic hematomas. Acute ones would often present with retinal hemorrhaging because of the trauma that caused them.)

Kurpiers asks about the fontanel, and Dr. Rodriguez explains that the fontanel "is a soft spot on top of a baby's head. Some babies are born with closed fontanels."

"This baby's fontanel was closed, right?" (It likely was as she was a year old.)

"I don't know," Dr. Rodriguez replies. "I didn't note this." I don't know where Kurpiers was headed by asking about the fontanel. A closed fontanel would seem to indicate that it would be more difficult to sustain an injury causing a brain bleed because the skull has closed up the only vulnerable soft area of the head. But this does not come up again.

Kurpiers and Rodriguez volley questions and answers back and forth regarding Maria's condition at the hospital. Kurpiers asks him if he checked for cervical spine abnormalities. (If apparent, this could indicate that Maria had been shaken.) But the doctor says, "I don't think we did."

Kurpiers asks, "Did you note that the caudate nucleus CT scan from Mease had a hemorrhage on the left caudate—a three-centimeter tear?"

"No. A *point*-three-centimeter tear. Many times I don't always agree with what the radiologists say."

Smirking at this response, Kurpiers says, "The left caudate nucleus is not in front of the brain. It's in a deep portion of the brain, isn't it?"

"Yes."

After this response by Rodriguez, Kurpiers drops the whole caudate nucleus discussion, and I wonder why it was even brought up in the first place. Was he trying to showcase knowledge of brain injuries? If it was something that would favor an argument by the defense, they didn't pursue it. Perhaps it was because the size of the tear was much smaller than Kurpiers stated that it no longer was a valid point.

"It was mentioned at the outside hospital that blood gas showed acidosis," Kurpiers states.

The doctor answers this statement by clarifying it. "It shows the acidity of blood, the oxygen levels."

"How long was this child without air?"

"I don't know."

Ron Kurpiers says, "No further questions," and returns to his seat.

There is a short redirect from the state where Dr. Rodriguez is asked if he had ever seen a hematoma of this nature. Yes, he had. Could it releak blood? No, there would be no lucid interval, which is classic of an *epidural hematoma*, not the acute subdural one that Maria had.

An epidural hematoma was the type that resulted when actress Natasha Richardson had a freak skiing accident in 2010. She was lucid after the accident, with no symptoms. Then after about an hour, she developed a pounding headache, eventually losing consciousness and dying after being taken off life support.[1] This bleed occurred between the brain and skull, not between the subdural lining and the brain as is the case with a subdural hematoma. The state wanted to make it clear that Maria's hematoma was not the type that could have allowed her to remain lucid for a while before losing consciousness.

Dr. Rodriguez again explains rebleeding; that with a chronic subdural hematoma, the body absorbs the blood so that on the scan, the area looks darker, not bright. (Bright would indicate fresh blood.) He says that you can get another bleed around it, but *that* spot does not rebleed.

Grissinger asks the doctor, "Is it possible that Maria Harris had that injury and then walked and talked and played and ate?"

"No."

It was time to stop. Both sides were worn thin with subdural hematoma types and volleying between chronic and acute.

The trial would resume in the morning. But prior to that, I stop in the courthouse cafeteria. I notice that Clyde, Patricia, and Esther are seated off to one side. Pat had already told me that it was best not to make contact with her either publically or privately until the end of the trial. We had known not to cross certain boundaries in our earlier interviews, and we had stuck to that, but now that the trial was underway, it was especially important that I did not acknowledge them. We did not want to jeopardize the trial in any way, regardless of how harmless a simple nod or hello might have appeared. For all practical purposes, my interviews with them were on hold until after the verdict when I could speak freely to them.

CHAPTER 9

I FIRST MET the Harrises when my husband and I were looking for another church around 2003. They were in the Sunday
school class of a church we rather liked, but it didn't have a permanent pastor in place since the former one had retired. We
didn't stay at that church and ended up joining the one where
we are members now, Bible Baptist Church in Palm Harbor. The
Harrises followed a couple of years later, and Pat and I became
fast friends. So it was with deep sadness that I tried to comfort
my friend through the tragedy of her granddaughter's injuries
and death soon after.

During the spring following Maria's death, I sat down with
Pat and Esther to talk about the idea of a book about her, and to
put some thoughts on paper. By mutual agreement in advance,
we would not discuss anything pertinent to the case because the
Harrises obviously did not want to jeopardize anything that the
police and their attorney, Brian Daniels, were working on. Holly
Grissinger had not yet been assigned to the case. What we did

talk about in that first meeting was a little bit of Harris family history.

Pat was born Patricia Lawson in March of 1954 in Bluefield, West Virginia, then a very tiny community. Pat was doted on by her parents because she was an only child. Her father worked the second shift on the railroad when she was young, so Pat and "Mommy" did everything together. Daddy felt badly that he was missing Pat's growing up years, so when she reached the seventh grade, he was able to give up the second shift and move to the first shift, allowing him to be home with his wife and daughter in the evenings. He especially enjoyed helping Pat with homework. It was harder on Mommy though, because she wasn't used to having him around and she was a strong and independent woman. When Daddy eventually retired, she went to work at the lunch counter at the local supermarket. She said jokingly that she took this job so she wouldn't feel like killing her husband for being underfoot, but she really didn't want to be home with him sitting around all day.

Pat was especially precious to her parents not only because she was an only child, but because they were married eleven years before Pat was born. Her mother was already thirty-two, and in those days, she was viewed as being almost past childbearing age since she hadn't gotten pregnant yet. Pat wanted to be an only child. She loved the attention and didn't want to share it with anyone. Mommy was advised by her doctor not to have any more children. Her delivery of Pat had been a labor that took four days and three nights, and it had nearly killed her. No treatments had been given. Years later, after Pat lost her mother, she wished she would have had someone to share that grief with, a sister or brother. Clyde couldn't understand the depth of Pat's sadness when her mother died. His family had never been that close-knit.

At one point, Pat's mother took a job caring for elderly people, just like Pat does now. Pat didn't like having her mother gone from the house while she was still in junior high, but she saw

God's hand in it and it helped both her and Daddy become more independent. It also planted in her a caring heart for the elderly.

Clyde, or Buster as all his family calls him, was born in February of 1955. He had a private family life. Like Pat, he was also born in Bluefield. In fact, they attended the same high school, but Pat didn't really know Buster personally. He lived on Stadium Drive, and she lived on Grassy Branch Road. He had also spent part of his growing up years in Florida.

Pat remembers seeing Buster's trophies in the high school showcase. He was very shy and she doesn't remember talking to him then, but she knew his sister, Sandy. Pat was friends with a lady named Pearl Grubb who was Buster and Sandy's grandmother. At the time, that connection didn't mean anything to Pat. But one day, she was at Pearl's home and she recognized Buster and Sandy among the people in photos on Pearl's wall. By this time, they had all graduated high school; Pat, the year before Buster. He was in the service. An idea occurred to Pearl. She asked Pat if she would be willing to escort Buster around and keep him company when he came home on leave. All his friends had left town, and there was no one around for him to talk to or hang out with. Pat, who was always outgoing and friendly, thought it would be fun to do this for her friend. But soon, to everyone's great surprise, especially Pat herself, they started dating! The families didn't realize that they were going to get serious so quickly since they were both so young and Buster was so shy. Pat was twenty-one, and Buster was twenty. They dated for three months, and then they got married! Buster jokes, "She paid me to marry her." They were, for all practical purposes, barely adults.

They wed on May 17, 1975, which was Buster's grandmother's birthday, at the church Pat grew up in and Buster attended as a teenager—Bailey Memorial Baptist Church. The preacher, Pat easily recalls, was Alton Jessie. (The church is still there, but has since changed names to Cumberland Heights Baptist Church.) Back then, Bluefield was a town of about twelve thousand people, and most everyone knew everyone else.

People did marry younger then, but since Buster was in the service, it looked like Pat would have to leave home. She was too young, and this worried her parents. Pearl was upset too. They needn't have worried about that though. Forty-five days after they were married, Buster left for Korea for a year, and Pat stayed behind with her parents. Her marriage seemed almost like a dream to her after he left.

But when that year was up, Buster's new station was at Little Rock Air Force Base in Jacksonville, Arkansas. Pat went there to be with him, and they lived there happily for three years. She would go back to visit with her parents for two to three months at a time each year. She loved being on her own with her new husband. But it was even better when he was finally out of the service after his four years of duty had ended. They moved back to Bluefield to start a home together and remained there for ten years. Buster got a good job with the Sanitary Board of Bluefield in wastewater management, a skill he was trained for in the military.

There was one thing though, for most of those years in Bluefield that concerned Pat. She, like her mother before her, was having a difficult time conceiving a child. In addition to this, Mommy fell ill to colon cancer and went through three surgeries over a period of years. Pat talked to her on the phone as often as she could when she was not with her. To this day, she still feels the urge to pick up the phone and call her mother, although she died in 1989 at the age of sixty-seven.

Mommy did have one wish. She wanted to live to see a grandchild. And she did live to see Christopher, who was born in July of 1987. Almost exactly like her parents, Pat's child was born twelve years after she was married, and she had spent almost all of the first year away from her husband.

Pat still had Daddy in her life, and she was grateful for that. In 1989, Buster got a wonderful job offer in Chambersburg, Pennsylvania, and the young family relocated there. (That fateful move, so innocuous at the time, would reach down through two future generations and ultimately be ground zero for the chain of events leading to the death of little Maria Harris.)

Daddy would visit his daughter and her family for three or four months at a time in the summer. He was able to do this for fourteen years! Daddy had numerous health problems, but he seemed to battle them as if they belonged to someone else. By the time he reached age eighty-one, he had acquired adult-onset diabetes, heart disease, thyroid failures, circulatory problems, and COPD from years of smoking. Yet, he could swim the length of a thirty-three-foot pool all underwater!

Daddy eventually died from complications of hip surgery. He still remains a powerful figure in Pat's memory. She loved both her parents dearly, and perhaps because of how they brought her up, sheltering her and showering her with love, she wanted to protect her granddaughter Maria in much the same way. Admittedly, Maria was quite spoiled, but this has no bearing on what happened to her. There is no excuse for ever abusing a child. Besides, grandparents spoil their grandchildren. I see it every day, and I will probably do the same.

Buster got transferred to Florida in 2002 with the fertilizer company that he still works for as of this writing. He is invaluable to them and has worked his way up within the firm as a dedicated and honest employee. He provided a comfortable, albeit not extravagant, lifestyle for his family and continues to do so. Pat followed him ten months later because she had to stay behind in Pennsylvania until the house sold and the children were out of school that year. Esther had been born in December of 1990.

Esther Marie Harris was supposed to have been named Rita Victoria, picked by Pat's father, but Pat's mother-in-law hated it. So in an unusual move, Pat and Buster asked their three-and-a-half-year-old son, Christopher, what to name her, and he said Esther Marie. The other choice was Kristin Hope, which would have been Christopher's name had he been a girl. So Esther was named by her brother. Not many people can make that claim! Unfortunately, she shares a middle name with the defendant, Stephanie Marie Spurgeon, in one of the many atypical features of this case.

CHAPTER 10

FEBRUARY 8, 2012

IN THE COURTROOM, the jury files in after Judge Newton has entered and asks for them to be brought in. They look tired, but other than that, their faces reveal nothing about what they have been exposed to so far in this case.

The state calls Dr. Jon Thogmartin, who would become a crucial witness later on after the trial has concluded in an unusual turn of events. Dr. Thogmartin is tall and gaunt, the imagined depiction of a medical examiner becoming reality before the courtroom spectators and jury. He has a balding, shaved head; wears wire-rimmed glasses that give him an intellectual look; and has the build of a runner. He does not appear wrinkled, but he is not young. He looks to be somewhere between late forties and early fifties. He has that science-guy look, and his sharp wit and ability to recall information will later put the defense on guard.

Dr. Thogmartin is the medical examiner for district 6. He came to Florida from San Antonio in 1995 when he finished his residency. He was involved in forensic science in Miami for a year. He is board certified in his field which includes forensic pathology (his primary practice), anatomical pathology, and clinical pathology. He has written several articles in his field.

Holly Grissinger asks him some pertinent questions regarding his experience as an ME. She inquires as to how many autopsies he has performed.

"Thirty-five hundred to four thousand," Thogmartin says without a trace of arrogance.

He has seen trauma, and he goes on to describe the five manners of death that are used by medical examiners. He notes that although there are five manners of death, there are infinite causes.

The most common manner of death is by natural causes. This is the result when someone dies from an illness or a heart attack, stroke, etc. The next manner is by accident, and numerous accidents result in deaths every day. They include car or motorcycle accidents, or falling off a ladder, a sports collision, or a freak accident to name a few. Suicide comes next, and of course, there are many ways for it to happen. Following suicide is homicide. The last category of manner of death is "undetermined," where it can't be determined how a body died or perhaps only a skeleton was found.

"In this case," Grissinger says, "you did an autopsy on August 30, 2008—on Maria Harris."

"Yes."

She asks him if he was given any information about Maria's case.

Dr. Thogmartin explains that it is a rare case where you just have a body in a field. "With Maria, you already have information that clinical physicians know. Medical records come in with the body. More than one hospital is involved. There are supplemental requests. Some end up being redundant. It is an ongoing process, but you don't go in blind."

Holly starts to say, "You have all the records—"

Dr. Thogmartin is anxious to explain that, "I can't say I have them all, but I have a big pack."

Holly indicates that this gives him the power to perform the autopsy.

He says, "It obligates anyone to have information to provide it, or it's a criminal offense."

"Did you document her height and weight?"

"Yes."

"She was approximately a year old?"

"Yes."

"What was her weight?"

Dr. Thogmartin looks it up in his bulk of information that he has brought with him to the stand. "It's not her living weight due to organ donation, swelling, etc. She was seventeen pounds and thirty-one inches tall.

"Did you do an external exam?"

"It's routine to start with an external exam. I note what they look like, bruises. They are treated pretty much like anyone else. Maria had a big surgical incision in her anterior torso. There were numerous things used for medical intervention...She had a head injury and brain death declaration. Her vascular organs had been transplanted to help out other children.

"She looked good. A head full of hair, no bruises or injuries from trauma."

"Would you have expected to see bruising after seven days?"

"My exam is much better. It is better if a person dies immediately. My exam becomes less valuable with each passing day. With blunt head trauma, there is impact. A bruise will fade, will lose value. There was nothing at the autopsy to indicate a bruise."

(Maria had thick black hair and a lot of it. It would have been easy to miss scalp bruising while she was alive. Also, scalp bruises do not easily show up externally, and if she struck a soft object, a bruise might not show even if her head had been shaved shortly after the injury, which it was not.)

Holly asks what organs were donated, and Thogmartin says, "The lungs were still there. The heart, liver, kidneys, and part of the spleen, and part of the pancreas were donated or were used for testing."

"Did this affect the determination and cause and manner of death?"

"Not in a case like this. Everything that was going on was in her head. Her lungs were not good—leave them." Dr. Thogmartin had reasonable assuredness that the organs in the torso were good.

"The lungs were left behind?"

"Yes, in general terms, they looked bad by radiography. They weren't well aerated. There were areas of pneumonia. When you are on a respirator for seven days, that's pretty typical."

Several years ago, I had gone into the hospital for surgery. I did not have pneumonia when I went in, but after three days on my back, unable to turn over, I did develop a mild case. It is not a stretch to imagine how this can happen due to immobility and exposure to so many germs in a hospital, combined with being on a respirator for seven days.

In the courtroom, Holly Grissinger inquires about Maria's internal examination at autopsy. "Was there an area on Maria's head that was flat?"

"Back-sleepers are flat-headed kids. For much of her life, she slept on her back. It's quite common."

"Were there any internal signs of injury?"

"No, not on the body."

"Were you aware that Maria was brought in with a subdural hematoma and acute retinal hemorrhages?"

"I am skeptical sometimes about them, so I am looking for them with experts to confirm."

Next, Dr. Thogmartin is asked to explain each photo in a series that he took at the autopsy. He talks about the photo on the top left, explaining that it is the front of her brain after bone and the top part of Maria's skull has been removed. There is dura mater protruding from the brain. The picture showed what the outside of the dura looked like.

The next picture is the same orientation without the dura present, showing blood that should not be there.

The picture on the lower left has the dura removed, and in the left meninges, there is a subdural clot present that should not be there. It is a subarachnoid hemorrhage. It should not be there, but Dr. Thogmartin says that it is typical to find the clot and the hemorrhage together.

The fourth picture reveals a subdural hematoma that had occurred earlier. It shows the typical bleeding between the hemispheres.

These photos are very graphic, but unless one is an expert, he would not be able to interpret what he is looking at. Dr. Thogmartin is good at bringing the information down to the level of most people who are not medical experts without insulting us.

Thogmartin explains that he sent Maria's brain to Dr. Nelson for further evaluation. The Lions Eyebank preserved Maria's eyes and sent them to an ocular pathologist.

Grissinger continues her questioning after the explanations of the photos. "There were no rib or spine fractures?"

Dr. Thogmartin shakes his head. "Normal development," he responds.

"When you are looking at medical documents at autopsy, do you look at it all together?"

"Yes. This case was not finalized until December thirteenth, two thousand and eight."

"What information—why did it take so long?"

"The slowest was the report on the eyes." Dr. Thogmartin explains that he then needs to re-review all of the information, and the police reports, and then certify the case.

Grissinger gets to the heart of the questioning by asking Dr. Thogmartin for his expert conclusions on subdural hematomas. "What causes a subdural hematoma?"

He relates to the court that he looked at the history and circumstances surrounding this case and that "accelerated, stopped, decelerated rapid movement of the head contributed to this case. I've never seen impact [evidenced by Maria's external appearance], but the object [she was shoved or pushed into] was not hard enough to cause a fracture." This theme would recur throughout the trial and gradually shift from the shaking back and forth to the actual suspected impact itself.

Holly clarifies, "You've ruled out all natural causes."

"She did not have chronic diabetes," he concludes. "She did have high glucose, but that's not unusual with stress trauma. The body pumps out glucagon." Dr. Thogmartin turns slightly and explains this directly to the jury. "There is insulin resistance due to trauma as a result of the brain bleed."

He has just demonstrated that it was not the high glucose levels that led to the brain bleed, but the injury and subsequent bleeding from the trauma that caused enough stress to significantly raise Maria's glucose number. The number did not stay high. Children in diabetic comas or states of unconsciousness are often so far gone that the number cannot be lowered even with emergency insulin treatment. Maria's number did come down, but she did not ever become alert again.

WebMD has a detailed description of subdural hematomas and what causes them. In the case of acute subdurals, diabetes is not even mentioned. What is mentioned is:

> A subdural hematoma is a collection of blood outside the brain. Subdural hematomas are usually caused by severe head injuries. The bleeding and increased pressure on the brain from a subdural hematoma can be life-threatening. Some subdural hematomas stop and resolve spontaneously; others require surgical drainage…Subdural hematoma is usually caused by a head injury, such as from a fall, motor vehicle collision, or an assault. The sudden blow to the head tears blood vessels that run along the

surface of the brain. This is referred to as an acute subdural hematoma.

(WebMD. "Subdural Hematoma: Symptoms, Causes, and Treatments. webmd.com)

Dr. Thogmartin tells the court that he is not a trauma surgeon or an endocrinologist. (Endocrinologists are the specialists who treat diabetes.) "Her blood chemistry was way off. [She was showing] fight or flight response. I see it all the time. Her subdural was not caused by diabetes."

Grissinger wants to know what the cause was.

"Blunt head trauma," Dr. Thogmartin states.

"What was the manner of death?"

"Homicide."

During this part of the trial, Stephanie Spurgeon was charged with murder in the first degree. No other conviction possibility had yet been introduced by Judge Newton. Everyone in the courtroom, with the possible exception of the attorneys and the judge, believed that Spurgeon would either get charged with murder or she would walk.

This belief made Dr. Thogmartin's testimony especially critical, as his information could become the reason that could cause Spurgeon to be sentenced to life in prison, the punishment for first-degree murder.

Thogmartin explains that he only has five choices for manner of death. "If there is no explanation, I don't argue for accidental death. She didn't do it to herself. So you are left with homicide versus accident. There were no reports of accidental head trauma. So by process of elimination, you are left with homicide."

(If Maria's injury had been an accident, Spurgeon, out of fear or just not realizing how bad it was, made the crucial mistake of not calling for medical assistance right away. Acute subdural hematomas, if treated early enough, can be relieved of intracranial pressure by draining off the blood, or by surgical removal of any large clots.[2] Delaying this treatment caused Maria's brain to swell within her skull to the point that it was too late to do anything to alleviate the pressure. Hours had gone by since she went down for her nap at noon or twelve thirty.)

Grissinger asks Dr. Thogmartin if he had viewed any photos of the scene.

"I am unfamiliar with the environment. The caregiver, I am unfamiliar with her. This is a walking, talking toddler. I am looking for an explanation for her to induce her own head trauma. There were [sic] none." He gives possible examples, such as Maria pulling down a television on her head, taking a "header" (a fall from a high enough place to injure her head), or pulling over a bookcase on herself. But "there were no abrasions. There was insufficient force to fracture the skull."

As I consider Dr. Thogmartin's testimony, I wonder if the jury will be able to see photos or a schematic of Spurgeon's home day care It would seem that this information would be quite helpful. Such evidence is usually presented so that a jury will be able to visualize the scene. Where was the Pack 'n Play situated? What other furniture was in that room? What other purpose did it serve? How close was it to the kitchen? How was Spurgeon able to keep her eye on multiple children at the same time if they were in different places in and maybe outside of the house? Such visual information would not be exhibited at this trial; however, I was very enlightened when I was able to find out a little about it later on.

In wrapping up her questioning, Grissinger hones in on the vital information that Dr. Thogmartin had mentioned in his testimony—the determination of cause and manner of death.

He states, "I can come up with cause without knowing anything about them [sic] or how it occurred. Manner of death is the circumstance. I need to know what occurred. If you don't know it, I do it by process of elimination."

"So," Grissinger asks, "it was homicide?"

"Yes," Dr. Thogmartin responds without hesitation.

"Your witness."

CHAPTER 11

I CAN TELL that Ron Kurpiers is overtly anxious to question Dr. Thogmartin, and he doesn't disappoint. "Your autopsy was on August 30, but the report was written on December 19!"

"Yes."

"Why the delay? Were you reviewing the records?"

"It was the eye bank. Generally they're the ones—"

Kurpiers interrupts. "Did you review the records [from Mease hospital]?"

"Yes."

"From All Children's Hospital?"

"Yes. When a person dies, we get those records with the body and they will be there."

"Did you get birth records?"

"I can't recall."

"Police records?"

"Yes." Thogmartin is not going to volunteer much information to Ron Kurpiers freely. He is making him dig for it.

"You based your opinion on reading the police reports?"
"No."
"You didn't interview anyone?"
"No."
Kurpiers then asks him if he had interviewed Stephanie Spurgeon, Patricia Harris, Esther Harris, or Clyde Harris, formed as an individual question for each person. Thogmartin responds with no each time, solidifying that word, *no*, in the minds of the jury.

Then Kurpiers obtains several more mostly negative responses from the medical examiner.

And then, "Did you review interviews of Patricia Harris?"
"Yes."
"Esther Harris?"
"I don't recall."
"Dr. Sally Smith?" (Who would soon be called to testify)
"No."
"Any of the doctors at Mease?"
"No, not directly."
"Any of the All Children's Hospital doctors?"
"No."
Kurpiers pins Thogmartin down with a question that he has been leading up to, one that goes off in a different yet familiar direction. "Ever heard the phrase, 'shaken baby syndrome?'"

Thogmartin here responds with a no. He must have assumed that Kurpiers meant it in connection with this case because he obviously would have heard of the term due to his line of work.

"Do you believe in it?" Kurpiers asks. (A less vague query might have been asked: "Do you believe that the syndrome is a real medical condition?")

Thogmartin hesitates, formulating his answer. "It would be bad to 'do a kid' that way. There would be neck trouble. Most of my colleagues don't use that term. Pediatricians use it but not in my field."

"You've never seen a shaken baby case?"

"I've never used one on a death certificate."

"Isn't it true that you've seen more lightning strikes?" (This area of Florida is known as the lightning capital of the world, so it would not be surprising to see several deaths a month resulting from lightning strikes or the after effects of them.)

"Yes, and bee stings."

Kurpiers asks Dr. Thogmartin about the cause of death he listed on Maria's death certificate—blunt head trauma.

"Yes, that's the wording I chose."

"Bruising," Kurpiers says. "You'd lost a lot of value."

"Yes. Artifacts created [bruises], heal. The exam has less value. It is critical to have the medical records."

"What do you deem to be essential?" Kurpiers is referring to the medical records.

"In her case, a pretty good thickness of them." Thogmartin goes on to mention that there was not a single bruise noted, but generally the doctors' exams are not as good as his. "Pediatricians are the primary diagnosers. They do not shave the head and do not examine the scalp. You cannot take them at their word."

"A host of doctors poured over the diagnosis of *this kid*...then it gets to you."

"Yes."

Dr. Thogmartin reiterates that there were no cutaneous or skin bruises noted pre or postdeath, and that there were no fractures at all.

The defense emphasizes that what happened to Maria occurred at least seven days prior to her death.

Dr. Thogmartin explains that "you can anatomically date a subdural hematoma within a range of days, but days become less valuable and...circumstances become more valuable." Here he is trying to downplay pinpointing exactly when the acute subdural hematoma occurred and emphasize that how it happened is more important in determining cause of death. "Anatomically, I leave dating of subdurals to the neurologist. In my opinion, it occurred on the day of unresponsiveness...common sense-wise, when she became comatose."

Kurpiers tries to pin him down by asking for the exact time of day that the injury occurred, but Thogmartin says that he doesn't know. Then he asks the medical examiner if he made any determination with respect to Maria having diabetes. Thogmartin tells him that there is nothing he can do to determine that because glucose levels fall after death. He explains that high blood glucose spills into the urine. It's not supposed to be there.

Kurpiers asks if there would be kidney damage.

"Eventually, after years."

"How would you know that?" Kurpiers' voice takes on an accusatory tone. "You didn't analyze the kidneys."

"They were removed. They are in someone else now. They are okay."

"How do you know that?"

"They were removed. They are okay."

Kurpiers does not give up on the kidneys. "How do you know that?"

At this point, the camera guy from a local affiliate who is one row in front of me turns around, looks at me, and rolls his eyes.

Thogmartin, not taking the bait to be goaded into becoming defensive, responds, "I don't. It's common sense. The transplant center would not use them if they were not okay. I would vote that it's much more likely that they are all right."

Kurpiers moves on to another area of questioning. I think his purpose was not so much to point out that Thogmartin could not prove the kidneys were "okay," but rather, to upset him or throw him off guard. It didn't work. Thogmartin has testified in hundreds of cases, and he is not easily ruffled.

Kurpiers asks him if he submitted anything to the endocrinologist and he replies that he did not.

"Did you analyze her eyes?"

"Someone else did."

"They came back and reported to you?"

"That's correct."

Kurpiers states that Dr. Nelson's report showed early organization of a subdural hematoma and massive cerebral edema.

"Yes, I saw that. It's typical of someone who has this injury." He then names other situations where the brain swells or doesn't swell.

"There was brain swelling," Kurpiers says.

"There was loss of oxygen. The key is yes, there was damage, herniation of the brain. It squeezes through the foramen magnum. (This is the area where the spinal column attaches to the skull.) All sorts of things happen. There is less blood flow. You end up with a swollen, mushy, soft brain."

"The brain weighed much more?"

"Yes. It is to be expected. Anyone who survives a head injury could develop edema. The subdural hematoma shown [*sic*] on the CT scan at Mease right after they brought her in. The edema later got worse and some herniation too. Edema is an evolving process."

The CT scan report is again placed up on the screen in front of the courtroom as Exhibit 4. It is dated August 21, 2008, the day of Maria's tragedy. Kurpiers states that there is a subdural hematoma and diffuse edema visible in the scan and wants to know what happened first.

"I don't know what happened first," Thogmartin responds. "If the edema causes the subdural...I don't have a physiological explanation for that. If the subdural causes the edema, the brain swells, pressure rises, blood flow decreases, and it leads to death. The brain receives blood from the carotid artery. The superior sagittal sinuses drain the blood—a clot was there."

Logically, it doesn't seem to make sense for an injury to cause swelling in the brain leading to a subdural hematoma. It cannot be ruled out, but it doesn't make sense to be injured to the point of causing brain swelling and not bleeding, with the bleeding coming later. In any case I've ever read about, there is a subdural hematoma brought about by trauma, and as time passes, swelling begins and increases, similar to a bump on the head on the outside.

Kurpiers finishes his questioning here, perhaps hoping to call attention to Thogmartin's inability to place a time of occurrence on the injuries. Grissinger rises to redirect.

"Is this shaken baby syndrome?"

"I've never used it [the term]. In the community today, they don't use it."

Kurpiers bolts up and shouts out an objection. He is overruled, and Dr. Thogmartin provides a lengthy response.

"It was formerly known as shaken baby. Abusive head trauma is now used, [when there is] a subdural hematoma, retinal hemorrhaging and edema present. With shaken baby, you would expect to see torso and neck injuries. Most children have a head trauma and that's what we see. My colleagues don't use it," referring to SBS.

Holly Grissinger clarifies the meaning of blunt head trauma. "Does that include rapid acceleration/deceleration?"

"Yes, you cannot cause tearing of the bridging veins [otherwise]. It must be a sudden stop with a solid object."

Remember that Dr. Rodriguez had testified that this injury was partly the result of shaking Maria? Here his testimony is practically negated by the medical examiner. But as would be the case throughout this trial, it would all boil down to semantics. When I think of "blunt trauma to the head," or "blunt force trauma to the head," even outside of the context of this case, I immediately think of someone's head slamming into an external object, or being whacked with an external object that is not sharp. It is not strong enough to cause a big lump on the outside of the head as would be the case if a person were struck with a baseball bat, for instance. No, the word *blunt* implies that it is a solid surface, but not hard enough, at least on the surface, to cause bruising. I keep reflecting back on the mattress in the Pack 'n Play and wonder if that is what happened to Maria. Was that the blunt object that her head forcefully came into contact with? At the time, it seemed plausible. But maybe something else happened to Maria in that room where the Pack 'n Play was kept.

The defense offered little in the way of any explanation as to how this injury could have been caused. They focused on illnesses instead, such as diabetes, to hopefully plant reasonable doubt in the minds of the jury. But was diabetes reasonable when she clearly had no history of it? And as it had already been pointed out, diabetes would only lead to a chronic subdural hematoma in a child, and even that would be extremely rare. Maria's bleed was acute, and accompanied with torn bridging veins.

Grissinger asks the medical examiner if the blunt force trauma has to cause a skull fracture. He tells her no.

"Does it have to cause a bruise?"

"It could have a bruise from repetitive force deceleration. Blunt force trauma. This kid had blunt head trauma of some sort. It conveys it to be more than a wild term not applied to an adult. The subdural hematoma has a tearing of bridging veins in the subdural space. [Bridging veins] are in the blood vessels, the dural sinuses, the jugular, and the heart. These spider web veins—they tear and blood leaks."

Holly asks Thogmartin, "How many times have you made a determination of blunt head trauma in a child?"

"A dozen or two," he says. "Most survive. It's not that common."

"With the violent trauma that occurred to that brain, would that child be walking and talking at the occurrence?"

Thogmartin looks at the jury. "In my opinion, if the subdural hematoma had predated August twenty-first, she would have had some *symptoms*, especially with the eye indications she presented at All Children's Hospital and Mease."

"You reviewed the medical records, the police records, Dr. Nelson's records, and the eye doctor's. You used all of that information including your autopsy and you determined [the cause of death to be] blunt head trauma, and the manner of death was homicide."

"Yes."

Holly Grissinger is showing a pattern to her questioning by getting each witness to show commonalities in their medical opinions. Each one states that there was some form of abuse to Maria, leading to homicide, or that she could not have been walking, talking, eating, etc., after the event. This is a good strategy because juries remember agreement between witnesses, and that cannot be overemphasized. There was room for doubt in this jury based on the testimony that they would hear throughout the trial, but Grissinger was making sure that the state showed the doubt to be unreasonable.

The next witness is Dr. Jeffery Bruce Hess, the pediatric ophthalmologist who examined Maria in the hospital. He is a private practitioner who is confined to the hospital. He has been practicing his specialty for thirty-three years, and he sees about two hundred children a week. He had reviewed the medical records of Maria's case.

Grissinger asks him if he sees blunt accidental head trauma in his work.

Dr. Hess says that he consults on such cases about two to four times a month.

"Do you do eye exams?"

"Yes."

"Do you consult with others?"

"Many times." He explains that the eye is like a camera, and the retinal lining inside of the eye, called the retinal sclera, showed superficial lining detachment. Retinal hemorrhages are about one-fourth to one-half a centimeter in size. He examines them routinely.

He responds to Grissinger's questions about testifying in court, saying that he has given his opinion about twelve to fifteen times.

"In 2008, did you examine Maria?"

"Yes."

"How do you conduct an exam?"

"At bedside, I dilate the eyes if needed, unless it's contraindicated. When patients are comatose, I don't need to do that. I used special equipment. An ophthalmoscope projects light beams into the eye. I focus on structures, looking into the eyeball through the pupil."

"Did you read the medical chart?"

"Yes."

"Did you talk to anyone then?"

"No, I don't believe that I did."

"Was Maria responsive during the exam?"

"No."

"Did you see retinal hemorrhages?"

"Yes, they were moderately severe." He relates that he saw many hemorrhages. They were large, covering good portions of the eyes, and the layers of the retina.

Grissinger asks him what can cause retinal hemorrhaging, and he rattles off a list, as he has probably done in court in the past in answer to this question.

"A bleeding disorder, the birthing process, high blood pressure, diabetes, infection of the blood, particles, eye trauma, and eye disease."

"Are retinal hemorrhages alone a sign of child abuse?"

"Usually other things are with it," the doctor says. "But retinal hemorrhages are strongly suggestive of abuse." He says that it's hard to tell how fresh they are, but in this case the retinal hemorrhages are fairly fresh.

Grissinger begins a line of questioning to show the cause of the injury is in line with the other witnesses' opinions. "Was it a single event or multiple ones?"

"Much all the same. It was probably one event. It's hard to tell."

"Would it change her ability to see or focus?"

"There would be visual compromise if she was running around."

Holly asks him more specifically if the retinal hemorrhaging would cause visual deficits, and Dr. Hess responds that it would.

"Could she pick up lint?"

"She would have trouble. It would be pretty difficult."

Grissinger rephrases her summary question that she has used on other witnesses. "You would not expect a child of twelve months of age to be walking around [with these injuries]."

"No."

"[Are the retinal hemorrhages] consistent with nonaccidental head trauma?"

"Yes," Dr. Hess replies.

"From rapid acceleration/deceleration?"

"Yes."

"Could intracranial pressure cause it?"

"Yes. The blood can appear in back of the eye. It's unlikely it's from a bleed in the brain."

"Maria's were extensive?"

"Yes."

"Is retinal hemorrhaging common with a subdural hematoma?"

"No."

"They are separate and distinct?"

"Yes. Just looking, I could see damage. There was no need for equipment."

"If you watched a child with this degree of damage, could you tell?"

"You would be able to tell that her vision was not normal."

These questions were asked no doubt to clarify that Maria would not be able to pick up tiny objects off the carpet as she was capable of the morning of the incident before she left home. Retinal hemorrhages are warning signs in a child because they are not usually seen in situations where there has been no abuse. And abuse is even more suspect if they are seen in conjunction with subdural hematomas because, as Dr. Hess explained, they are not normally seen together. There is a wealth of information online from various professionals and organizations that have documented the reasons suspected for these two injuries to be seen together in young children. The result is that they are, together, almost always linked to abuse. In fact a government document, published in 2003 by PubMed.gov, the US Library of Medicine, states that:

> a prospective study was conducted from January 1996 to September 2001 on 241 consecutive infants hospitalized for a subdural hematoma to determine the frequency and the type of ocular abnormalities encountered. The results showed that, [retinal hemorrhages] were significantly more frequent in non-accidental head trauma than in infants with head impact. (The document concluded with), When associated with a subdural hematoma, they [retinal hemorrhages] are strongly suggestive of shaken neglect. They are rare in pediatric accidental head trauma.
>
> (Kahn et. al., Ophthalmologic Findings in Suspected Child Abuse Victims with Subdural Hematomas, Opthalmology, Sep 2003)

The point here is that it is the rapid acceleration/deceleration of a child's head that leads to the retinal hemorrhaging, and whether that implies SBS or blunt force head trauma, both are nonaccidental and are abusive. The study itself showed no instance of retinal hemorrhaging in the seven children examined that had proven accidental severe head trauma. These results are pretty conclusive in demonstrating that abuse causes retinal hemorrhaging in children and accidents as a rule do not.

Throughout this trial, the defense kept changing course in what they speculated might have caused Maria's injuries and also to detract guilt from away from their client. First, they tried to convince the jury that perhaps the well-baby vaccines or a diabetic condition were the cause. Then later, they implied that, well yes, it could have been abuse, but nobody saw Spurgeon do it, even insinuating that Patricia Harris caused something to happen on the ride home. Other possibilities are suggested as well. Not only were none of these credible, but so many trial balloons were being floated before the jury for alternate causes of Maria's demise that it may have been worse than not suggesting any at all. In my mind, I would be asking, *Was it abuse or an accident or an illness? Did someone in her family do it? What do they want me to believe?* The defense did not focus on any one of these in particular until after the trial in a twist of events that would seem stranger than fiction.

CHAPTER 12

NOW IT IS the defense's turn to query Dr. Hess, and they spend a lot of time doing so.

Ron Kurpiers begins by asking the eye doctor about visual problems from the retinal hemorrhages and indicates that there would be problems. This is done to introduce Dr. Hess's deposition, which causes the state to object and the attorneys to approach the bench. His deposition had been admitted to the records back in May of 2010. This was actually before Kurpiers and Brunvand were the defense attorneys on the case, so neither they nor anyone on their legal team had questioned Dr. Hess in his deposition. It had been the first legal team who had deposed Hess, the one that had been let go by Spurgeon.

Kurpiers returns from the bench and takes an accusatory posture since the objection was overruled. "You wouldn't be able to tell to what extent—"

Hess interrupts. "That's just what I said."

"Why the change?" (From the deposition).

"There is no change," Dr. Hess insists. "I said there would be some visual problems. I wouldn't know the extent."

With a dramatic flair, Kurpiers says, "Under oath, in May of 2010, you said a child could still look at objects."

"No, I didn't say that," Hess replies adamantly. He explains that he had said that a child could not see details. Kurpiers drops this path of questioning, and I cannot tell if he got the answers that he was hoping for.

He continues on by telling Hess that he had indicated that the retinal hemorrhages looked fairly fresh. "Give us an hour," Kurpiers demands, knowing this is not an answerable question.

"Several days to a week or so."

"On August twenty-second, 2008? Several days to a week prior?"

Dr. Hess explains that increased intracranial pressure causes retinal hemorrhages to form. "With a normal vaginal birth, you wouldn't expect to see them a year later."

Kurpiers doesn't persist in attempting to pin Dr. Hess down on a time for the retinal hemorrhage formation to have occurred. He has received the answer that he wanted—a wide window from days to a week. In fact, wide enough so that, according to Dr. Hess's testimony, they could not have happened the day before he examined Maria. This is not good for the state because he is their witness. Holly Grissinger stands to redirect her witness and focuses instead on the probable cause of the injuries to Maria's eyes.

"To have retinal hemorrhages of this extent, there would have had to have been quite a trauma for them to occur."

"Force," the doctor replies.

"What type of force?"

"Usually acceleration/deceleration. The head goes back and forth." Hess indicates that it is the most common type of force, resulting in the striation between the vitreous fluid and the retina.

"In your world of medicine, ophthalmology," Kurpiers states on redirect, "there is not a single study showing how these occur!"

Dr. Hess says that attempts have been made to study them, but there is nothing definite.

Grissinger asks a couple more questions, since she has the last word in the state's side of the case. She brings the reason for the retinal hemorrhages back into play.

"They don't just pop up out of nowhere, do they? There has to be some trauma to the head for her eyes to bleed."

"Yes."

It is important to note here that a trauma to the head would not necessarily cause a subdural hematoma along with this retinal damage, but it can occur on its own as a result of nonaccidental causes. As mentioned in the earlier case study, it is not common to find them together, but when they are seen together, the cause is almost always non-accidental in nature, undermining illness and metabolic reasons as well, especially when torn bridging veins are present.

The next witness for the state is their expert radiologist, Dr. Kevin Potthast. His name in the pediatric radiology section of doctors at All Children's Hospital is Dr. Joseph K. Potthast. He appears youthful but has a very serious disposition. He specializes in radiology with subspecialties in neuroradiology and pediatric neuroradiology. He also teaches radiology. He analyzes on average about one hundred MRIs and fifty to one hundred CT scans per week.

Grissinger begins by asking him if he has seen a CT scan of a subdural hematoma. He replies that he has, "thousands of times." He has spent seven years at All Children's Hospital, three years at Tampa General Hospital, and eleven years at the Trauma Center, giving him numerous opportunities to analyze subdural hematomas in radiological studies.

Grissinger asks him to clarify where a subdural hematoma is found.

"[In the] empty space between the brain and the skull."

She asks if he had seen the CT scan of twelve-month-old Maria. He responds that he was not involved in the actual initial interpretation of her CT scan. It was taken at Mease Hospital, not All Children's, where he is on staff. The CT scan pictures of Maria's brain are introduced as Exhibit 2 on the large monitor at the front of the courtroom. It is the same exhibit previously shown of the scan from Mease Hospital. There are three series of scan pictures visible.

The jury has been very attentive throughout the trial, but they are even more so as Dr. Potthast begins his animated explanation of the pictures.

"The thirty slices outside the brain look normal," he says, sounding like a professor giving a lecture. "These slices are the part of the CT scan that starts at the top of the skull, working down to the bone and before showing any brain matter."

He then describes the middle aspect, which does show brain matter, and he describes what he refers to as "a bilateral brain injury."

"There are dark areas that don't look so good." He indicates them with a pen. "There are whole stripes that don't look so good." He explains that a very white area indicates blood between both hemispheres of the brain. The dark areas show more water than usual which means that swelling has occurred. There is cell injury and cell death. He describes it as direct head trauma and, significantly, as "nonaccidental."

Dr. Potthast explains that a normal structure of the brain would have no white areas.

"Can you tell if this is acute or chronic?" Holly Grissinger asks.

"This has the typical appearance of acute or a very recent subdural hematoma."

"The acute subdural hematoma that you are seeing, how long after an event would it be possible to see on a CT scan?"

"Within minutes after a patient bleeds. The heavy part went to the bottom."

"What if the injuries occurred around noon? Would you be able to see this subdural hematoma?" Grissinger asks, referring to the exhibit.

"Yes."

She asks if the dark areas are a swelling injury.

"Yes," Potthast explains that this is usually the result of hypoxia. Hypoxic means low oxygen delivery to the cells. Oxygen may get to the brain but not to the cells. This is seen in a stroke. It is a pattern of darkness typical of a hypoxic injury. There wasn't enough blood flow to the brain cells.

"Could the subdural hematoma cause hypoxic injuries?"

"No," the doctor responds. "Either they occurred before or at the same time."

Grissinger wants to know if they are the result of two separate traumas, and again he responds with no. He goes on to say that they are most likely from the same injury but in different parts of the brain, so the brain responded differently to the same injury.

"Would Maria have been walking and talking with this subdural hematoma?"

"This is a global injury," Dr. Potthast says emphatically. "In my experience, [this child would be] comatose and on life support. She would be very ill with no significant level of consciousness. There would be very severe long-term brain damage."

Grissinger asks the doctor if the injury could have been caused by rapid acceleration/deceleration of Maria's head.

"Yes. It is acute and global. It involves much of the head."

"Are there any other abnormalities or injuries in the CT scan?"

"There is a little white dot," Dr. Potthast says as he points to it on the image. "It may be another hemorrhage, but nothing major. (This white dot is the 0.3-centimeter tear that Kurpiers had brought up earlier in the trial.)

The injuries predominantly are hypoxic and subdural. Some hypoxic areas could be direct bruising of the brain."

Now, with the jury and gallery all watching intently, the scan switches to the MRI from All Children's Hospital, named Exhibit 3. Even from where I am seated, the images are much sharper and look almost three-dimensional in definition. Dr.

Potthast tells the jury that since there is no radiation, the MRI shows a lot more information. He explains how there are ten to fifteen different ways to look at the same slice of brain by using different brightness levels.

He notes that there are bruises and contusions (which are deep bruises). They show as bleeding spots in the frontal lobe. He talks about how the cells are dying due to cytoxic edema. The dead cells show as very dark on the MRI, which is the opposite of how they appear on the CT scan. There is a lot of water, which indicates swelling. He sums up what we are looking at as "a debilitating severe brain injury."

Grissinger clarifies that Potthast sees no other disease processes going on other than what has been discussed, and he agrees. I am curious to see how long the defense will take upon cross-examination with Dr. Potthast, as he is very savvy and knowledgeable in his field. He is also skilled in his ability to explain these complicated medical issues in such a way that not only does the jury seem to understand him completely, but they appear to be very interested. He is portraying Maria's injuries to be very severe and to have affected the entirety of her brain.

Potthast is illustrating now how a subdural hematoma runs from the front of the brain to the back.

"Can you date that subdural hematoma in hours?" Grissinger asks.

"From twenty to thirty minutes to several days." (This window of time is narrower than Dr. Hess's was for the retinal hemorrhaging). "The subdural blood may not in itself have caused loss of consciousness."

"Your witness," Grissinger says to Ron Kurpiers as she walks back to the prosecution table.

"Doctor, you are unable to tell us what it [the hematoma] looked like prior to 4:21 p.m. on August twenty-first, 2008," Kurpiers states, rather than asks.

"Bridging dural veins ooze. They don't gush."

"How briskly?"

Dr. Potthast takes on a defensive posture. "I wasn't there."

"Exactly." Kurpiers pauses for effect. Then he begins speaking very boldly, trying to persuade the jury that there is a flaw in Potthast's statements. "I'm not trying to trip you up here."

Potthast relates that it depends on how much information you have about the injuries.

"Could it have happened at 3:21? An *hour* earlier?"

Potthast is not new to giving testimony. In a lawyerly fashion, he answers Kurpiers' question without really answering it. "It's an opinion based on my experience."

"An hour, or as far out as twelve hours? Twenty-four hours?"

"That's right."

Kurpiers has latched on to something he can use. He attempts to introduce reasonable doubt by showing that Dr. Potthast cannot pinpoint the time of the injury by less than twenty-four hours.

"You're not telling the jury that it only could have occurred at noon."

"No."

Kurpiers asks him if he sees any progression in the injury.

"Injuries are more obvious and extensive on an MRI," the doctor responds.

"The findings related to the injury are worse [than they appeared on the CT scan]?"

"Yes."

"Yes?" Kurpiers echoes. Then he states with a hint of sarcasm that there is a different technique being used and that "an injury doesn't stop." He doesn't really ask a question.

But the doctor responds by explaining that in the brain, once the cells die, they spill out, and the swelling becomes worse.

Kurpiers wants to know how long it would take for the injury to show up in the case of a stroke.

Potthast does what attorneys dread. From his position on the witness stand, he answers the question with not one of his own, but several.

"How good is your equipment? How old is your patient? The dark areas are subtle and get more obvious. How still was the patient? How keen was the person looking at [the injury]? How big was it? Many lesions are seen within two to four hours. Some not for twenty-four hours."

Kurpiers tries to pin him down. "You said hypoxic injury or stroke" (meaning not necessarily a nonaccidental head trauma).

"I used stroke in a specific sense: a sudden onset of a specific injury to the brain where oxygen didn't get to it."

"You are seeing a global hypoxic injury."

"Yes."

"[There was] a substantial period of lack of oxygen?"

"Yes."

Kurpiers then asks if Maria could cry and if she could go in and out of consciousness.

Again, Potthast shifts to a generalization instead of directly answering Kurpiers' questions. "It's a really sick patient that is gonna die or have a long term brain injury."

Kurpiers states that Maria had various levels of consciousness. He asks Potthast which came first, the subdural hematoma or the global hypoxia.

"I'm not sure which one did. I don't know that the child stopped breathing. In this type of injury, they are typically seen together." This response indicates to me that it didn't matter which one came first, but that they were both the result of a trauma to Maria's brain. She had stopped breathing at least twice before even arriving at the hospital—once in Esther's arms, and once en route to the ER. Hypoxia could have been the result if she had stopped breathing for as long as Esther indicated. There would have been little or no oxygen to the brain for several minutes. But she could have already had a bleed. The CT scan of the subdural hematoma was taken within an hour of when she stopped breathing in the ambulance. Dr. Potthast, however, was apparently not aware that she had stopped breathing at least twice. He was at the second hospital, All Children's, and perhaps had not reviewed the paramedics' records from Mease Hospital.

This becomes clearer when Kurpiers asks him, "What indicated that the child stopped breathing?"

"No," Potthast replies, "I didn't say that she stopped breathing."

Kurpiers introduces yet another possibility for Maria's injuries. "Someone could have strangled her."

But Potthast immediately discredits this idea, which does not come up again. "Lack of oxygen is not the same as lack of breathing. Lack of oxygen could be low oxygen."

This is an odd place for Kurpiers to end his questioning of Dr. Potthast, but he apparently wants to stop his own figurative bleeding. He has shown that he lacked an understanding of hypoxia by introducing strangulation as a suggested cause of Maria's injuries. Also, strangulation would indicate a finished crime. Attempted strangulation would have been the more accurate way of stating his speculation. These were honest mistakes, but Kurpiers probably went too far with that concept, causing the doctor to correct him regarding causes of lack of oxygen at the end of the cross-examination. Also, there were no marks on Maria's neck indicative of any attempt at strangulation. It was an odd suggestion anyway, because who would have attempted to strangle Maria if she came out of the Spurgeon home unresponsive?

On redirect, Grissinger asks Potthast if a subdural hematoma can result from a traumatic injury, and he agrees that it can. She narrows the next question down to whether it can result from a global hypoxic injury, meaning that the whole brain is involved in loss of oxygen, and again he agrees.

"Can they be from the same event?"

"Yes."

"Can the event cause a change in consciousness?"

"Yes."

Grissinger starts leading up to her now well-established summation. She wants to know that if a child is still breathing but unresponsive, and then stops breathing normally, if it could cause the child to become hypoxic. Again, Potthast agrees.

"If the child was walking, talking, eating up until noon, would you see that subdural hemorrhage in that child's brain?"

"No."

Grissinger has driven home the theory that the injury could not have occurred twelve to twenty-four hours earlier, since at that time, Maria was fully awake, aware, and behaving normally. A child who is symptomatic for hypoxia would not be able to be alert simply because of the lack of oxygen flow to the brain. She would be unable to get enough oxygen to the brain cells that would be necessary for her to walk, talk, eat, etc.

The state now calls Dr. Stephen Nelson, the chief medical examiner for the tenth district court, which encompasses neighboring counties. He works in a similar capacity as Dr. Thogmartin, and they occasionally consult one another for opinions on cases. Like Thogmartin, Dr. Nelson is a medical doctor. His specialties are anatomical pathology, neural pathology, and forensic pathology. He is board certified in all three and has been a medical examiner (ME) since 1987. He has written numerous articles and given lectures. He, like Thogmartin, has performed thousands of autopsies.

Holly Grissinger approaches the witness stand from her place at the podium and asks him how many autopsies he has performed involving a child's brain.

"Not that many, hundreds."

She follows up by asking Nelson what he does when he is asked to give an opinion on an autopsy done by another medical examiner. "What information do you get [from the other ME]?"

"Some," he replies, "not much, so that we are not jaded in offering an opinion. On some others, we need more information."

"When you receive a brain, is your purpose to do cause and manner of death?"

"No," Nelson responds firmly. "In an examination of the brain, they have legal authority." He explains that he functions as a consultant and that the brain is delivered to him via a chain of custody. It is transported in a solution of formaldehyde.

Dr. Nelson explains what happened to Maria's brain once he received it. Her brain arrived on September 16, 2008. He examined it on the twenty-second. When he weighed her brain, he determined that it was 1,110 grams, which is slightly outside the range for a child of Maria's age.

"Did you find a subdural hematoma?" Grissinger asks him.

"Yes."

Then she inquires as to whether the ME has prepared a PowerPoint presentation. In rapid response, the defense asks for an approach to the bench, which leads to a fifteen-minute recess. I speculate that this may be because the defense was unaware of this PowerPoint and they would have liked to have reviewed it first. But it may have been due to something else altogether.

Upon returning to the courtroom, Dr. Nelson shows his presentation of a cross section of a scalp down through the layers of brain. He explains that blood accumulates between the yellow membrane and the surface of the brain, which is the subdural area. Specifically, he indicates that seventy-five percent of subdural hematomas are caused by trauma.

Dr. Nelson then explains what can cause these injuries: alcoholism, boxing, and child abuse. He indicates that he is referring here only to subdural hematomas and not epidural ones, which occur between the dura mater (the outer membrane of the central nervous system) and the skull. Subdural hematomas, which occur beneath the dura mater and the outer membrane of the brain itself, show tearing of veins, lowering of pressure, and the oozing of blood. He differentiates between veins, which ooze blood, and arteries, which spurt blood. There is a big difference.

Subdural hematomas, he notes, "occur in front of the head and on the sides." He tells the court that approximately 80 percent of subdural hematomas in children are present on both sides of the brain. They are very rare in the back of the brain and/or in the spinal cord. If there is more than one hundred cubic centimeters of blood resulting from a subdural hematoma, then it will definitely lead to death. And since there are three hundred cc's of subdural space in a child's head, there is brain stem herniation in one-third of the cases. If it remains untreated, the blood will start pushing the brain out of the way. Death depends on how fast it forms and the size of the hematoma.

Dr. Nelson continues on with his minilecture, explaining that a hemorrhage is an irritant. "The body wants to wall it off and reabsorb it. We can estimate how long it has been there." He talks about red blood cells being present up to the first day, and then after twenty-four to forty-eight hours, neutrophils are present. Cells in the dural layer attempt to come out, and the surrounding area attempts to reabsorb it.

After his detailed explanation is complete, I contemplate whether the jury has made any sense of it. Because I have some background from college in biology and anatomy, I was able to understand his presentation, in part because he spoke slowly and in the manner of a professor. I silently prayed that the jury understood it because understanding this particular information is critical to understanding the timing of the injuries.

Dr. Nelson talks about Maria Harris's information from her autopsy that he had received from Dr. Thogmartin. He explains that the cell layers are two to three cells thick. There is no iron present, and it is unorganized; therefore, it is an early subdural hematoma. There is a new membrane that he points out that is very thin. This also indicates that it formed very recently, its purpose being an attempt to wall off the subdural hematoma. This explanation becomes critical later on as the defense witnesses will place an earlier date on the subdural hematoma, trying to demonstrate that it occurred before Maria arrived at the Spurgeon home. But Dr. Nelson's detailed analysis in and of itself is not directly refuted by any defense witness.

He also indicates that there is anoxic ischemic encephalopathy, which means brain death is happening everywhere. At the time of death, he says that this hematoma was probably a week old. No cellular changes had taken place.

Grissinger stops him here to ask if this rules out any infections in Maria's brain.

He responds that there are no infections.

She asks if it is an acute hematoma.

"There is evidence of fresh blood."

"Could a child twelve months of age, having sustained this subdural hematoma, walk and talk?"

Nelson responds, "I don't believe so, no." It is not the solid answer that Grissinger has received from prior state witnesses, but it is in line with their responses just the same.

On the board at the front, two pictures are displayed showing two kinds of hemorrhaging. The dark reddish black area indicates blood.

Dr. Nelson tells the court that this hemorrhaging would be caused by the blunt trauma that was inflicted.

"Blunt trauma?" Grissinger asks. "What do you mean?"

"Sharp force."

"Blunt trauma consistent with rapid acceleration/deceleration?"

"Yes." Dr. Nelson explains the injuries are caused separately, like gunshot wounds.

Holly asks him about the higher than normal glucose level in Maria's blood.

"Stress from the head injury increases glucose levels. Yes, there would be various electrolyte changes."

"Were you asked to do additional testing in December of 2008?" Grissinger gets this question out on the table to take the wind out of the defense's cross-examination, since she figured it would likely be brought up then.

There was a test performed, according to Dr. Nelson, to ascertain microscopic changes that are very specific to trauma. He explains that there is a stain for that test, but the literature does not say that the stain was positive for trauma. He, in fact, cannot say that this stain test is infallible if it shows up as positive for trauma.

Grissinger steers him away from the stain test, now that it has been introduced as a reason for further testing and instead asks the doctor, "Can you tell the jury that the subdural hematoma was a result of a violent episode?"

He cannot. "We don't have an explanation." He relates that the brain was that of a one-year-old child. She could have been in a car crash or fallen down the steps. Of course, Dr. Nelson did not know the circumstances of Maria's injury based on where it occurred and what the diagnosis was when she was still living and breathing and her brain was inside her skull.

Grissinger states that, "You have a subdural hematoma. It is seven days old. What do you do at that point?"

"Prepare a report and provide it to the individual who asked for it."

"Do you rely on information given to you when you make your findings?

"No," he answers, "the findings. It wouldn't have any effect on what my findings are."

On cross, Kurpiers wants to talk about the stain test again, and I can't blame him. This test seemed to be an aberration because if its ability to demonstrate that a hematoma was caused from a violent episode was not conclusive, then why do it? Dr. Nelson was asked to do this test, but it is not clear who requested it.

Kurpiers mentions that the doctor did the brain examination on September 22, 2008, and wrote the report on October 6, over two weeks later. Then he says that "for some reason," an additional report was done on December 17. He asks if the study done in October was insufficient.

Dr. Nelson tells him that it did not have the additional special stain testing. Nelson goes into detail, explaining how the stain reveals damage to axons in the nerve cells and is supposed to indicate if there was trauma to the brain. But he could not reach a conclusion as to whether this was a diffuse axonal injury; in other words, a specific type of trauma event.

Nelson continues talking about his findings. He explains that when there is a global brain injury (as was the case with Maria's subdural hematoma), "It makes postmortem handling a challenge. The brain will start to dissolve the moment there is incomplete profusion of the blood. Brain dead is dead. Even though the child is not pronounced dead, a type of decomposition is already occurring. Normal brain weight is 655 to 918 grams. For a twelve-month-old child, the average is 786 grams. Maria's brain weight was 30 percent higher than normal.

"You attribute this to the swelling," Kurpiers states.

"Yes, because it had already started to undergo dissolution."

As this discussion between the defense attorney and the medical examiner continues, I am struck by the total disassociation of their words. Maria had been a beautiful child, a creation of God in his image, and they were talking about her brain as if it were a carburetor. She may be gone from the living, but she still is a little girl in the hearts of her loved ones, and it is so hard to imagine that people can become so inured to the fact that that they are talking about a person who had died so very sadly. I suppose medical examiners need to be aloof, or they would not be able to do their jobs. Having seen dead bodies in anatomy labs, I can understand that even though I couldn't possibly have chosen that sort of career. There is a huge gap between examining a body donated to science that is prepared and preserved, and taking a Stryker saw to slice through the skull of a recently deceased person's body to remove the brain after the rest of the organs have been examined. It takes a very unique type of person to become a pathologist. These people must often even inject humor into the conversation to keep from dwelling on the body or what happened to it. My hope is that they never insult the deceased but always perform their duties with respect, handling the body with care. Pathologists that I have spoken with have a different mentality than a doctor. They usually do not need to be in a hurry; the patients have already died and there is no urgency to save lives. Also, the patients can only hopefully tell their story to the ME purely by a meticulous examination. They cannot speak otherwise. Authors William R. Maples and Michael Browning discuss some of these feelings in their book *Dead Men Do Tell Tales: The Strange and Fascinating Cases of a Forensic Anthropologist*.[1] At any rate, it would be a daunting task to constantly work with the dead. The souls are gone, and the shells are all that are left to hopefully reveal clues as to why and how they met their ends.

In Maria's case, fortunately, there is much more information at hand since she was able to be examined for an entire week prior to her death. Numerous doctors and specialists were able to scrutinize her hands-on and consult with each other on her deteriorating condition. This opportunity shed light on much more information than they would have had if she had died immediately after her injuries. It also gave these witnesses the chance to see her and touch her and know first-hand what was happening, as opposed to the defense witnesses, who only had documents and comparative studies upon which to base their testimony, as will be demonstrated later.

Now, Kurpiers questions Dr. Nelson about the timing of the injuries, and the doctor is vaguer than some of the earlier witnesses. "Seven days? About a week? It could have been longer."

"Six and a half to eight days?" Kurpiers tries to narrow it down.

"About a week," Dr. Nelson repeats.

"If you will tell the jury the time it was," Kurpiers persists.

"About a week."

The defense certainly would like it to be longer because that would put the injuries outside of the time frame when Maria was at the Spurgeon home. But thus far, there has been no conclusive evidence that she was sick or injured in any way before that day. To the contrary, she had been alert and active, and even Stephanie Spurgeon had apparently admitted in the police report that Maria seemed fine when she arrived. Also, remember that when Dr. Nelson was examining Maria's brain, he did not know the timing or the sequence of events that led to her death.

Next, Ron Kurpiers wants to know about the oozing veins. "At what speed were they oozing?"

"We know the person was still alive. We know when veins are cut, they ooze," Nelson replies.

Oozing is a nonspecific term, and Kurpiers wanted to know if it could happen rather swiftly or very slowly. When I think of oozing, it could be applied to the sticky resin that very slowly comes out of trees, or it could be mud oozing through a riverbed that is drying up. Both are correct, but one is extremely slower than the other. The bottom line is that a cut vein oozes, or bleeds quite slowly when compared to an arterial bleed, which pumps with the heart and can kill a person very rapidly if a major artery is severed or punctured.

Kurpiers asks a leading question: "Oozing causes uncon-sciousness, right?"

"No," Nelson frowns. "In children, there is not a mass effect to produce them, but they are a marker [severed veins]. It doesn't work like a mass effect like in an adult."

"How quick did that thin film [membrane] happen?"

"It depends on what a child does clinically. A day. I don't expect a child with a subdural hemorrhage to act normally."

"This is trauma?" Kurpiers asks.

"Yes."

"What kind?"

"Blunt trauma"

"What kind?" Kurpiers asks again as if he did not hear Dr. Nelson's response.

"Blunt trauma," Nelson repeats defensively.

Kurpiers asks if the injuries could have resulted from a fall, and Nelson tells him that there is no evidence of that.

Then he asks if there could have been a metabolic reason for the injuries.

"I don't think that was your question," Dr. Nelson says curtly, implying that it was off topic from discussing blunt trauma as the cause. He had already answered that query twice.

Aggressively, Kurpiers challenges the witness. "Have you ever *seen* it?"

"No." Now Dr. Nelson appears angry. It is possible that this was the result that Kurpiers wanted from the interrogation, but I'm not sure how well it went over with the jury. Sometimes an angry witness appears out of control and defensive to the jury, and other times he or she appears to be bullied by the attorney. The tension in the room builds, and it will not be the last time the defense attempts to corner a witness in this trial.

Kurpiers ends the cross-examination by bringing up the stain test once again and how it is supposed to indicate a type of trauma. Dr. Nelson says that the stain test was consistent with acceleration/deceleration of the head.

Neither party is able to successfully prove or refute the validity of this stain test. It would have been better to not have performed it, but again, Dr. Nelson was never asked who requested that it be done. It is a loophole that is never closed.

CHAPTER 13

DR. SALLY SMITH, the state's next witness is no stranger to courtroom proceedings involving child abuse cases. In fact, she had been a witness in the recent trial involving the death of a child in foster care mentioned earlier where foster mother Tenesia Brown was acquitted. She testified for the state, and the defense attorney who questioned her in that 2010 trial was none other than Ron Kurpiers. Dr. Smith and Ron Kurpiers have a history in the courtroom, and it is not a pleasant one. Kurpiers probably feels that he has the advantage not only because he won the prior case, but because Dr. Smith was part of the losing side and she is an advocate for abused children. She is fiercely protective of her role in exposing child abuse, and this attitude clearly comes across during her testimony.

Dr. Smith is a graduate of Georgetown University. She received her medical degree in St. Louis and is now a pediatrician at All Children's Hospital in St. Petersburg, where Maria Harris spent her final days. She is board certified in pediatrics and child abuse pediatrics. Dr. Smith spends half her time in private practice and the other half as part of a child protective team. She is on the active medical staff at All Children's, and she was the pediatric director there from 1990–2002. Smith is still active in all trauma cases admitted to the hospital and is a medical consultant for trauma services. She has evaluated 1,500 to 2,000 cases of suggested child abuse. She sees seventy to one hundred cases a year of head trauma. Some are accidental, others abusive.

I list her credentials in some detail because, as it will become clear later, Dr. Smith's credibility as a witness is challenged by some of the defense's lines of questioning. What I note that separates her from the norm in pediatrics is the considerable amount of time she has spent in her career focused on child abuse cases. A person can only become an expert in something if they truly practice in the field, and Dr. Smith's experience is quite extensive. She has a commanding disposition in spite of her small stature and young appearance. On the stand, she looks more like a police detective than a doctor, perhaps in part because she will be answering questions on child abuse. She takes her seat in the witness box, sitting forward stiffly, but she relaxes a bit when asked by Grissinger to talk about head trauma.

Dr. Smith relates that she sees abusive head trauma, resulting from physical abuse to the brain and head. Some of the children have skull fractures and even broken bones on their faces. Some of the injuries are primarily to the brain, and not much or nothing is visible externally.

She says that shaken baby syndrome is not used much anymore because it is hard to tell if a baby has been shaken or thrown. There are not injuries specific to certain events such as a fall out of a window or a car crash. With an acceleration/deceleration inflicted on a child, there is strain and stress of the small blood vessels on and in the brain. This can lead to serious neurological abnormalities.

She continues explaining about how abusive head trauma is determined. There are exams that have been in use since 1990.

She looks at CT scans, MRIs, and X-rays. This is the radiology side. Some of the radiologists don't know what to look for if they are not familiar with child abuse. But at All Children's Hospital, pediatric radiologists and neuroradiologists do know what to look for. They are specialists, trained in this type of trauma.

Grissinger asks her if she has testified in head trauma cases. "Yes, forty to fifty times."

"Do you review medical records?"

"In 2008, most of it was paper."

"The EMS report," Grissinger says, "what happened prior to them getting to the hospital?"

Dr. Smith tells the court that a consultation will usually occur early when the records get to the hospital. "On August twenty-second," she states, "at 10:00 a.m., I talked to the maternal grand-parent and the mother. She [Maria] was not responsive. She would not move at all." This was during Dr. Smith's exam which took thirty-five to forty minutes. "There were some movements with blood testing. She was on a ventilator, so there were no inde-pendent breaths."

She says that the external exam showed that she weighed about twenty-two pounds. She was 9.7 kilograms, which was about twenty-one pounds. She had no known medical condi-tions. In fact, her history is pretty well documented. Her mother had an uneventful pregnancy and delivery. There were no prob-lems at all until "this visit" in August of 2008.

Next, she is asked about retinal hemorrhaging. "You look through the pupil into the back of the eyeball to see evidence of retinal hemorrhaging. Ophthalmologists can see the whole eyeball, whereas my instrument has to be moved around. When there is bleeding, the inside of the back of the eye looks bright red. I saw retinal hemorrhages in both eyes."

Later, Kurpiers will try and discredit Dr. Smith's testimony that she had actually observed retinal hemorrhages in both eyes. This is important because, as the government article that I referenced earlier stated, "[retinal hemorrhages] are rare in accidental pediatric head trauma."

Dr. Smith continues to explain her diagnosis of Maria. "The CT scan at Mease had evidence of fresh bleeding between the interhemispheric fissure and areas on the surface of the brain on both sides. When there is damage to the gray/white differentiation, it doesn't look normal. Blood flow and fluid between blood cells in the brain are abnormal. It went from the surface all the way deep into the brain. This is characteristic of abusive head trauma. It's not like a child had a fall, which is only on the surface of the brain. This is why these children are so neurologically damaged. The hemorrhages on the CT scan also showed on the MRI. The MRI shows better detail of abnormalities. It had progressed overnight."

Grissinger asks, "Is it normal for it to progress?"

"Yes, in these cases. As cells die, they bring in more fluids." She explains that this is known as "pruning," and it is normal for the main cells to be replaced or actually switch to perform different functions. "Factors associated with pruning are different in children than adults." (This explanation will also become critical later as interpretations of the CT scan and MRI by defense expert witnesses will not differentiate between children and adults.)

Dr. Smith then describes what is different about a hematoma when it is in the subdural area of the brain. "There is not much blood. It is not a pressure-related problem. The bleeding demonstrates what happens to the brain itself. It is not because of the blood. It's because of the global injury to the brain."

Grissinger asks Smith if a child with a subdural hematoma could walk, talk, and eat, and Dr. Smith says no.

"There would be no normal level of consciousness. There would be swelling and lack of oxygen increasing over time." Dr. Smith says that all these things that Grissinger asked her about would not be possible with this deep brain injury.

"Did you come to certain findings in the case of Maria?"

"Mease hospital records noted 'stupor, seizures, limited response'. There were lots of seizures and abnormal brain waves. Abnormal neurological findings. It had happened abruptly." She describes deep abnormalities of the brain substance, global in nature, as well as retinal hemorrhaging, which is very rare in other routine traumas.

Dr. Smith notes there is physical abuse associated with trauma to the head when there are these deep abnormalities. She reads a great deal about the subject, attends lectures, and works with other clinicians in pediatric child abuse cases.

Grissinger hones in with a key question to lessen the impact when the issue comes up on cross-examination. "To your knowledge, based on your experience in pediatric child abuse, are there those who believe it is not a medical diagnosis?"

Dr. Smith doesn't believe so in the area of pediatric medicine. Abuse exists and can be diagnosed.

"Can a child be pushed multiple times into a soft object? Is that physical abuse?"

Smith indicates that a mattress used to stop a child's head subjected to rapid acceleration/deceleration with sufficient force and frequency, in other words, repetitive, can cause extensive injury to the brain. Other reasons for abusive head trauma can be ruled out. "We don't randomly say, 'This is abusive head trauma.' We look at a broad spectrum of alternate diagnoses and rule them out."

"Is it an American Association of Pediatricians–accepted diagnosis?"

"Yes. In my field, approximately 25 to 30 percent of cases are not child abuse. Mine are higher for child abuse because of my position. Sometimes we need additional testing to check the metabolic screen to make sure everything else is ruled out, [such as] no sign of bone abnormalities or fractures. At this age, we often see severe brain injuries without skull fractures or other fractures. We sometimes see them, but often we don't."

"How is it that her brain could have sustained the injuries she sustained without a skull fracture?"

"Throwing on a bed is one of the main scenarios for severe injury—blunt force trauma to the head. The best way to tell when an injury occurred is when the neurological changes occurred."

Holly Grissinger ends her direct examination of Dr. Smith's testimony with a culminating question. "Based on your opinion and your training and experience and information and statements from family and law enforcement, can you say whether or not this injury was accidental?"

"It was *not* accidental. It was an abusive injury."

That evening, I went online and did a bit of research on the combination of shaking a child with impact and found that there was an abundance of information from doctors around the world. The following information in particular, seems to summarize Maria's circumstance well:

> Previously known as "shaken-baby syndrome," many experts now feel that severe deceleration injuries (i.e., swinging the head against an immobile object such as a wall) are often involved. Clinically, varying degrees of brain injury are noted, associated with acute subarachnoid, subdural and retinal hemorrhages. Some children may present with acute subdural hematoma and chronic, proteinaceous extra-axial fluid collections suggestive of multiple traumatic episodes. Acute management of shaking-impact syndrome involves operative removal of significant intracranial hemorrhages when these are present. The role of intracranial pressure monitoring and ventricular drainage is controversial in young infants with widely open sutures and fontanelles. Unfortunately, infants with injuries severe enough to cause prolonged coma and cerebral edema commonly have devastating neurological outcomes in any case.
>
> (Frimm and Gupta, Pediatric Neurosurgery, Jan 2006)

CHAPTER 14

RON KURPIERS AND Dr. Sally Smith have faced off before. There is no love lost between them, and Kurpiers is champing at the bit to get in front of Smith and interrogate her. She is obviously uncomfortable, and her body language indicates a defensive shield.

He goes on the offensive right away. "Do you hold any other certifications?" Not waiting for a response, he continues. "You are not board certified in ophthalmology or radiology or the subspecialties that you talked about?"

"That's correct," Smith responds curtly.

"You no longer use the phrase 'shaken baby syndrome,'" he declares loudly.

"I use it, but that terminology has its limitations."

"Five years ago, that wouldn't have been your answer," he goes on to say, making statements rather than asking questions.

"Maybe ten years ago—"

"When did you change the role of shaking versus impact versus one or the other?"

"There are various kinds of trauma. [We use] a broader term—abusive head trauma." The entire time Dr. Smith is speaking, she only looks directly at the jury, not at Kurpiers.

"There are no studies done with live children?" Kurpiers' question would backfire later with one of the defense's own witnesses.

"Yes, that's correct. There is a videotape of an adult in prison being shaken."

Ignoring this, Kurpiers continues. "You say that you saw retinal hemorrhaging in this child on August twenty-second at roughly 10:00 a.m. When you did the exam, it was not with a scope?"

"It was done with an ophthalmoscope. There are two types, the one ophthalmologists use and the one pediatricians use. I saw retinal hemorrhages." When Dr. Hess testified earlier, he stated that he was able to see Maria's retinal hemorrhages without any equipment at all, so Kurpiers knew better than to continue down this road. So instead, he jumps to the time-frame issue.

"When did they occur?" he asked sharply.

"The appearance evolves over a couple of weeks. The exact minute or hour or day—related to August 22, 2008—I can't tell you that. You can't specifically give a date to a retinal hemorrhage due to its appearance."

Here, as he has tried to do consistently, Kurpiers attempts to insert doubt by trying to get the witness to pinpoint a time on the occurrence of an injury. The key is, is there reasonable doubt if all of these separate witnesses give a rather narrow time window and also agree that abuse occurred, and that the injury was not due to a preexisting illness or accident? They all agree that a child could not behave normally after such an injury and would not be able to walk, talk, or eat. This consistency among witnesses, most of whom did not know each other, is crucial to the outcome of this trial. It is often the discrepancies between testimonies for either side that can cause a case to collapse, leaving attorneys scrambling for a foundation on which to base their closing arguments.

"Did you see the Mease records?" Kurpiers asks.

"Yes."

He then asks her if she saw seizures.

"I was reviewing the chart. There were posturing episodes—that's not seizures—they gave her seizure meds."

"Look through the paperwork, and I believe it says seizures."

He then asks if the records indicate retinal hemorrhages.

"I don't know that they looked for retinal hemorrhages," Dr. Smith replies.

Then Kurpiers shifts into attack mode, firing off a rapid statement, but not questioning the witness. "You work hand in hand with the state attorney's office. You meet during the investigative stage and you meet on a weekly basis with law enforcement."

"Every two weeks, at least by telephone. I don't know about weekly," she responds.

"In this particular case, you do not know what was done to Maria Harris, *do you?*"

"No," she says quietly, still looking at the jury. She continues responding to Kurpiers' closed-end question. "I have a very good idea what *was* done to her—acceleration/deceleration blunt force trauma." Dr. Smith is visibly upset at this point.

Ron Kurpiers asks Dr. Smith to review her deposition taken back in February of 2010. I would like to know why it took so long to depose her if Maria died in August of 2008. The case was filed in a timely manner. The deposition was given to Olney's legal team, not Brunvand's, as it had not taken over the case yet.

"Look at pages 12 through 13." She is asked to read a highlighted section.

"I have no idea what was done to her to cause this." Dr. Smith becomes angry. She says indignantly, "I don't think that it is appropriate to quote me out of context! I said plenty leading up to this statement!"

"You also said that you might speculate that she had a combination of forces, written on that page. Is it consistent with shaking and a single impact?"

"I don't know."

At this point in Dr. Smith's testimony, I note that several of the jury members are frowning when Kurpiers is speaking. Do they think that he is bullying the witness? It isn't so much the questions, but the tone he is using. A powerful scenario is being played out, and it truly shows the animosity between these two people. I am cringing inwardly, and I cannot imagine being on that witness stand.

"Where would the impact have been?" Kurpiers asks, a hint of sarcasm in his voice.

"I don't know," Smith responds, sharply.

"Other than child abuse?"

"No."

"Your comment, 'child abuse' is speculation," he states.

"No! It's not!" The witness and the attorney glare at each other. The tension in the room is palpable. Everyone in the courtroom is frozen waiting to see when it will resolve, if at all. Then Kurpiers continues firing questions at Smith in rapid succession, barely waiting for her responses.

> Kurpiers: "The subdural hemorrhage you saw, was it in consultation with another doctor?"
> Smith: "Yes."
> Kurpiers: "Was it Dr. Potthast?"
> Smith: "I don't know."
> Kurpiers: "Did you consult at any time with Dr. Luis Rodriguez?"
> Smith: "I don't know."

And finally, the conversation veers away from whom Dr. Smith may have consulted with and back to Maria's injury. Voices drop to more normal volume levels.

"Can we age subdural hematomas?" asks Kurpiers.

"Not within an hour or so, but we can narrow down the age."

"Was this an acute subdural hematoma?"

"It's fresh."

"Is that the best you can do?" Kurpiers wants to know, emphasizing the doubt he has in the accuracy of her responses.

"Yes."

Dr. Smith is a doctor. No doctor is going to give an exact answer on the timing of an injury any more than a forensic team can pinpoint an exact time of death if it is not known in advance. It is a window. Here, it was a reasonable window. The exact timing is less important in my opinion than the fact that Maria went into the Spurgeon home in an alert and healthy state and came out lethargic and limp, then unresponsive. This is the gorilla in the room that the defense doesn't want to talk about. Kurpiers consistently points out throughout the trial that no one saw Stephanie Spurgeon hurt Maria. That fact does not exclude the underlying foundation that there is no other reasonable explanation for what happened to her, and all the rabbit trails that the defense continues to present, both during and even after the trial, are unreasonable. The jury doesn't have to agree that Spurgeon absolutely and positively caused Maria's death; they only have to agree that she did it beyond a reasonable doubt. Unreasonable doubts are just that. Not plausible. The fact that no one saw her do it does not make her innocent by any stretch of the imagination. Yet, that is the only argument they maintain. Everything else keeps falling off the map.

Kurpiers now brings up one of these conjectures that are on another road to nowhere. "If something had happened to this child on the way home from the day care, would the medical findings have been the same?"

"No," she answers, firmly.

Referring to her deposition to close out his cross-examination, he has her state what she had said back in February of 2010. "They might be."

To quell any lasting implications of this drama-infused cross by Kurpiers, Grissinger quickly steps up to redirect Dr. Smith back to the known facts.

"The fact that this child had a violent, traumatic injury to the brain, does it matter that it happened on the front or the back? On one side or the other?"

Dr. Smith says that the problem is the rapid acceleration/deceleration and sudden stop.

"So," Grissinger continues, "whether her face was forced into a mattress or the back of her head was forced into a mattress, it doesn't matter."

"No. I've been doing this for over twenty-plus years. The pattern of injury that this child had has a long experience in pediatrics. It has been well-established for over twenty years. Subdural, arachnal, double retinal [injuries] are due to rapid acceleration/deceleration. This child had all those things. She had no other reasonable explanation for all of her other constellation of findings."

Holly now attempts to undo any damage caused by Kurpiers' statement that the injuries could have happened on the way home from the day care. She says that Maria was unresponsive to her grandma when she tried to wake her up.

Patricia Harris had already testified at this point, and the jury had a pretty good indication of what kind of grandma she was to Maria. After hearing Pat's testimony, it would be pretty incredulous to even imagine her harming her child in the car somehow, then calling EMS because she didn't know what was wrong and was hysterical at the scene at her home. Again, the validity of reason must come into play when these injuries are considered.

Dr. Smith says, "The timing of the injury was related to the timing of her symptoms. There are clinical findings with certain types of injuries and medical diagnoses, and the thing that pinpoints the injuries are [sic] the symptoms. We can be specific based on the child's neurological condition. She had neurological symptoms at the time her grandmother picked her up. She wasn't normal when she left. The family members recognized the serious condition she was in. She was unresponsive within seconds of the trauma."

Kurpiers has a couple more questions, to the dismay of Dr. Smith.

"The ride on the way home, who did you get that description from?"

"The grandmother."

"So you based your opinion on—"

Dr. Smith interrupts. "The babysitter gave the same description to [Detective] Lyons."

There is a bench approach now, most likely because the law enforcement officer was mentioned. It is brief, and Kurpiers continues wrapping up his questions.

Then Dr. Smith confirms that she spoke with Patricia and Esther Harris at the hospital, and that Patricia Harris had driven Maria home. The only three people in the house (before EMS arrived) were Patricia, Esther, and Maria Harris.

I didn't understand why the drive home was so important to the defense. Patricia had stated Maria's condition upon pickup when she had testified, and this was never disputed. The fact that Pat said that Spurgeon also told her that Maria was tired and had played hard was also never disputed. Of course, Spurgeon couldn't dispute this herself because she would not be a witness in this case against her. But it was probably in the police report. The state had demonstrated through Pat's testimony that Maria was not normal when she was picked up, so the ride home could not have done the damage that was already progressing in a semi-comatose child.

But now, it was the defense's turn to try and discredit all the state's witnesses because at this point, the state rests!

CHAPTER 15

DR. SALLY SMITH was the state's last witness. Because of the heated questions and answers between Dr. Smith and Ron Kurpiers, she would become a memorable witness, if not a good one. The jury would not forget how Kurpiers handled his questioning of her.

My thoughts at this point were that the state had left out a lot of information. How can this be their entire case against a defendant accused of murdering a child in a home day care? I realize that these are the state's attorneys, and not private ones, who have more time and resources to devote to investigations and research. But I am still, out of concern for the Harrises, worried that too much has been neglected. Again, I wonder about the phone records from Stephanie's cell phone and/or landline that fateful day. Who did she talk to that day, and when and for how long? It was also my understanding that her husband, a U.S. Post Office employee, was on disability. Was he unable to work at all? If not, where was he? Why wasn't the jury permitted to know this information? It seemed like an awfully short period of state testimony when it involved a case of first-degree murder against the defendant.

There was additional critical information that was intentionally omitted from the trial. There had been a witness to another incident at the day care, and the hearing for that situation had occurred on May 5, 2010. It was debated under something called the Williams Rule, which goes to the character of the defendant in a case. The Williams Rule allows evidence to be introduced from past crimes or wrongdoings of the defendant if those crimes are relevant to the current case.

Because I was out of town at the time, a friend of mine, Scott Nichols, attended that hearing for me and contacted me each evening after the two days of testimony to review what was covered:

Spurgeon's family is present on the defense side of the courtroom. On the state's side, there are several law clerks. Of course, since this is only a hearing, there is no jury. The state calls several witnesses, the first is the person who would be notably absent at the trial itself—Detective Kelly Lyons, who was then an employee of the Pinellas County Sheriff's Department.

She walks to the witness stand with confidence. She is blond, perhaps in her midthirties, and well-dressed, carting a truckload of documents with her. During the investigation, she is the one who interviewed everybody. The state questions Detective Lyons about the events of August 21, 2008. The detective recounts that Maria never talked on the phone to anyone, but it was Spurgeon who had indicated that Maria was doing fine, and Spurgeon had never been challenged on this matter according to her own statement to the police.

This admission is critical, and it would not be brought up by the state at the trial. It goes to show that Spurgeon said that she observed nothing unusual in Maria's behavior at the time she spoke to Patricia Harris on the phone. If there was any "preexisting condition," it would surely have been evident to Spurgeon, but she had stated that all was fine, and this information confirms that Maria was not acting abnormally in any way during the time she was awake at the day care.

At this Williams Rule hearing, Detective Lyons relates how Maria never woke up when Mrs. Harris picked her up. She notes that even as Mrs. Harris and Stephanie Spurgeon talked in the room or when Pat was holding her, she never woke up. She never woke up in the car. She was like a rag doll. She establishes that Stephanie was the only adult in the home that day. She says that some things did not look right—how Maria was sleeping on her stomach without her binky in her mouth and the drive from the day care. Mrs. Harris only had Maria with her during the fifteen- to twenty-minute drive from the day care.

What amazing testimony this could have been for the state had Detective Lyons been called to testify. In the grand scheme of things, it probably didn't matter, but it would have perhaps solidified the case more in the minds of those who were hesitant to render a verdict. But the detective was nowhere to be seen during the trial, and in fact, no longer lives in the state of Florida.

During this particular hearing, the defense tries to establish that Maria had a blank stare when she was at the day care based on a statement made by a parent of another child. After this statement, he says that she was "okay." This man, whose testimony at trial the reader will note later, changed entirely and this "blank stare" was never mentioned. The state maintains that she was playing with the kids according to Spurgeon, disputing this man's information right there at the hearing. The two sides battle back and forth before they even get to the Williams Rule testimony to establish prior conduct of Spurgeon.

Then the state brings out some interviews from eight years prior, in 2002. Daniel and Sharon Anderson* had filed a complaint against Spurgeon on March 29, 2002. Their child, Lindsay* had been interviewed. At the time of this hearing, she is fourteen years old, making her six years old at the time of the following event.

On March 29, 2002, Lindsay was at the day care with her three-month-old sister, Gabrielle.* In a shocking revelation, the interview stated that Lindsay had witnessed Stephanie Spurgeon pick up Gabrielle, shake her violently, and throw her in the crib. She had heard her sister crying and saw Spurgeon yelling. Spurgeon grabbed Gabrielle to stop the crying and shook her, continuing to yell at her the whole time. Then she threw her into the crib causing her to hit her head on the backboard of the crib.

The defense said it did not happen. What is so revealing to me is: what are the odds of being accused of doing the same sort of thing twice in two completely different years, but in the same setting with the same reaction and being innocent of the accusations? The first time Spurgeon apparently got away with it. Would she with Maria Harris? This is damaging testimony against Spurgeon. If a jury gets to hear it, the case against her would likely be a slam dunk.

The prosecution says that they have evidence that it could have happened within a certain time frame and that she has a history of this behavior. There was a short investigation in 2002, but it there was never any follow up.

Kelly Lyons' testimony was solid, and the defense would have an uphill battle trying to dispute it. They try their best at this hearing to point out inconsistencies regarding Lindsay and Gabrielle, but they cannot trip up the detective. Because this hearing took place in May of 2010, the attorneys for Spurgeon would be her first team and would no longer be part of this case at the time of the trial. That meant that Brunvand and Kurpiers would have had to deal with these reports during the trial, and it would have been quite interesting. But it was not to be.

This defense team notes that the word *shaken* was never included in the report by the Andersons and that the case was closed. Kelly Lyons indicates that the police department's child protection investigators did not do a good job investigating this event.

The defense points out that Lindsay had never given a sworn testimony of any wrongdoing by Spurgeon. They note that there are inconsistencies in the testimony of Kelly Lyons. Lyons then states that the reason for the inconsistencies is because Lindsay was "freaked out" and scared to speak up. Detective Lyons has not seen Lindsay's deposition. Lindsay had said in the deposition that she saw Spurgeon shake her sister with a "long, angry shake."

The prosecution notes that the variations in Lindsay's testimony were due to her being at an older age during the deposition and able to articulate better. (Even when she was a small child, she would have really had no motive to say that Spurgeon had done such a horrible thing to her sister. The harmful situation was not "introduced" as a possibility to Lindsay by anyone. She voluntarily told her mother what had happened and that's why the police were notified at the time).

The state then calls Dr. Sally Smith, the pediatrician from All Children's Hospital, whose testimony was important at this hearing. She outlines what she saw at the hospital on August 22, 2008, in a similar manner to what she would later do at the trial. She notes that the reason Maria had been transferred to All Children's Hospital from Mease Hospital was because she had a brain injury and could not breathe on her own. Mease was unable to treat this type of situation in a child. She discusses the abusive head trauma, including the subdural hematoma and retinal hemorrhages. She concludes that it was physical abuse, high force acceleration/deceleration, and that bruises are not always seen.

The state then allows Smith to point out that a child could be shaken severely but not die from it. Trauma to the brain can sometimes be sustained, and the child can go on to lead a normal life with only some minor learning disabilities. She rules out anything that could have happened to Maria accidentally. She says that "Maria lost consciousness immediately after receiving the injury."

To dispute her testimony, the defense notes that there were no obvious injuries on the outside of her body, no broken bones. There was no way to determine how many successive shakes Maria received or impacts and shakes received. (Does that really matter? One is too many.)

After a fifteen-minute recess, Lindsay Anderson is questioned, the intent being to see if her testimony will be allowed at the trial under the Williams Rule. Lindsay is fourteen years old with reddish hair, looking the typical young teen. At the time of the incident, she was six years old, and her sister Gabrielle was not even a year old yet. She states that Gabrielle was in a walker. She was crying a lot. Stephanie picked up Gabrielle and yelled at her and shook her. She jerked her out of the walker and shook her, shaking her head back and forth about four or five times. Stephanie was angry. Stephanie dropped her in the crib, which was also a playpen, she notes.

"Do you remember these things?" She is asked.

"Barely."

The state tries to strengthen her testimony and mitigate the fact that Lindsay "barely" remembers it. She certainly remembered it at the time because there was a CPI report filed. It would have had a traumatic effect on her, and she would not likely forget it, although it is possible she could be blocking it out to some extent because it frightened her so badly.

The defense states that they are not sure if it was ever established that Stephanie tossed Gabrielle up in the air and caught her by the arm, pulling her arm out of its socket. Maybe this is the way Lindsay saw it, but it could have been a possible injury caused by jerking her out of the walker by her arm. The defense relentlessly attacks her testimony. She begins to cry. She says she does not remember speaking to the child protection investigator when she was six years old. "I don't remember...maybe I got mixed up." She responded, just as many adults do, that she does not remember specifics to many of the questions that she is asked. She may also be afraid of the ramifications of revealing what she saw, but more likely, she has blocked out the traumatic effect it has had on her.

On redirect, the state shores up her testimony, and the important pieces still hang in the air. Gabrielle was shaken and thrown/dropped in the crib. Spurgeon was angry.

The state then calls Sharon Anderson, Lindsay and Gabrielle's mother. To protect her identity, I will not describe her, except to say that there is nothing unusual in her appearance. The attorney asks an odd question. "Did Lindsay have any anger issues?"

"Yes, to some degree." I tried to rationalize why this question was asked. Possibly because the defense already knew the answer, the state wanted to get it on the table. Also, it may go to show how the rough treatment of her sister at the Spurgeon home had affected her personality in a deep-rooted way.

"Were there any other adults in the home that day?" Mrs. Anderson is asked.

"I saw no other adults there."

She talks about how that day caused trauma to Gabrielle for about three or four months. She had to hold her constantly and not put her in a walker or a playpen. This behavior would be consistent with an infant who has been abused.

Then the defense reviews her testimony. They do not seem to take issue with what Mrs. Anderson has said but that she seems unconcerned with any abuse having occurred. (Obviously, she had been concerned or the child protective investigations would not have been contacted). Then there was some discrepancy about whether Gabrielle was picked up by one arm or by two hands under her arms.

A friend of Spurgeon's, Marcia Gadson,* says that she was there that day, and that nothing wrong happened to Gabrielle or her sister. This disputes Sharon Anderson's testimony that she saw no other adults there that day. Gadson contends that Stephanie was a good caregiver and patient with the children.

Since the Anderson children were at the Spurgeon home on more than one day, it is difficult to lend credibility to Gadson's statement, unless she was also there every day and minute that the Anderson children were. This is just my own observation. The prosecution does not spend much time on cross because there is really no way to prove she was there that day, and at least one witness has said that she saw no other adult there.

This ends the hearing for the day, and everyone leaves wondering if any of this information will show up at trial.

CHAPTER 16

FIRST THING THE next day, the defense calls Daniel Anderson, stepfather of Lindsay, and father of Gabrielle. He states that he never heard Lindsay say when she was six years old that Stephanie did anything bad. (Of course, this is her stepfather, and most young girls will normally discuss things with their mothers that they would never talk about with their fathers or stepfathers.) He only confirms that Lindsay said that she saw Stephanie jerk Gabrielle out of the "saucer, walker, or something." The defense points out the differences between a six-year-old's testimony and a fourteen-year-old's, attempting to cast doubt on Lindsay's current sworn testimony. The defense also points out that Gabrielle is above average in intelligence and that she is healthy.

The prosecution establishes that the action of Spurgeon upon Gabrielle was a violent action from a sitting position to the held position. All other testimony aside, even Lindsay's father has stated that Lindsay had talked about this action.

Next, the defense calls a woman who was formerly employed by the Pinellas County Sheriff's Child Protection department. It is Sandy Cielo,* a Hispanic woman in her forties. She was an agent for the Child Protection Investigations Department and was on the investigation team regarding the incident involving Gabrielle. Sandy was investigating in March of 2002, and she had noted then that there were no marks on Gabrielle and that there is no recorded testimony stating that Gabrielle had been shaken at the time.

The prosecution then questions Cielo, indicating that she cannot exactly state word for word what she had said back in March of 2002, but that she can only refer to her notes in giving testimony in this hearing. In her notes, she has written that Gabrielle was thrown into the air and caught. The prosecutor points out and Cielo agrees that often children leave out facts and details until the second interview. The attorney asks why Marcia Gadson was not interviewed until June when the incident took place in March. (This is a great question because Spurgeon would certainly have wanted any witnesses present who noted her innocence to be interviewed as quickly as possible. But here we have a three-month delay. Did Gadson just show up out of the woodwork?). No acceptable answer is given. Gadson just didn't think it was necessary to indicate she was there immediately since she "knew" Spurgeon didn't do anything wrong. I contend that she was not there when the incident occurred.

As this hearing winds down, the prosecution points out that there is sufficient evidence and case history to allow Lindsay's testimony to be admitted into evidence for the trial. Other cases are referenced that back the need to introduce the Williams Rule into the trial so that the court can be aware of Spurgeon's pattern of behavior.

The defense contends that Gadson's testimony that nothing happened should be enough and that because she saw nothing happen, that the Anderson's incident should not be allowed into trial. They also indicate that the degree of shaking related by Lindsay would have caused some injury to Gabrielle, but she is fine. They review the inconsistencies in Lindsay's and Sharon Anderson's testimonies. Their arguments sound strong.

However, with respect to the degree of shaking, they will negate that SBS even exists when the trial is underway. To be fair, it is an entirely different defense team that will state this at trial, but it is a direct contradiction to the premise mentioned here by this defense. Either SBS exists as a component to abusive head trauma and would have contributed to the injuries, or it does not and thus would not.

But now, at this point in the hearing, the judge interrupts the defense and says that it was Lindsay's testimony that Gabrielle was grabbed, shaken with both hands, and then thrown into the air and caught by one arm and then thrown into a playpen or crib. She wants the record to show that it was not just shaking alone that allegedly occurred. (The similarities between this situation and what apparently happened to Maria are eerie).

The defense then highlights that the minor inconsistencies are very major considering that Gabrielle never bumped her head in the crib. (This is not a known fact because, if there was padding in the crib on the backboard, or if she actually hit her head on the mattress itself, a bump or bruise likely would not be evident).

The defense mentions Lindsay's mental issues and continues to argue against allowing the information from this hearing in court. They define the Williams Rule by indicating that it is for the victim being the same victim, and Gabrielle and Maria are two different victims. It sounds odd to admit on their part that these two little girls are both "victims." It is also their interpretation of the Williams Rule. Definitions indicate though that it does not necessarily refer to the same victim, it definitely applies to the same defendant.

Locatethelaw.org defines the Williams Rule as:

character evidence in the evidence code. It allows similar fact evidence of other crimes, wrongs, or acts when relevant to prove a material fact in issue such as:

1. proof of motive;
2. opportunity;
3. intent;
4. preparation;
5. plan;
6. knowledge;
7. identity;
8. absence of mistake or accident;
9. other special circumstances as specified in case law.[1]

According to this definition, the rule would apply to the character of Stephanie Spurgeon in other acts or wrongs to prove a material fact in issue, which would include intent and possibly opportunity, above. The prior acts, so similar in nature that took place in the same location (the Spurgeon home) against the same type of victim (a very young child) validate the application of the rule in this case. But would the prosecution use it if they are granted the right to do so?

The judge states that there will be a written order regarding her decision on the Williams Rule in one week.

It would all be for naught, because even though Judge Newton issues an order allowing for the Williams Rule to apply and for all this testimony to be admissible at trial, the prosecution decides that it is too risky to use it. They want a solid conviction without likelihood of an appeal. Using the Williams Rule because the judge allowed it could be grounds for appeal later by another judge who might conclude that it should never have been allowed. The same source, locatethelaw.org notes that it is not a good idea to use the Williams Rule in a trial. The prosecution needs to consider the following:

Weigh your Williams Rule evidence carefully. More of our cases are reversed on this issue than any other. Since the Williams Rule is one of admissibility, the burden is on the defendant to raise an objection to show that the evidence should be excluded. Once the defendant raises his objection, the burden shifts to the state to show relevancy and to show that the evidence is not being offered to show propensity to commit crimes. Be careful not to make the Williams Rule evidence the feature of the trial. It may be reversed.[2]

So the prosecution, even though they disagreed amongst themselves on this issue, ultimately does the safe thing and chooses to keep this information tucked away. But now that the trial is over, here it is, with names changed to protect those involved, in order to present a more complete picture.

CHAPTER 17

FEBRUARY 9, 2012

BEFORE THE DEFENSE begins to make its case in the trial, Ron Kurpiers makes a Motion for Acquittal based upon the alleged innocence of his client. This standard procedure is expected by both the judge and the state. In response, Judge Newton denies the acquittal and states her reasons for doing so by giving a synopsis of her view of the case so far.

The judge concludes that the evidence is most favorable to the state and enters the information into the record, summarized here.

There have been eleven witnesses presented by the state. Maria Harris was a year old at the time of her death. There were numerous expert witnesses all testifying to abusive head trauma. The manner of death was homicide. The cause of death was blunt head trauma. Judge Newton's summary is further paraphrased here:

On August 21, 2008, [in the morning] the victim was a healthy, normal, one-year-old child who went to the home of Ms. Spurgeon. At 2:45 p.m. that day, when she was picked up by her grandmother, she was nonresponsive, limp, not awakening, foaming from her mouth, vomiting, and rushed to Mease Hospital, not at any point to regain consciousness.

She passed away seven days later. The doctors at All Children's Hospital discussed a variety of injuries, subdural hematoma, retinal hemorrhages, abruptly developing neurological abnormalities. All these things were present. The conclusion was abusive head trauma. Dr. Sally Smith referred to it as physical abusive trauma to the head. "For all of these reasons, the court denies the Motion of Acquittal."

Although Kurpiers by necessity needed to ask for this acquittal based on the proposed innocence of his client, it may have caused more damage than he could have imagined. The jury heard the judge's summary of the state's presentation of the case, and although she may have not stated the events with 100 percent accuracy, she did get the most meaningful parts right and they were: the condition Maria was in when she arrived at and when she left the Spurgeon home, the agreement of the witnesses as to abuse causing her injuries, and the manner and cause of death. The very word *homicide* stuck in my mind because this manner of death was ruled on by the medical examiner, Jon Thogmartin, and he doesn't rule lightly on these things. He had even sent Maria's brain off to another ME who specializes in examining brains in head trauma cases.

If I couldn't shake the fact that the judge has put the manner of death as "homicide" out there for all to hear, what would the jury be thinking? Of course, they would now be able to hear everything the defense could throw out there to refute the charge that Stephanie Spurgeon had murdered Maria Harris.

Ron Kurpiers tells the court that he suspects he will call three paramedics and three doctors as witnesses. One doctor is not a medical doctor, but has a PhD in Physics.

But the first person Kurpiers calls is none of these six people. Instead, he is the parent of another child who was at the Spurgeon home that day. Ronald Chola,* father of two, takes the stand. He looks a little frightened, but is anxious to speak just the same.

"In August of 2008, did you explore putting your son Carter* in a day care?" Kurpiers asks.

"I found Ms. Spurgeon through an ad on Craigslist and went to her house to observe her." He said that he went there three times to "basically see how she handled herself with children. I was impressed. I did go with my wife on the last time. I wanted my wife to say, 'This is the person.'"

"Did you bring your son?"

"Yes."

"Did he interact with other children?"

"Yes."

Kurpiers says to Chola that he then made the decision to place Carter in the day care and Chola agrees.

"August 21, 2008. Do you remember the date okay?"

"Yes."

"What time?"

"7:15."

"Were there any other parents there?"

"No."

Chola did not know it but Patricia Harris was there, sitting in her car where she had parked it on the side of the Spurgeon home, crying and praying inside.

"Were there other children there?"

"Yes."

"Prior to going there, did you know there would be a new child there?"

"Yes. My wife told me."

"Tell us what you saw."

At this point, we are never told how many other children are at the home, just that Chola responded affirmatively when asked if there were other children there. This response indicates that there was at least one other child there besides Maria. I was hoping that on cross-examination, the state would ask Mr. Chola how many other children he saw there since Spurgeon was the only caretaker, but he was not asked. It was just one more element missing from testimony regarding what could have been gleaned from behind the closed doors of the day care: just how many children were at the Spurgeon home that day that she was solely responsible for, and how many there were when Chola dropped off his son.

Chola relates, "When I walked in the house, there was a child in a fenced-in play yard. Stephanie Spurgeon was putting stuff in the fridge. The child was really loud and disorganized and unfocused. Her head was going back and forth. She did reach out for my son, and my son ran away. She made no eye contact." (This Mr. Chola was the same man who, at the Williams Rule hearing, stated that Maria had a blank stare. It was not to be repeated at the trial, and that statement seems to be contradicted by what he describes as Maria's behavior here.)

Kurpiers asks if Chola knew her name.

"Not at the time."

"Loud. What did you mean by that?"

"Just a loud child. More yelling, I'd say. Not crying, could have been happy, yeah."

He is asked about how long he observed her.

"Possibly three minutes...probably. I was there a total of five minutes." He then says that he tried to personally interact with the little girl and say hi. "You know, that was basically it...say bye...done for the day."

On cross-examination, Brian Daniels says, "You saw the child standing."

"Yes."

"Conscious."

"Yes."

"She reached out for your son."

"Yes."

"She saw him."

"Yes."

Daniels asks him if she had made what sounded like a happy squeal, and Chola responds that he didn't know the child; he had never seen her before.

"Do you remember the evening of August 22? [Being questioned by] Detective Todd Green? Do you remember describing it as a happy squeal, not crying, not in distress?"

"Yes."

"And she was able to stand?"

"Yes."

Their next witness is Lt. Daryl Meil, a firefighter from Palm Harbor Fire Rescue who has been on the job for twenty years. When Kurpiers asks him about when he responded to a call at the Harrises' address in Palm Harbor, Meil says that he would like to look at the report.

"What time did you answer?" Ron asks.

"It shows it at 15:01, no, 15:26."

"The same as 3:26 in the afternoon?"

"Yes."

"What do you recall when you first arrived?"

"We were looking for the correct address. There was a young lady at the front door holding a baby. The door was open. [The baby looked] kind of lethargic. She was holding the baby up to her chest. The baby's color was not looking good. Her arms were kind of out."

"What was your primary role?"

"We have a paramed. As a lieutenant, I'm responsible for the safety of the scene. The two people in the house were highly upset. I took them into the kitchen to get basic information."

"Were they upset to the point of interfering with the care of the baby?"

"Yes."

"Your role was to get the baby away?"

"Yes, and also to gather information on the patient: medical history, medications, allergies."

"You were taking information in a location inside the home away from the baby. Did you bring the baby inside the home?"

"No. Sunstar brought a stretcher to the front door. An assessment was done in the doorway."

"Did you stay with the mom and grandma until the ambulance went to the hospital?"

"They wanted to be with the child."

So far, Meil's testimony is in harmony with Patricia's and Esther's. There is nothing unusual mentioned up to this point. Even the timely arrival of the ambulance is noted, only minutes after EMS had been called.

Kurpiers continues with his questions. "Was there ever use of a defibrillator?

"No." Meil explains that there were patches applied to Maria's chest area to check her heart rate so they would be able to tell quickly if they needed to shock her heart. That was not done.

"Did you ride in the ambulance?"

"No. I took the fire truck and followed with the crew."

"Did you hear the baby make any noises?"

"No."

"When you arrived at the hospital, were you close to the baby?"

"I was outside the curtain in the ER. The staff was working on the baby."

"Did you hear the baby cry then?"

"Yes."

"Was this a relief to you?"

"Yes. I conveyed this to the mother and grandmother. They weren't intentionally interfering with patient care, but they were upset. They appeared to be under a great amount of stress." (Recall earlier that Kurpiers had tried to pin Esther down on being under stress, and her denial of that. Again, she obviously didn't mean that she wasn't stressed out, but that she was having a far greater emotional reaction. She was closer to hysteria. Meil's testimony confirms this.)

"They were highly upset," Kurpiers states. "Did the stress continue while you were there?"

"I tried to calm them down."

"They were under stress the whole time? Is that a fair statement?"

"Yes."

The state feels that there is no need for cross-examination. The amount of stress exhibited by the Harrises was not unusual. Any mother and grandmother would be extremely emotional if their child/grandchild was in the emergency room being worked on by a medical team, after having been delivered there by an ambulance for an unknown condition (at the time).

Also, the information that Meil provides about Maria's crying is not unusual. It is not uncommon for a child with a severe blunt head trauma to respond to pain by crying out and then slipping back into unconsciousness. No one noted that the crying continued for any length of time. That would have been a question for the state to ask had they wanted to cross-examine Meil, but it was not important enough to do so, if they did not have an idea of what his response would be. His testimony with Kurpiers was likely rehearsed, but cross-examinations never are, and it can be just as risky for the attorney doing the questioning as for the witness if the answer is unknown. In the case of this witness, his testimony did not harm the prosecuting side at all, and confirmed the emotional state of Patricia and Esther, as well as the fact that there was no delay in calling EMS after Pat's arrival at home with Maria.

Ron Kurpiers calls a Palm Harbor firefighter to the stand next, Rudolph "Tony" Mercer. He is a fairly young man, with a lean muscular frame and thick dark hair.

Kurpiers asks Mercer if he remembers responding to a call in August 2008, at around 3:00 p.m.

Mercer answers that yes he does.

"What did you see?"

"A grandmother and a mother described a baby in distress and needed help."

"What was your role?" Kurpiers asks Mercer, following a similar line of questioning to the one he asked of Meil.

"To care for the baby and get the baby to the hospital." Mercer then describes how he took vital signs including Maria's pulse, hooked up the pads, and got her on the stretcher and into the ambulance.

Kurpiers asks what tools were used during this time, and Mercer tells the court about Broselow tape, which is a tape that is laid out beside the baby to measure and in order to be able to tell what dosage of drugs to administer. (It is also useful to gauge what size equipment is necessary for emergency resuscitation procedures).

Kurpiers asks Mercer if he rode along in the ambulance with Maria, and the paramedics and he said that he did. There were no noises from Maria in the ambulance. Mercer was in close proximity to Maria's station in the emergency room.

"Did you hear crying in the ER?"

"Yes."

"Do you recall it vividly?"

"Yes," Mercer responds. "It was music to our ears, yes. A good sound for us."

Too Brief A Candle

"Was the baby breathing at the scene?"
"Yes."
"Your primary focus was the baby?"
"Mostly, yes."
"Not the mom or the grandma?"
"Not specifically, no."

Kurpiers asks if Mercer observed Patricia and Maria Harris and if they appeared to be under stress, and he said yes.

Again, the state chooses not to cross-examine this witness. The fact that Maria cried does not seem to be relevant to them, especially since—even if she slipped into consciousness momentarily and cried out for a few seconds while she was being worked on—she lapsed back into an unresponsive state shortly after, never to awaken again, according to the doctors' testimonies who examined her.

The defense's next witness is Helen Conroy, who was a paramedic with Sunstar in 2008 and had been so for about five and a half years.

Kurpiers asks her if she recalls responding to the scene at the Harris's address.

She says that yes, she does, that she recalls arriving there in the afternoon sometime after 3:00 p.m.

"About the same time as fire rescue?"

"Pretty much the same time. I pulled up the stretcher. The medics went inside. I couldn't see anything. I could hear someone say, "What's wrong with my baby?" Conroy said that the person sounded very upset.

"Were you driving the ambulance?" Kurpiers asks.

"Yes."

She notes that she saw paramedics enter the home from both Sunstar and from the fire department.

"Did you see the baby?"

"Yes."

"Who was carrying it?"

"If I remember correctly, it was one of the paramedics. She appeared to be unresponsive. She was very pale, breathing. She had a wet spot on her shirt."

Kurpiers asks if the spot was vomit, and she says that yes, it was vomit. She then related some testimony that was rather vague about the grandmother providing information about the vomit, that the baby had been whimpering, vomited, and went to sleep.

This testimony did not align with what Patricia Harris told the court during her testimony. She did not know that Maria had vomited until she arrived home with her in the car, and she could not have known that she "fell asleep" after vomiting because she had no way of seeing her when she was driving based on the position of the car seat.

Kurpiers then establishes that Conroy drove the ambulance to Mease hospital and entered the ER. She had no contact with anyone after she moved the stretcher over to the bed.

On a short cross, Brian Daniels asks Conroy for the name of the paramedic who treated Maria. It was Chris Chumbly.

Next, a critical expert witness for the defense is called, Dr. James Ipser. He is a distinguished gentleman with thinning white hair, and he has quite a remarkable background in his field. He enters the courtroom with a very large container of what I assume are documents in tow. Dr. Ipser has a PhD in physics. He is not actively teaching now but is a professor emeritus. He taught at the University of Florida for thirty years and spent ten additional years at the University of Chicago's physics department. He has taught both undergrad and advanced graduate students, and studies the motion of objects.

"I developed a course in accident reconstruction and biomechanics for physics students."

He also has published articles in seventy-eight publications and journals. He says that his specialty is biomechanics, but most of his publications are about astrophysics. He is a member of several societies related to accident reconstruction and physics. He has testified as an expert about 150 times in criminal, civil, and federal courtrooms in Pinellas County. He says that he is willing to take a case from any source, including the state. He has testified on shaken baby cases for the defense and the state about four or five times, "equally split."

Kurpiers stands tall and prepares himself for what will become a lengthy testimony from his witness. "When a case comes to you, what analyses do you form to reach your opinions?"

"I look at documents—police reports, medical reports, statements made, depositions. I go out and collect information that I myself need in order to do the calculations that I am asked to perform."

"In this case, how many hours did you spend?"

"Eight."

After this point, Dr. Ipser's testimony becomes extremely scientific and complex. I'm afraid he is beginning to lose some of the jury. Although I took many science courses in college that had nothing to do with my degree, to be frank, Ipser lost me several times. But the importance of this testimony would become even more critical *after* the trial when a sudden development occurs, so I will include all the relevant parts of his testimony here, outside of where he repeats himself. Kurpiers wants to know what records were reviewed in this case.

"Let me look at my stack here as an aid...Mease Hospital medical records, autopsy records—"

"Did you review the records from All Children's Hospital?" Kurpiers interrupts.

"Yes, I did."

"What are you looking for in medical records that you will need?"

"I want to identify the damage that has occurred and if there is any evidence that can tell us about any of the forces applied. One of the things I'm especially interested in is external forces."

It dawns on me, sitting there in the back of the courtroom, that this physicist has never laid eyes on Maria, living or deceased.

What he is basing his entire testimony on are the records that he has brought to the stand with him that he has to dig through to find what he being asked about. In no way am I belittling his knowledge, because he obviously must be extremely intelligent to have a PhD in physics, but all the knowledge in the world cannot replace being able to examine the actual person who was injured. I wonder if the defense will be calling any people who actually examined Maria, outside of the paramedics. I would have to wait and see.

Kurpiers asks the professor if he "saw" any external trauma.

"No," he responds, "none was found whatsoever." (Of course, he couldn't personally have observed any external trauma, which is why he had to respond in this manner. None was found, not, "I didn't see any.")

He answers Kurpiers questions that this sets the baseline, and the fact that there was no visible external trauma would play an important role, as well as the size, height, and weight of an individual.

Ipser discusses the weight of a body. "The heavier the body, the larger the force that must be used to move the body. The fundamental area of physics is mechanics. It deals with the motion of an object, which is changed by forces greater than the force. The more rapid the motion, the greater the weight, the more force is needed to generate the motion."

Kurpiers steers Ipser to where he gets his information from. "Do you use government studies?"

"The government has developed the criteria, say, in automotive design, to reach damage to the head or the brain. The name for the criteria is the Head Injury Criterion Index. HIC Index. It relates the force acting on the head to the damage that force can cause—permanent damage to the brain."

For me, as an uninvolved listener, it is hard to interpret what his testimony means, not because the meaning of the words are difficult to interpret, but because of the way that Dr. Ipser phrases his sentences. I wonder what Kurpiers is thinking as he questions him.

Kurpiers asks if the HIC is used on adults or children.

The doctor says that it can "go all the way down through the age groups. There are other studies which involve the rotational motion of the head also. There are two ways in which damage can be caused: the head moving into an object and stopping very suddenly. Another way is rotational motion back and forth rapidly, has the potential to cause problems."

Broken down, in my mind, the professor has just noted that blunt force trauma to the head and rapid acceleration/deceleration are the two methods that can cause damage to the head. So in calling this witness, the defense is conceding that SBS could exist and could cause damage. Unfortunately, the state never makes the link so that the defense has to own up to this fact or deny their own witness's testimony. But on the bright side, it really wouldn't carry too much weight. I want to mention it, however, because such a big deal is made throughout this case by Spurgeon's supporters and the defense that SBS is not a reality.

Kurpiers tries to negate SBS here. "Shaken baby syndrome?" he asks Dr. Ipser.

Ipser replies that he has studied little on this phenomenon. He says that he uses physics to calculate the value of these (government) indexes. In this case he notes that we are dealing with a twelve-month-old child who weighed approximately twenty pounds. He tells the court that he is not a radiologist and he is not offering medical opinions, but he is a physicist and he's talking about forces that can cause physical damage.

Personally, I could find no information about this HIC index online outside of the realm of automobile crash evaluation (often using crash test dummies), or for evaluating helmets for cyclists. The whole concept of a head injury in this scope does not even apply to nonaccidental blunt force trauma. If it did, these statistics would be evident as well as statistics for falls, fights such as boxing, etc. The application of this index to Maria's injury is not only misleading, but it makes no sense. It is apples and oranges. Automotive crashes don't even vaguely come close to nonaccidental blunt head force trauma. Some of the same injuries might be present, but one would have to discount the speed of the vehicle, whether it was struck by another vehicle or whether it struck an immovable object, and other factors that have no connection to a one-year-old child becoming comatose at a day care and exhibiting no external injuries, unlike a car accident.

Kurpiers asks Ipser how much force would have been necessary to shake Maria.

"To cause brain damage, you want the force to be less than a certain value. I can calculate the value that you want to remain below. Let me put it this way: the government has told us through experiments what forces are safe. Force would have to be applied to the head to get into a dangerous area." Then he talks about shaking a head back and forth and the amount of force required on the head.

I fail to see the connection between what he is trying to explain and Maria being slammed into an object such as a mattress. Ipser said that the government has done experiments. It would seem logical that these were not done on live people, but instead on crash test dummies. My assumption would turn out to be correct. Can subdural hematomas be mimicked in crash test dummies?

Ipser is now indicating something on a diagram. He is showing some connection between a value that the government uses to assess danger "and the number of Gs that you have to use in force to make the head go back and forth." "One G," he says, "equals the weight of an object. We all live in a one-G environment. Pounds of force equal the number of Gs times the weight of an object."

I look at each jury member in turn. Only a couple of people actually look like they have a clue as to what Dr. Ipser is talking about. This doesn't make them ignorant jurors. It just makes them wonder what any of this testimony has to do with child abuse and whether it was done or not. Maybe he will get to that relation-ship next.

Dr. Ipser takes his lecture up a notch. "I know this doesn't mean anything, but I'm going to give you this number without going into the calculation. I can calculate the number of Gs that can be applied to the head, 350, that is safe—the recommended value that we stay below because twice that is always when dam-age has been observed to occur. To get at the upper limit of the safe zone, 50 Gs acting on the head, you have to be holding the whole body. That's fifty Gs for the whole body."

What? I think to myself.

"If we want to exert force by shaking," Dr. Ipser continues, "fifty Gs times twenty pounds [Maria's weight] equals one thou-sand pounds. To reach the upper limit of the safe zone, you need to reach the upper limit of the safe zone." (*What?*) "I don't know any *adult* who could do this." (Remember this last statement as it will be very important posttrial.)

"This is the safe zone. You would need about 50 percent more force than this for a subdural hematoma to occur." (Again, I won-der what tests have been done to prove this theory as live people had not been used in experiments to see how much force was necessary on their heads to cause a subdural hematoma to occur.)

Dr. Ipser reaches this conclusion: "You can't do it by shaking back and forth. There are other ways you can do it. Other ways, it can be done." (Maybe by blunt force trauma to the head?)

Kurpiers wants to know about these other ways. "How can it be done?"

"You could make the head hit something very hard. [If you] took a child and slammed her head against this table, or any hard surface. The head is going to stop immediately, then the aver-age person could hit their [*sic*] head hard enough." (He switches from child to average person in this comment, making his answer ambiguous to the jury.)

"Would you expect to see external trauma?"

"There would be some evidence of impact. A cracked skull—that's what you would have had to do—threw it down, slammed it. By shaking, there is no way." (Dr. Ipser is a physicist, but yet he is claiming that there would be a cracked skull from blunt force trauma. Again, what experiments have been done that prove this result, especially with live children?)

"You talked to us about the force that would have been necessary," Kurpiers exclaims, "in excess of one thousand pounds."

"Yes. Typical force is one hundred pounds."

"It would be like a crushing force."

"If you hold the child," Ipser says, "the shaking of the body causes the head to go back and forth, but that is through the neck—that would severely damage the neck. An adult would only need 15 Gs to damage the neck." (So now we introduce the neck, which was never a consideration in Maria's case as she had no neck tissue damage. And where do the 15 Gs come from? Was this tested on people as well?)

Kurpiers asks the physicist if he formed an opinion "to a reasonable degree of scientific possibility given the lack of no sudden impact [sic]."

"No one could achieve it [by shaking], and even if they [sic] could, there would be severe damage to the neck."

"Shaking without blunt impact on a hard surface would be sufficient to cause this damage?"

"Shaking and impact on a soft surface—well, you need a hard surface. A soft surface doesn't have enough force to cause the damage to sufficiently stop the head." (Where is the evidence to back this statement?)

I am surprised at this point at all the testimony proffered at face value, and I am anxious to see how the state will handle it upon cross-examination. I wouldn't have to wait long, and they do not disappoint me.

Holly Grissinger wants to know immediately from Dr. Ipser who told him that someone shook Maria Harris's body.

"It was the claim of Dr. Smith?" he asks, as if he is unsure.

"Did Dr. Smith say she [Spurgeon] picked up this child and shook her?"

"Yes, I think that's what she implied."

Grissinger asks him if it is true that Smith had said that it was a shake and/or a repetitive force with impact.

"Yes, it could be." He admits.

Grissinger then gets Ipser to state that he performed eight hours of trial preparation, and received $250 an hour. He is not a medical doctor, which he admits without hesitation, and he has never handled a baby's brain. What he does is analyze vehicles versus objects and the effects of change of motion of objects in the vehicles. But he also admits that 95 percent of his articles are about astrophysics, not mechanical physics.

Finally, the government study origins come out in the open. The HIC index, Ipser explains, was developed in the 1970s with primates! "It is fair to say that no one gives up their children to perform these tests." (I think it is also fair to say that apes are not exactly built like children. They have longer arms and wider shoulder spans, shorter necks, and smaller brains. They probably have thicker skulls too, especially if that horrible testing was done on adult apes. To add to these variances, these tests, according to Dr. Ipser himself, were done in moving vehicles, not with a living creature being slammed by a larger living creature into a solid object either once or repeatedly back and forth. Thank God that wasn't ever done, at least that we know of! It certainly wouldn't say much for the compassion of mankind for the animals that we are given dominion over. The original HIC tests on primates were abusive enough.)

Next, Dr. Ipser defends his theories on the safe number levels. "You make a determination. I'm taking the records—forces that had to be applied to cause damage [to Maria]. I used the value that is deemed to be safe, not a precise value. It's a range. Three hundred and fifty is a safe value way below the levels to be found to be associated with this type of damage."

Grissinger discusses an article on biomechanics with Ipser that states that almost nothing is known about biomechanical levels of the injury tolerance of subdural hematomas in children. Dr. Ipser says that it does go out and say what is deemed to be a safe level. (But how? If almost nothing is known about the levels, how can he know what a safe level is?)

Grissinger mentions that the levels that Dr. Ipser refers to are the result of a single incident of a shaken child—one event over a short period of time.

Dr. Ipser talks about studies he uses that reference contact with soft objects and that the value of the index with soft objects can be extrapolated. (How?)

The attorney wants to know if the study included limitations. "They are not using live infants, they are using dummies."

"The values produced are so far away from what is deemed to be dangerous. The studies won't mimic an infant's neck exactly. If you shake a baby rapidly, you risk damage to the neck itself...they can't...the damage to the surrogate neck can't be determined."

Dr. Ipser may have unintentionally or even intentionally have drifted off the track of the questioning, which was, I believed, about blunt force trauma to the head, not SBS. He keeps talking about damage to the necks and how it can't be ascertained with accuracy because they can't test with live infants. That's not what Holly is asking him about.

She now questions him about what percentile Maria's head was in.

"I only know that her brain was larger than the midpoint. I don't know what percentile. No, not exactly. What's important is the overall weight of the child."

Grissinger catches an important contradiction in his statement. "It makes absolutely no difference if the child's head is larger in relation to the body?"

"Well...yes, but we are not talking about a giant variation between head and body for a child of twenty pounds."

When I reviewed these notes later, they did seem contradictory, because it should be obvious to most people that there is a significant difference in the proportional weight of a one-year-old child's head to her body compared to, say, the head of a twelve-year-old child to her body. Children have to "grow into their head size," and it is even evident in photos of young children how much larger their heads are in proportion to their bodies than older children. It doesn't have to be a "giant variation," but only one large enough to make a difference when considering certain nonaccidental injuries and how they can occur. I speak as a layman and not a physicist, but I only want to point out that the head size and weight of a toddler in proportion to the body should not be trivialized. It is a very important consideration. For instance, when referring to twenty pounds, a three-pound head would be fifteen percent of the entire body weight, which is a much higher ratio than that of an adult, or my head would weigh almost twenty pounds!

Grissinger wants to know if Dr. Ipser is viewing Maria's injuries as a single shaking episode, and he says that yes, he is focusing on that.

"You did not consider repetitive force and impact?" This is a great question, because in an automobile accident, there are typically not repeated crashes and impacts on the head, but only one. The professor admits that he did not consider these.

"You did not do repetitive force [experiments] into an object?"

"No."

"That's your opinion, correct?" Grissinger refers to his previous testimony.

"Yes."

"You're not a medical doctor."

"No."

"Is it a fair statement that crash test dummies aren't accurate because no one can determine damage to the neck?"

"Grossly speaking, it's the same amount of force on the total body," he responds. "It's going to be the same, regardless of the neck. The head is going to experience that same loading too."

"Shaking a baby and shaking an adult is the same?"

"Yes, the head is going to respond," Ipser says, evading the actual question.

This answer takes me aback, even though Ipser doesn't give a definite yes or no response. Earlier, the professor had talked about weight and Gs and the amount of force necessary to inflict injuries on a twenty-pound child and a safety zone number. Now, it sounds as if he is saying that weight doesn't matter because the head will respond regardless of who is shaken or has impact. Even if Maria was not subject to repetitive shaking back and forth, but instead, a backward shake and then an impact—I believe the impact happened twice in a row because of the admitted "two pats" on the back—wouldn't a child's head in general, if the child is shaken, respond more vigorously because the neck is weaker, and the head weighs more in proportion to the body than an adult? These are my conjectures, but the physicist has not proven otherwise. He talks about the mechanics of motion. It would seem to me that a heavier object attached to a lighter and more flexible one is going to move back and forth with a greater degree of motion leading to more potential damage. Also, one must take into account, the strength and anger of the person doing the shaking. I contend that this part of the equation has never been measured.

Grissinger again confirms that Ipser is not talking about a cumulative effect, and he says that, "No, I'm talking about one isolated effect." This is perhaps because his experiments are with auto accidents and demonstrate results from single effects.

Dr. Ipser discusses an SBS study. He says that he had already formed his own opinion, and this study confirmed it. The study used a constructed "model" of a one-month-old infant that was placed in an accelerometer. He does not go into detail about his opinion, just that this study confirms it.

Grissinger notes that it is an imperfect science, and he says that yes, it is, but that dealing with adults is not perfect either.

The defense decides not to offer any questions on redirect, which is probably a good idea. They likely want to minimize the verbal damage caused by this confusing testimony. Dr. Ipser could not link Maria's injuries directly to any of his studies. In hiring him as an expert witness, the defense had hoped to get some answers indicating that there was no way that Maria's injuries could have been caused by an adult of Spurgeon's stature. In interviewing him to consider him as a witness, they had not done their homework, because, even though he did his best to explain the mechanics of motion and strength in single impacts, he no doubt confused the jury and his testimony had little to do with Maria Harris's situation.

Keep in mind that he specifically said, "I don't know any adult who could do this." He was referring to Maria's injuries. This is an odd statement because when one considers all the abusive cases that have occurred and brought to trial, some with defendants who admitted to the crimes, it would mean that none of them could have possibly committed them if the child had injuries similar to Maria's, especially if the child died from them. That is not plausible. Also, remember this statement, because after the trial, the defense would change its position entirely based on a single possibility that they would claim they had no knowledge of.

CHAPTER 18

THE NEXT DEFENSE witness is a medical doctor, Dr. Diana Carbonero-Canuzzi. She works at the Mease Hospital emergency room, and had been there for the last six years. She sees patients in all conditions. She says she was on staff the day Maria was brought in. Kurpiers asks her if she remembers seeing twelve-month-old Maria in the emergency room.

"When were you first notified?"

"When they walked in or EMS. I don't remember, it could be either one. I probably followed the child into the room." She goes over her standard procedures when a patient is brought in by ambulance. She examines the patient to make sure he is breathing, checks for responsiveness, etc.

State Exhibit 4, the Mease medical records, are introduced.

"Is there any indication of external injuries?" Kurpiers asks.

"I'm taking a moment..." The doctor flips through the records. "No obvious sign of head injury based on my record. A CT scan was ordered. I would have ordered that."

"Was the child conscious or unconscious?"

"Not conscious. Not responding purposefully." The doctor notes that Maria cried out upon deep palpation.

"Yes, she cried. She did."

Apparently, she only remembers this from reading the records, because earlier she said that she doesn't remember who brought Maria in and that she "probably" followed her into the room. She also notes that a CT scan was ordered. She says she would have ordered that. If she was the doctor on staff that day, then yes, she would have ordered it, but another person, perhaps a physician's assistant, could have examined Maria. Doesn't this doctor know for sure if she ordered the CT scan? Wouldn't her authorization be on the record itself if she did?

"She came in at what time?"

"It says here, 15:50. 3:50."

"How long was she in the care of Mease?"

"I don't recall. Fairly brief." She explains that they test, stabilize, and make phone calls.

Kurpiers asks her if she recalls making the calls to transfer her to All Children's Hospital, and she says that she does remember. Then he asks if Maria remained in her care from 3:50 until 7:30 p.m.

"Once a patient is stabilized and accepted, generally not. I don't continue to care for the patient. I don't remember if I went back into the room or not."

"Prior to her arrival, was her blood glucose pretty high?"

"I don't recall."

Kurpiers asks about the blood glucose test done at the hospital and if it was pretty high.

"I think it was 290," she says.

Kurpiers asks if the glucose and ketones in the urine could be related to the stress of the situation.

"It could be the cause," Dr. Carbonero-Canuzzi responds, helping to rule out diabetes even though she is a defense witness.

On cross, the doctor explains that Maria was transferred to All Children's because she had a head injury and Mease doesn't have the proper critical care for pediatric patients. She is the only actual doctor that "saw" Maria Harris alive who was called by the defense. She was a weak witness for them in this regard because she remembers very little specifically about Maria and was just doing her job as an ER doc in getting her stabilized and sent off to the hospital that could handle her injuries.

There is one more defense witness today, and he would turn out to be quite interesting. Dr. Mark Herbst, a radiologist who has worked for himself since 1998, reads images for independent imaging centers through the Internet. He then prepares his reports online, and doctors download and read them.

Dr. Herbst has an extensive curriculum vitae including holding the position of head of MRI departments at two hospitals. Eighty percent of his analyses are now MRIs. He has published a few articles, all concerning radiology. He explains how radiology is more sophisticated today with films being downloaded onto CDs.

Dr. Herbst has testified over two hundred times, and of these, twenty to thirty were regarding head trauma. He is energetic and a bit quirky, perhaps in his early forties, with glasses and thinning brown hair. When I did a search for him later, I found that he is or was an adjunct professor at St. Petersburg College, and that he is listed as a radiologist, lecturer, and expert witness on LinkedIn.

Upon questioning by Kurpiers, Herbst explains that he uses a system that makes the information on the images anonymous. He has no outside information on where it comes from. It will have a patient name and an attorney name if there is one. "I go through the images and write down everything. Then I call the attorney and tell them [sic] what I found, and then I can tell if what I found helps you or hurts you."

It goes without saying that Dr. Herbst is another witness of the defense who neither saw Maria nor her body, nor photos of her body. He only saw two reports of MRIs and CT scans and used these to draw his conclusions. This does not make him a bad analyzer, but it does suggest that he did not have the complete information necessary to reach the correct conclusions. And he would soon have a courtroom epiphany concerning what he suddenly notes on one of the images of Maria's brain that I researched later and was able to find refuting evidence for.

Kurpiers leads him to the studies that he looked at, Exhibits 2 and 3, a CT scan and an MRI.

"I looked at them in chronological order, so I looked at the CT scan first from August 21, 2008."

"How do you analyze a CT scan?" asks Kurpiers.

"The lowest slice out of thirty-two slices—the level of the eyeballs right through the eyes into the top of the head. White is bone, gray is soft tissues. Two main things I compare the images to: a database of normal in my head, and I compare symmetry on the picture." (He must be really good to have an entire database of what is normal in his head. I'm not saying that this isn't possible, but I've heard no such other commentary from any radiologist.) "There is no external injury; no swelling," he notes, indicating the images that are up on the lighted display. "There is nothing outside the skull."

"What inside the skull alerted you that something may be abnormal?"

"Starting from the very first slices, there are areas of the brain that are darker than they should be. [This is] not normal. As I go through, I'm seeing these dark, splotchy areas in the brain... indicate water in the tissues that is between the tissues. Swelling. This is a lot of edema. This is so obvious! Any edema is abnormal. Very abnormal!"

"Edema indicates—as a radiologist, what, to you?"

Dr. Herbst lists out some of the things that can cause swelling in the brain, including trauma, stroke (infarction), drowning, aspiration, tumors and masses, and infections, which include herpes of the brain, fungus, and parasites.

He says he does not see any evidence of any of these *except trauma*. He points at an area between the hemispheres of Maria's brain on the CT scan. "This bright center line like dripping candle was—that *is* blood that is less than a week old. After a week, it decreases in density. After a week, it is the same color as the brain or even darker. So I know this blood is somewhere between an hour and a week old."

Kurpiers asks him if he can tell where the bleeding is coming from.

"I can't tell you exactly what blood vessel is bleeding. I can tell you that the area where the bleeding is happening is the subdural area, so it is a vein that is bleeding in there."

"Are veins fast bleeders?"

"No. Veins tend to ooze and can stop bleeding with pressure."

Herbst notes that every single slice of the CT scan shows abnormal edema and the subdural hematoma. Kurpiers asks him if he also evaluated the CT report from Mease Countryside Hospital and compared his findings to that report.

Herbst responds by saying that there was a little blood visible *inside* the brain. He says it is a shear injury when the brain is injured with impact, also known as a diffuse axonal injury. He is apparently referring to the Mease report here, but that is not clear. I wonder, though if the jury heard that Herbst has stated that this brain was injured with impact!

Kurpiers attempts to clear this up. "When would the injury to the brain that showed up on *this* CT scan have occurred?

"Two things," Dr. Herbst responds, "one is the edema, and one is the subdural. The subdural hemorrhage [can show up] immediately and up to seven days later. Usually, edema doesn't show up for a whole day. Usually, [the scan] is normal for the first twenty-four hours. It could be up to twelve hours ago. If it were less than twenty-four hours, you wouldn't have edema yet. This edema is more than likely more than twenty-four hours old." He goes on to say that it could be one day or two days and up to seven days. Then, he retracts the twenty-four hour statement and says that it would be between twelve hours and seven days for just the appearance of the edema. My head is swimming with alternate time frames now.

This entire conclusion about edema bothered me because at first, he says "usually," and then he eliminates the word "usually" and says that if the time that had passed was less than twenty-four hours, then there would be no swelling in the brain. Then he lowers the time to be a twelve-hour minimum before edema appears. So I went online when I got home and found numerous cases of edema occurring very rapidly after a brain trauma. In particular, I located a tragic news story of a sixteen-year-old football player who died only a couple of hours after a collision on the field and sustaining a subdural hematoma and massive edema in his brain. This brain swelling certainly didn't wait over twenty-four hours or even twelve to appear.[1]

After discussing bridging veins and oozing, Ron Kurpiers steers the testimony in an entirely new direction. "Are you familiar with lucid intervals? Have you seen them with subdural hematomas?"

"I'm well aware that lucid intervals occur in subdural hematomas," the doctor responds.

I note here that Kurpiers did not differentiate between acute and chronic subdural hematomas, and I remember that lucid intervals are usually connected with chronic ones, which are not fresh or new, or as traumatic. I also realize that Herbst does not directly answer the question. He does not say that he has seen lucid intervals, but only that he is aware that they occur.

Kurpiers asks him to look at the MRI images now and they show up on the display. The MRI, Kurpiers notes, was taken on August 22, 2008. "Do you see anything different?"

"No, just a different color scheme. The blotchy white areas are abnormal parts of the brain."

Dr. Herbst is now discussing how CT scans are a better imaging technique for picking up blood. "Any progression of subdural hematomas or edema has no significant difference because we are comparing apples and oranges." He is talking here about comparing CT scans with MRIs, and this makes a lot of sense. Not only are they two completely different methods of imaging, but the images they show are in drastically different shades of gray or contrast, depending on whether one is looking at an MRI or a CT scan.

The doctor discusses an impact injury, which he refers to as a shear injury. (This is where the bridging veins that connect the lining under the skull to the lining over the brain tear and ooze. It has been documented that this injury occurs upon rapid acceleration/deceleration of the head, which causes the brain to move rapidly within its dura casing, tearing these veins, and ultimately resulting in a subdural hematoma if there is enough bleeding before the oozing stops.) Dr. Herbst is saying that the brain "has gray matter on the outside and white matter on the inside." "This is oversimplified," he says. "Like two different Jell-Os with different hardnesses, the gray matter and white matter move in relation to each other, causing a shear. That one spot with the little splotch above the right is that junction." He indicates this spot on the image.

When he talks about shearing and moving in relation to each other, it almost sounds like tectonic plates moving at different speeds or in opposing directions. But regardless of how a person compares shearing to something he is familiar with, whether it is earthquakes or Jell-O, the point is that it is something that can result from a specific type of trauma.

As the doctor continues in his animated fashion, he begins to become even more excited, and I realize that this may be something that was not rehearsed at all with the defense. Or perhaps it was.

He starts describing the blood on the images. "If it's white, then it's less than seven days old. There are ways you can age the blood more on an MRI. Deoxygenated blood is at first blue. It breaks down in a very predictable way. It's white on the T-1 weighted images, which only occurs after three days—which means this blood is three days old. Now I see! It's more than five days old! Before it breaks down, it's black. I can tell you for sure *that* blood is greater than five days old!"

Dr. Herbst is nearly jumping out of the witness chair with excitement. But if he is such a brilliant expert witness, and all he does is read scans, why didn't he notice this "darker" blood before? He just now, in the courtroom, has this amazing revelation? Again, I went online later to look for how radiologists interpret blood shading in MRIs because it was the MRI that the doctor was viewing, and these are his areas of expertise.

Sometimes you find things that contradict what you are looking for, but thus far, I had not, and I felt justified because both times, Dr. Herbst had claimed his accuracy and he was adamant about it. This gave me good cause to look for exceptions to his rules. Also, I speculated and then found on several sites that water (edema) also shows up as darker on MR imaging. This is not to say that what Dr. Herbst saw was water, but only that he did not rule out that these darker areas could have been water as well.

I actually located a government abstract that discussed infantile subdural hematomas due to traffic accidents. In the article, it differentiates between some of the results caused by accidental versus abusive situations including SBS, although it may not necessarily apply here. As with the information provided to refute Dr. Ipser, the last sentence in this abstract is particularly interesting in relation to Dr. Herbst's claim about the different ages of the blood dating the hematoma as older than five days: "The fact that a single and recent trauma can result in mixed-density ISDH can be of great importance in forensic medicine."[2]

What this sentence is saying is that a single event can cause different densities of blood. The state's witnesses were in agreement that Maria's injuries happened when her symptoms showed up, in other words, at the day care. That would be the single and recent trauma. There would not have been an old trauma that would have continued with fresh bleeding to the point of sudden unconsciousness, retinal hemorrhaging, vomiting, an inability to breathe independently, and ultimately, death. It would have had to have been an acute, very recent, and very traumatic injury. By definition, acute subdural hematomas are very symptomatic.

> Subdural hematomas are usually the result of a serious head injury. When one occurs in this way, it is called an "acute" subdural hematoma. Acute subdural hematomas are among the deadliest of all head injuries. The bleeding fills the brain area very rapidly, compressing brain tissue. This often results in brain injury and may lead to death.[3]
>
> (nlm.nih.gov/medlineplus)

Then there is this very complex statement that, when broken down, means that different shadings in blood in an MRI can be a result of a variety of things. These things are mentioned here in this article on neuroimaging of brain hemorrhages from Harvard Medical School (emphasis mine):

> An acute hematoma may have high, low or mixed signal, *depending on its age, its hematocrit, the local pH and oxygen tension, and the field strength of the imaging system.* With higher field MR systems (1.0–1.5 Tesla), such images have significant signal loss (proportional to the square of the field strength) in portions of the lesion because of the abnormal magnetic susceptibility of hemorrhagic tissue. Magnetic susceptibility is a reflection of local interruptions of the homogeneity of the magnetic field, and such interruptions produced in parts of a hemorrhagic lesion make the image black. Deoxyhemoglobin has been reported to contribute to the increased magnetic susceptibility, but the chemistry of acute hemorrhage is extremely complex and this is reflected in the variability of observed signal changes.[4]
>
> (K. Johnson and J. A. Becker, Neuroimaging of Brain Hemorrhage, *The Whole Brain Atlas*)

I also came across numerous references and journals that said that dating of a subdural hematoma by MRI imaging alone may not be reliable in children because of the variations in hematocrit levels. The amount of iron a child has in his or her blood can alter the brightness of the blood on the MRI. It should only be viewed in conjunction with the CT scan, blood work, a physical exam, and the onset of symptoms in order to narrow down a time for the onset. These articles, many of which are pretty recent, are too many to list here, but I invite the reader to do a little research by doing a Google search of these words: "hematocrit variations child acute subdural hematoma."

At this juncture of the testimony, Kurpiers has let Dr. Herbst give his opinion with a dramatic flair. But now he asks him what causes subdural hematomas. I'm not sure if he does this because Dr. Herbst's testimony came out of the blue and Kurpiers wants to gain control over the questioning or not. Possibly he is afraid if he doesn't that he would have no idea what the doctor will say next. The testimony itself didn't seem to hurt the defense in any way, but perhaps the way in which it was delivered was a little over the top. Like I said, Dr. Herbst is a little quirky.

He responds to Kurpiers. "Typically, it's some kind of trauma [that causes subdural hematomas]."

"Can you tell what kind?"

"No." Herbst compares them to a dent in a car fender. You cannot tell what caused it.

"You didn't see any evidence of external impact to the head?"

"No. It doesn't mean it wasn't impacted, but I don't see any."

Kurpiers probably felt that a simple no would have been enough.

On cross, Grissinger tries to discredit Dr. Herbst's testimony step-by-step. "You don't work for any hospital."

"Correct." he responds.

"You don't work with children."

"Correct."

You predominantly work for the defense in criminal cases?"

He agrees.

"For this trial, you were contacted on January 20, 2011, and went through the process you described. Is it fair to say you don't consider interviews of witnesses before interpreting your scan?"

"Yes, it is in a bubble, yes."

Grissinger walks away from the podium, questioning as she paces. "Had you previously stated that there was some kind of trauma?"

"Yes."

The attorney asks if the trauma could have been caused by Maria's head hitting something, and he agrees. His answers have become very cursory. Dr. Herbst has been cross-examined many, many times.

Holly asks about the age of the subdural hematoma and the resulting edema. He answers that the hematoma is about a week old, and the edema was a minimum of twelve hours and more likely twenty-four. Again his testimony changed. He had initially stated the edema was between twenty-four hours and seven days old! I hope that the jury is paying close attention to this paid witness.

Grissinger says, "You're not taking into account any circumstances."

"I'm just saying about a week old. There are lucid intervals with chronic subdurals."

"I'm talking about an *acute* injury, then the onset of unconsciousness," Holly states sharply. "Your definition of acute is up to seven days."

"Lucid intervals can occur with subdurals," he restates, leaving out the word *chronic*.

"If someone receives an *acute* subdural hematoma, they can then have a lucid interval?" Grissinger asks with disbelief.

"Yes." (However, no proof has been provided by any defense witness as to the validity of this statement.)

She decides to drop this line of questioning after making sure it was on the record. "Is the difference between a CT scan and an MRI the resonance?"

"Yes."

"Are you looking for different things?"

"You're looking for the same things, but they look different on the different scans—dark versus bright. A radiologist ignores that and looks at pathology."

"You were deposed less than a month ago."

He admits this is true.

Then she brings up the question of the blood in his testimony with Kurpiers. "You were never asked to do that?"

"That's right."

"You indicated that it was consistent with a Jell-O example. Do you see global edema on the CT scan?"

"Yes."

"What came first, the subdural or edema?"

"I can't tell which came first."

No other person in this trial with a radiology background besides Dr. Herbst has indicated or would indicate with such absolute certainty the dating of blood on an MRI scan. "*I can tell you for sure that blood is greater than five days old!*" He admitted that he was not a medical doctor, and he was not affiliated with any hospital. He had never seen Maria alive nor at autopsy.

I stood with the rest of the gallery as we were dismissed from the courtroom after Judge Newton's exit. For just having sat there almost all day, I was exhausted.

Pinellas County Criminal Courthouse.
Photo, courtesy of J. M. Barlow

Fountain in Town Square, Chambersburg, PA.
Photo, courtesy of Borough of Chambersburg

Cumberland Heights Baptist Church,
WV where the Harris's were married.
Photo, courtesy of church website.

Stephanie Spurgeon with her attorneys
behind her during jury selection.
Photo, courtesy of Zuma Press

Brian Daniels and Holly Grissenger
at the Prosecution table.
Photo, courtesy of Zuma Press

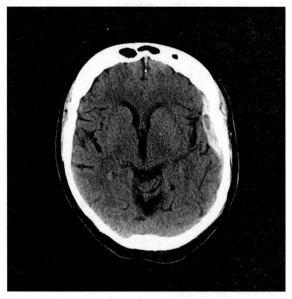

Image of subdural hematoma.
Photo, courtesy of Wikipedia

Stephanie Spurgeon's former home where she had her day care.
Photo, courtesy of J. M. Barlow

Dr. Jon Thogmartin, the Pinellas County medical examiner.
Photo, courtesy of Zuma Press

Kurpiers, Spurgeon, and Brunvand, right after
the reading of the verdict.
Photo, courtesy of Zuma Press

Flowers in memory of Maria Harris at church.
Photo, courtesy J. M. Barlow

Curtis Krueger, court journalist for the Tampa Bay Times.
Photo, courtesy of Curtis Krueger

Maria Harris's gravesite
Photo courtesy of J. M. Barlow

CHAPTER 19

FEBRUARY 14, 2012, VALENTINE'S DAY

IT IS 8:10 a.m. when I enter the courtroom for what is likely the last day of what would become a short trial. I start to think that I am off base with this observation, but it was a first-degree murder case, after all, and this was only the fourth full day of testimony by witnesses. There had been recent cases involving crimes of a far less serious nature that had lasted well over a week and sometimes two, just for testimony. I am surprised that no character witnesses have been called for either side. It would have been a credit to Spurgeon's defense to have parents of other children whom she had cared for over an extended period of time, say, several years, to testify to her caretaking ability. On the other side of the coin, it would also have been of possible help to the Harrises to hear from people who have watched Esther and Pat care for little Maria. They could have been folks from Esther's old high school day care at the YWCA, and/or people from our church. And of course, there was the glaringly missing testimony from law enforcement. Instead, we just heard snippets from police reports. (At one point later on, during deliberations, the jury would ask to have a portion of the transcript of Patricia Harris's testimony given to them. They would be denied that request. I believe that a judge's discretion in not giving transcripts to a jury is always good because without the entire transcript, the words might be taken out of context and interpreted incorrectly. The verbal manner in which the words were expressed is absent as well.) As for the police reports, they were never admitted into evidence by either side, so the jury was not able to ask for them. If I were on this jury, those records would be what I would want to see—not the ones that are available as public record, but the ones that are in the case file. Of course, that would not have been possible, and this request would have been denied as well.

The day begins on an unusual note. Without the jury present, the state begins arguing that a rebuttal witness should be allowed to remain in the courtroom during the defense witnesses' testimonies. The defense never asked for any witness to be precluded. They argue that just because they didn't ask for him to be precluded doesn't mean that he should be allowed to remain in the courtroom. The witness in question is Dr. Alexander, a pediatrician. The defense wants him out of there. They say that he was brought here specifically to respond to the testimony of their witness, Dr. Leetsma.

The two witnesses the defense plans to present today are a forensic pathologist and a neural pathologist. "Not a pediatrician!" Kurpiers snaps.

Judge Newton asks for the state's argument to show that he is an essential witness. They argue that transcripts both outside and at trial have indicated that metabolic disorders were present or a

217

possibility in Maria. Dr. Alexander could show that those disorders are not possible in the causes and effects of Maria Harris.

Kurpiers is angry. He says, "This guy jumps up and down about shaken baby syndrome!" Kurpiers goes on to mention that Dr. Alexander would bring up all the triad of symptoms of SBS. "Oh, I've reviewed the transcripts. They are completely disingenuous—irrelevant! Live people, dead people—apples and oranges! How do we know what the focus of testimony is going to be until we have it?"

Grissinger is the angry one now. She raises her voice. "They are the ones that made shaken baby syndrome an issue in this case. *We* never said that!" She says that their (the state's) focus has been on violent acceleration/deceleration.

Judge Newton doesn't take long to reach her decision on whether to allow this rebuttal witness to remain in the courtroom during defense witness testimony. She rules that he is not considered essential. "I'm not comfortable making this finding." She says she has an appeals concern. So the state loses a critical battle preventing Dr. Alexander from remaining in the courtroom during the defense witnesses' testimonies. He can be questioned based on reasonable hypotheticals presented by the defense, according to Judge Newton, but she says that he must remain outside of the courtroom until it is time for his testimony. But Dr. Alexander is never called upon to testify.

Dr. Jan Edward Leetsma is the pathologist who is next called by the defense. He is from Chicago and graduated from Hope College in Michigan in 1960 before going to medical school at the University of Michigan. He attended the University of Colorado at Denver for his pathology specialty, studying anatomic and neuropathology. He also attended the Albert Einstein Medical School in New York.

Dr. Leetsma was in the US Air Force Med Corp, serving at Walter Reed Medical Center and performing pathology services for the military. He was honorably discharged in 1971.

His additional credentials are extensive, most of which are his experience and professorships in Illinois. The last segment of his career was spent at the Neurosurgical Institute, which is contained within a private hospital in Chicago. He spent about twelve years there doing pathology work, and then he retired. He is grandfatherly and kind in appearance, yet his eyes betray a sharpness that reveal an intelligent and detail-oriented mind. He bears a striking resemblance to former Vice President Dick Cheney.

He gives the definition of neuropathology for the jury. [It is] "the study of mechanisms of diseases of the nervous system; the brain, spine, eyes, muscles, and nervous system."

When asked by the defense, Dr. Leetsma details his practical experience in his career. He examined brains and nervous systems of people who had died in the hospital. His role was to determine what caused their deaths, what diseases they had. He tried to resolve conflicts between varying diagnoses. This work frequently involved complete autopsies, but even more often, total brain dissection and lab studies were required.

He would often go to the operating room during brain surgeries to render a diagnosis and give guidance during the operation. He did not normally make decisions involving cause and manner of death, but contributed to the findings of the pathologist as it related to what was found in the brain.

Dr. Leetsma has testified as an expert "a couple of hundred times" in trials including a few that have made headlines such as the Phil Spector murder trial and the Michael Peterson trial in North Carolina, not to be confused with other Peterson murder trials of late. Leetsma recalls that he thinks he testified in a court nearby in Tampa.

Kurpiers gets to the meat of his questions. "Did you make an assessment in this case?"

"Yes."

"When?"

"A year, maybe two years ago. The attorney contacted me. He said, "I've got a case." I said, "Tell me about the case." He told the attorney that he thought he could help. "That's what happened as far as I can tell". (There is no mention of whether it was an attorney from Spurgeon's first legal team or the current one.)

"I use the objective evidence. Anyone can use it, and they can't be charged by anyone. CT scan, scene evidence, autopsy, microscopic study slides..."

"Did you examine the CT scan?"

"I did not. I have a report. The CT scan was not available."

"Did you examine microscopic tissue slides?"

"Yes."

"What was the most important evidence that you examined?" Kurpiers probes.

"The microscopic tissue slides," Leetsma says with emphasis. Then, using a PowerPoint presentation that is introduced as the defense's Exhibit 2, he describes an infarction (the death of tissue resulting from failure of blood supply) of the cerebral cortex with cellular reactions outside of the brain where most of the nerve cells are. There is pink "stuff" on one of the slides, and he says that this stuff is what the brain looks like. "The blood vessels become congested with blood cells. This is not uncommon at death, this backing up."

He describes the cerebral cortex (the surface layer of gray matter covering the brain) shown in his presentation as being broken up into little pieces with little dots, which are areas of inflammation. "This part of the brain is essentially dead. The blood supply is interrupted. It fell apart." He refers to this as necrosis. "It takes time for nerve cells to fade away. It takes about five days for this necrosis to occur." So far this information is consistent with what was happening to Maria.

He explains that if the person remains alive, that the part of the brain where the necrosis occurred will never function again. "It clearly indicates a circulatory deficit to this part of the brain. It can be an obstruction in an artery or vein so that blood can't get out or in. It can do it in anything that can prevent [blood] flow. Just looking at this slide, I don't know which is operating."

He is telling the court that he doesn't know what caused the cell death in that particular section of the brain simply by looking at the slide. Perhaps if he had been able to look at the CT scan that he had not been able to examine, he would have been able to isolate the cause of the cell death.

Dr. Leetsma continues to explain the necrosis. "It takes several days for nerve cells to fade out and several more days to look like this—from the time of death."

With interest, Kurpiers asks, "It tells you something was happening in the brain a week earlier?"

"Yes."

"The slides that we're looking at, where did they come from?"

Dr. Leetsma explains that a 1 × 3 inch slide is prepared with a thin slice of brain on it, and then a digital picture is taken of it.

Next, he is reviewing a clot, which he calls *an organizing thrombus*, in the superior sagittal sinus, the area above and behind the brain. It allows blood veins to cross over from the top of the head to the back of the head.

He goes into detail on this slide and a few others about blood clots. "If this were just a blood clot, we'd have just red blood cells, but...we have all this blue stuff." The main focus of his discussion is that when a blood clot forms in this area, it can cause a reaction that makes it stay there. Blood comes in and cannot get out. The tissue becomes damaged, and prior to death, there is clotting.

He explains the anatomy of the venous (vein) system of the brain, focusing in particular on the main venous channel. "If it gets obstructed, it could result in the backup of a lot of blood into that system and find its way into another venous channel." (This is a conjecture on Dr. Leetsma's part because he had not seen the CT scan, which showed that there was not much blood in this area. Apparently, he did not know this). He does state that there are different types of infarction, but both cause blood to stop flowing.

Leetsma indicates a venous infarction on his presentation. "It's like a sewer plugged up in your house. It backs up, leaks, blood vessels become distended. They may break—the older vessels first. There is focal bleeding, cerebral edema in the brain, a hemorrhage leaking into subdural space causing a subdural hematoma. The symptoms are not so easy to determine at first."

He rattles of a list of symptoms: headaches, irritability, poor feeding, too much sleep, not enough sleep, brain swelling, comatose, not breathing. He says that the time it takes to form a clot or to become comatose can vary. It occurs to me at this point that this description sounds much more like a person who has had a stroke and a secondary event of a chronic subdural hematoma. This does not sound like a description of someone had a sudden abusive head trauma, or even an accidental one that was violent enough. Dr. Leetsma is a very sharp man, but it is quite possible that he was working with far too little information. Microscopic slides of Maria's brain were only part of the puzzle—a very small part.

He also mentions that clotting in a vein can have a spectrum that ranges from immediate all the way to something that may be missed until autopsy, and though it is similar to adult clotting, it is much more common in infants and young ones. (Dr. Thogmartin, the medical examiner, had seen actual clots in Maria's brain at autopsy, and he mentions them in his testimony. He also said that they are often seen together with subdural hematomas).

When Ron Kurpiers asks him when the event happened, Dr. Leetsma says that it was about a week old. "The blood vessel is reacting to the clot that is not supposed to be there. About a week before death. Yes...not precise." This testimony would date the injury comfortably in the range of when Maria was at Stephanie Spurgeon's home.

Dr. Leetsma offers his expert opinion on what he thinks caused the clot. "Like most everything else in medicine, a large component of it is "We don't know" or "We can't figure it out." He suggests some possible causes, saying that these are prevalent in 75 percent of the cases: dehydration, viral infection, blood more viscous (too thick), sticky, fever, infection, bacteria in the blood, toxins, inherited disorder of bleeding, or clotting." The last cause, he says, can be tested with modern genetics, but from a slide it cannot be determined. He also mentioned that if she was vaccinated recently, there could have been a serious reaction. The genetic testing would have to have been performed on Maria's blood when she was living. He cautions that the fact that Maria appeared healthy ten days earlier does not mean anything and that pediatricians can miss "stuff" on examinations.

I note that he has mentioned absolutely nothing about other possible causes for what he observes on the slides. Why would he not even mention an accident? Dr. Leetsma is obviously avoiding any mention of trauma of any sort as a cause of the hematoma or the clotting. That is not reasonable, and I hope that the jury senses this. I remind myself that he is a paid expert witness for the defense, and he has not seen any scan of Maria's brain, never saw her alive or deceased. and did not see much of the information in doctors' reports. He is basing his deductions solely upon microscopic slides of brain tissue. Where did the 75 percent figure come from when he mentions what causes could have led to these brain abnormalities? Is this a figure he concocted based on his own conclusions, or is it actually documented in a medical journal? It would be enlightening to find out the answer. Also, Dr. Leetsma is from out of state and is very good at testifying at trials. Will the defense introduce any more local expert witnesses, or have they drained that pool?

Ron Kurpiers asks him if it is fair to say that the clot grew, but at the early stages there may not have been any symptoms.

Leetsma points out some white striping called Lines of Zahn in the clot and says, "It could have been developing and until it closed up this venous channel, you wouldn't know."

He is still treating the clots like they were occurring very slowly and silently, as in a stroke victim. Clots in carotid arteries, for instance, are silent until they close off the artery altogether, blocking blood flow and causing a stroke. Obviously, I am not a doctor, and a little knowledge is dangerous, but note that Leetsma said that, "It *could* have been developing." If so, and if it was not from abusive head trauma, where did the bleeding stem from? In contrast, all the professionals who testified for the state said that the hematoma was acute (fresh) and that the onset of symptoms was immediate.

There is a blog site about SBS that I monitor because it is full of information about cases and shifting views on this condition. The site itself is biased against SBS; however, in all fairness, they do have some good information about the research and the progression of studies that have indicated the causes of injuries in young children. Some of these injuries that were suspected to be caused by SBS turn out to be from something else. But the fact is, in many cases, abuse is not ruled out as the cause, but only SBS. A quote from the blog site from an ME illustrates this fact concisely. However, I will credit the actual source where the quote was derived from so that it is not taken out of context, rather than from the blog itself. (The blog site is mentioned later on because I posted on it myself and was restricted further access).

> Dr. Vincent DiMaio, the chief medical examiner of Bexar County, Texas, and the editor of the American Journal of Forensic Medicine and Pathology, calls shaken baby an unproven hypothesis. "I'm not saying these deaths are from natural causes," he clarifies, "I'm saying that these children are not just being shaken. They are *also* being hit on the head or thrown against something. It's an impact injury."
>
> (Melissa Fletcher Stoeltje, "Does Shaken Baby Syndrome Exist?" mysanantonio.com, July 2011)

As Dr. Leetsma's testimony continues, I try to keep an open mind. He shows several more slides and provides detailed descriptions of what we are looking at. One is a slide of a subdural hematoma with a blood clot, showing a new membrane. This new membrane is there because it is part of the healing process of the subdural hematoma. Obviously, it did not heal.

Leetsma describes a subdural hematoma as a blood vessel that has ruptured above the arachnoid and above the brain but below the dura. He says it occurs due to the backup of blood. "We can age and date the process by what components of neo-membrane are present." He is the second professional on either side to mention the formation of a new membrane and using that membrane to determine the age of the subdural hematoma. He had earlier dated the clot as approximately a week old at the time of death.

It is at this point in Dr. Leetsma's testimony that things begin to get a little weird. He pulls out a report called "Aging and Dating of Subdural Hematomas" from 1936, which he had transformed into a chart. He says he thinks that it shows "a hundred and some cases. The trick is to know how old they are, and they knew when the fall occurred. And they wrote this paper, about forty pages as I recall, about what they saw."

Then he relates that there is not much going on in a subdural hematoma in the first few days. As it ages, red blood cells staining characteristics change from red to lavender. A neo-membrane will be a half to a third of the thickness of the original dura, "and that's about where we are. Then it gets a little blurry after a three to six months subdural hematoma."

Hold on! Not even the dramatic radiologist, Dr. Herbst, had mentioned anything about a hematoma that was three months old! That evidence would point to a chronic bleed, not a sudden, violent, and acute one. No one had challenged the fact the Maria's brain injury was recent, and here was this doctor, who had not seen any scan, talking about images showing a three-month-old subdural hematoma. Where is the relevance? Will the state pursue this on cross?

Kurpiers asks Dr. Leetsma what this suggests as to when Maria's hematoma started. "Go to the area that is the most

advanced," he answers. "The oldest component of this process."
He compares it to a pebble in a pond. "It depends on where you
take your microscopic section from. You have to put it into context. I have to take what they give me. The oldest that we have is
on the order of a couple of weeks."

Well, there it is. The slide was prepared after Maria's death. The
state maintains that Maria's injuries occurred at the Spurgeon
home. That was eight days before her death. After she died, Dr.
Thogmartin examined her brain, and then sent it to Dr. Nelson
who most likely prepared these slides. All these events occurred
within the span of approximately two weeks, in complete harmony with what Dr. Leetsma has concluded in spite of his rabbit
trail about three- to six-month-old hematomas. The jury must be
able to discern the difference.

He also notes that his chart, which is formulated with that
data from 1936, is a pretty good estimate of what a subdural
hematoma is under a microscope. (Isn't there any more recent
data on this information? If so, does it run contrary to what Dr.
Leetsma is saying, which is why he chooses not to use it? The
state has no time to check this out, but using data from over
seventy-five years ago is a little strange when we are talking about
modern medicine, which includes MRIs and CT scans).

At this stage, Kurpiers interjects a question that would usually
be posed at the beginning of a witness's testimony. "Have you
published a book?"

"Yes. *Forensic Neuropathy.*" Leetsma indicates that it is the
first place where this chart that he made from the data occurred.
The second edition was released in 2009. He tells the court that
the book is used by his fellow neuropathologists and forensic pathologists.

When Kurpiers asks him if the book is used in medical schools,
the state objects and this objection is sustained. Kurpiers moves
on to ask him if he taught as a professor at medical schools.

Dr. Leetsma said yes, that he had done so and he used this chart all the time.

"That's the guide that you use to find the age of a sub-dural hematoma?"

"Yes."

As the defense nears the end of its questioning of Dr. Leetsma, he talks about something called *intracranial pressure volume dynamics*.

Kurpiers wants to know, "How could you have a subdural hematoma and not be symptomatic?"

"The total volume inside the brain compartment is rigid," Leetsma responds. He lists the materials inside the brain and spinal cord: meat, tissue and water, a volume of blood and vessels. He also mentions the amount of cerebral spinal fluid (CSF) in a child as fifty milliliters and in an adult as one hundred milliliters. It is produced twenty-four hours a day, seven days a week, by the brain and surrounding structures and it needs to be absorbed.

He describes next an experiment in a baby where two millilit-ers of saline solution was injected into its spine. It was not toler-ated well. In a hematoma, there is four to five milliliters. "You get a sick baby. You have a compensatory mechanism, but it's fragile." (Well, no argument from me on this point, but I don't understand where this fits in to how his testimony aids the defense.)

Dr. Leetsma gives a summary of his final opinion, reaching these conclusions:

1. He clearly notes a superior sagittal venous thrombosis where blood is coming in but cannot get out (a clot).

2. There is bleeding around the vein and in the subdural space which "can" come from that thrombosis as well.

3. At some point, the brain experienced infarcts; "a crum-bling house of cards."

4. The body attempts to heal itself while this mechanism is occurring. "This is what happened to this child functionally."

He drew these conclusions from looking at microscopic sections of Maria's brain on slides that were prepared from brain slices several days after her death. As he said, "*I have to take what they give me.*" There is nothing here in this summary that indicates that an abusive trauma did not cause her fatal head injury. These descriptors are just the mechanics of what was happening inside her brain as a result of something abnormal happening externally. Dr. Leetsma, who never saw Maria in any capacity, did not disprove that her injuries occurred at the home of Stephanie Spurgeon on August 21, 2008.

CHAPTER 20

THE STATE DECIDES to question Dr. Leetsma with an adversarial approach by trying to punch holes in his credentials.

Holly Grissinger says, "You are not board certified in pathology."

Dr. Leetsma says that he got his board certification in neuropathology—in 1970.

She then asks if he got recertified, and he explains that he was grandfathered in and exempted from recertification. He has no other board certification. In other words, he has not applied for or received any board certifications in his field or in any related field in over forty years.

"Have you ever treated children?"

"No."

"When was your last autopsy?"

"In Munich, Germany, two years ago."

"Have you ever performed a forensic autopsy of a child?"

"Never have. I may have participated. I was never the primary."

He tells the court that in criminal cases his usual role is that of a witness for the defense, but he had also testified for the prosecution in the past for a number of years. He reveals his fee to be $400 an hour outside of court and $600 an hour in court, but he is not sure of his total fee in this particular case. He earns 100 percent of his income from consulting.

He says that he attended the National Conference on Pathology. Grissinger asks him if the conference was concerning abusive head trauma. He responds, "I don't know, exactly."

He also attends an annual Academy of Forensic Sciences and does quite a bit of publishing about viruses. He has done brain exams in hospitals, but retired in 2003 from practice. The other areas that he has examined or been involved in are autopsy reports, microscopic slides, and Dr. Plunkett's reports. Dr. Plunkett would be the next witness for the defense. Dr. Leetsma says he may have worked with police reports, but he can't recall. He is also asked if he provided a letter to the defense, and he says that he has done so.

Grissinger asks if this letter is fair and accurate. Leetsma asks her if she would like to see it, and she tells him no, that she already has one.

There were four items he received that he actually reviewed. There were photos of Maria that were included in these items. But there were no police reports reviewed. Leetsma says that he may have received them, but he hadn't looked at them, and he had no history on Maria. He told Grissinger that the CT scan and the MRI films were unavailable.

Next, Leetsma says that he did not consult with Dr. Plunkett, even though he had read his reports. But he did say this regarding talking to Dr. Plunkett: "Not to formulate my opinion, we talk all the time and of course we talked about this case."

He restates that the thrombosis (clot) in the superior sagittal sinus was approximately a week old, and yes, this was consistent with Maria's time spent in the hospital.

"That [clot] caused intracranial pressure?"

"Yes. It certainly can."

"In your opinion, superior sagittal sinus thrombosis (SSST)—it contributed to it?"

"Venous congestion and SSST caused infarctions to increase. Intracranial pressure—yes." He explains that SSST can lead to subdural hematomas, but he can't date the clotting beyond a week. Then, even though this never came out during the direct questioning by the defense, Dr. Leetsma says that Maria's subdural hematoma is older than that (a week). "It could be there. I just don't know."

He has just contradicted himself and Grissinger knows it! She wants to confirm if the SSST could have caused the subdural hematoma because, after all, that's what Leetsma's previous testimony just suggested. He attempts to strengthen his words by saying, that it could have, or "it could have been independent as to when the child got sick."

Grissinger asks, "If a child's been dead for several days, is SSST normal?"

"No!"

"So you would not expect to see it."

"In a brain-dead person? Yes, you could see it."

Grissinger knows the jury must be confused here, and she takes advantage. "Wouldn't it be quite shocking to find a person with brain death without SSST?"

"No. You could find that. There would be a percentage that occurred while a person was on a respirator."

"Can an infarction cause a subdural hematoma?"

"Yes."

"Where in relation to the SSST did this occur?"

"A venous infarction is pretty extensive to a large part of the brain up above it and close to the sagittal sinus."

Grissinger asks if this resulted in swelling in this case.

"Some of the symptoms." (He is referring to his list of symptoms resulting from SSSTs). Leetsma explains that intracranial pressure can result in a person becoming comatose. The cause of the clot is a large component of that pressure and could be on that list that he mentioned earlier.

Wisely, Grissinger asks him, "If the child has none of the conditions on the list, what else could it be?"

Leetsma pauses. "Diarrhea." At this odd response, any bored people on the jury probably snapped to attention. Dehydration encompasses diarrhea, I would venture to guess, and it was one of the conditions that Leetsma had mentioned. "I covered the majority. It could be others."

"So for 25 percent or more, we don't know why." Grissinger says aloud what I have been thinking.

But, almost unbelievably, Dr. Leetsma suggests that symptoms can "randomly" develop and lead to death. Again, he has studiously avoided the obvious: trauma. Most children admitted to the ER with subdural hematomas have had some sort of trauma occur, but not one of the incidences on Dr. Leetsma's list suggest trauma resulting in a brain bleed. The source of his list is still unknown.

Grissinger reiterates that Leetsma said that Maria's pediatrician "messed up" when he pronounced her healthy at her well-baby exam.

"Yes, it can happen. It does happen." In effect, he is saying that her pediatrician did a poor job examining her because he missed symptoms of an acute subdural hematoma. How many neurological specialists would consider this likely?

Grissinger gets to that seventy-five-plus-year-old study and says that it was done on 105 people, all of who were all adults.

Leetsma's response is, "[With a] subdural hematoma, you don't see much for three to four days." I fail to see how this answers her question.

Grissinger looks astonished. "You wouldn't see it on a scan? For three or four days?"

"No. You might see it immediately, or it can be visible within minutes or hours of the injury." Leetsma explains, immediately contradicting his prior answer.

Pausing to make sure the jury caught the inconsistency in Leetsma's testimony, Grissinger then states, "A child's brain responds to trauma by increasing cerebral blood flow."

"Yes. For reasons unknown."

"A trauma to the head increases blood flow, causes swelling and pressure quicker than in an adult?"

"Yes. A child's response to cerebral blood flow contributes to it. It's malignant cerebral edema." (Recall that Dr. Herbst said edema doesn't show up for at least twelve to twenty-four hours after the trauma. The confirmation of Grissinger's statement by Dr. Leetsma appears to contradict Dr. Herbst when referring to children).

"You believe that SSST takes weeks to evolve into intracranial pressure and lead to symptoms." Grissinger is becoming passionate about the fact that Leetsma appears to be tripping over his own testimony.

"All I have said is about a week—at the time of hospitalization. It contributed to the cause. It *is* the cause of death."

So Dr. Leetsma has just concluded that Maria's cause of death is not abusive blunt force trauma to the head, but instead is a blood clot that developed while she was in the hospital! He has reached this conclusion from looking at microscopic brain matter on slides.

Grissinger asks, "What are the signs and symptoms of blunt head trauma?"

"Bruise, headache, listlessness, poor feeding, crying, sleeping too much, collapse, respiratory failure, coma."

That ends the brunt of Dr. Leetsma's testimony. As he leaves the witness stand, he nods to people on the defense side of the room and exits the courtroom.

It occurs to me that Leetsma's testimony would have carried a lot more weight if several important situations were different. Here are ten that come to mind:

1. If he would have had to actually get recertified in his field with continuing education as people have to do now in many fields, including medicine, instead of being grand-fathered in since 1970, over forty-two years ago

2. If the source of his list of causes of SSSTs and subdural hematomas was a valid and revealed one

3. If he used a study that was current and representative of a mixed-age population instead of one from 1936 comprised of only adults

4. If he did not indicate that SSSTs lead to subdural hematomas and then suggest that it was the other way around with Maria

5. If he had more information from which to glean his conclusions outside of microscopic brain slices on slides

6. If he was familiar with the case itself and not merely a paid but retired consultant from out of state

7. If he didn't claim that he did not consult with Dr. Plunkett on the case and then say that he had only talked to him about it

8. If he would have differentiated between acute and chronic subdural hematomas in his testimony and which one he thought applied here and why

9. If he could have admitted that trauma is a common and valid cause of subdural hematomas in children instead of avoiding it like the plague in his testimony which was quite disingenuous

10. If he could have linked why he felt that Maria's pediatrician "messed up" regarding her injuries and ultimate death and why he believed that was much more plausible than blunt force trauma to the head as a valid reason for her death

Dr. John Plunkett, another pathologist, will now take the stand for the defense. Perhaps he had more resources at his disposal in order to reach a conclusion in this case. Regardless of whether he did or not, he had talked to Dr. Leetsma about Maria Harris as we have already been told.

CHAPTER 21

THERE IS MORE to Dr. John Plunkett than meets the eye. At a glance, he is, like Dr. Leetsma, a kind-looking elderly gentleman with intelligent eyes. He is a board certified pathologist who has published several articles in general and forensic pathology journals. Since 1998, all of his articles dealt with issues of forensic and infant head injury. He has taught physicians, nurses, law, and defense attorneys about these issues, and he has testified as an expert witness over 200 times. However, because this defense team hired him from Minnesota, he has only testified in the state of Florida approximately six to eight times.

When I did a Google search for Dr. Plunkett, the first site that I found was an interview he did for CBC television (Canada). It was for a show called *The Fifth Estate*, and it aired only a month before this trial, on January 15.[1] The broadcast was supposed to be about SBS and whether it was real or just an invented condition, but somehow Dr. Plunkett took total control of the interview away from reporter Gillian Findlay and steered the conversation from SBS and instead toward a study that he did from 1988 to 1999 involving playground accidents. It became a well-known study often referred to in courtroom cases by the defense concerning head trauma, but it was not a well-respected study in the medical community because of the small size of the known sample.

In this televised interview, the very first question posed to Dr. Plunkett is, "Can you shake a baby to death?"

He responds, "Yeah. I think you can. I think it's possible to shake a baby, cause significant neck damage, and kill 'em, you know. I haven't seen one. I haven't read of one, but I think it's at least theoretically possible—at least a small infant—zero to three months."

But in an article published in April 2007 in *USA Today*, there is this information:

> "It doesn't exist," Dr. John Plunkett, a Minnesota pathologist who began openly questioning shaken-baby following the 1997 involuntary manslaughter conviction of British nanny Louise Woodward, the case that put SBS on the map. "You can't cause the injuries said to be caused by shaking, by shaking...That's just nonsense."[2]
>
> —Breed, Allen G.
> "Studies Split on Shaken Baby Syndrome" USA Today

In future interviews and articles that are readily available online, Plunkett would sway with the breeze on the topic, but would mostly say that SBS does not exist as a condition.

Many pediatricians disagree that it does not exist.

"People confess to it. So it has to be possible," Dr. Suzanne Starling, director of forensic pediatrics at Children's Hospital of The King's Daughters in Norfolk, Virginia, counters.[3]

The next question Dr. Plunkett is asked in the CBC interview is, "If it is theoretically possible to do it, then what's the problem with the syndrome?"

"Well," he says, slowly, "the syndrome is subdural bleeding, retinal hemorrhaging, and brain swelling. That's the syndrome. In fact, if you are able to cause injury or death, it's not by causing subdural bleeding, retinal hemorrhaging, or brain swelling. It's by causing structured neck damage and death because you interfere with the brain stem centers that control breathing."

I consider this information with respect to Maria Harris. She had what is now called the classic triad of symptoms of SBS: subdural hematoma, retinal hemorrhaging, and brain swelling. She had no visible neck injuries, but she did have problems breathing and in fact had stopped breathing at the Harris home for a short time. She was placed on a ventilator at All Children's Hospital because of irregular breathing. She also had seizures, even before arriving at ACH, which can be a direct result of edema in the brain. Was Maria shaken? She had shearing of the bridging veins connecting her dura mater on the surface of the brain membrane to the area under her skull. That would indicate some sort of momentum. Most likely, she was both shaken and thrown or slammed into a rather soft surface. The shearing has been proven to result from rapid acceleration then deceleration of a child's head. Would she necessarily have to have had visible damage to her neck? Perhaps not externally. What about at autopsy? Maybe not at that point either. Whiplash usually shows no visible injuries but is very painful to the injured party.

Dr. Robert Reece, a well-known clinical professor of pediatrics at the Tufts University School of Medicine, defines SBS as:

> a term used to describe the constellation of signs and symptoms resulting from violent shaking or *shaking and impacting* of the head of an infant or small child. The degree of brain damage depends on the amount and duration of the shaking and the forces involved in impact of the head. Signs and symptoms range on a spectrum of neurological alterations from minor (irritability, lethargy, tremors, vomiting) to major (seizures, coma, stupor, death).

TOO BRIEF A CANDLE

These neurological changes are due to destruction of brain cells secondary to trauma, lack of oxygen to the brain cells, and swelling of the brain. Extensive retinal hemorrhages in one or both eyes are found in the vast majority of these cases. The classic triad of subdural hematoma, brain swelling and retinal hemorrhages is accompanied in some, but not all, cases by bruising of the part of the body used as a "handle" for shaking. Fractures of the long bones and/or of the ribs may also be seen in some cases. *In many cases, however, there is no external evidence of trauma either to the head or the body.*[4] (Emphasis mine).

(Allen G. Breed, "Studies Split on Shaken Baby Syndrome," *USA Today*)

Dr. Reece also lists the signs and symptoms he has grouped together as a result of violent shaking on a website. The reader is free to agree or disagree with his findings. The site can be viewed at dontshakejake.org/didyouknow.html.

In the CBC interview for *The Fifth Estate*, the topic now switches to Dr. Plunkett's study. He completed the study in 2001, but the results accumulated were from the eleven-and-a-half-year period between 1988 and 1999. He wanted to see for himself if there were instances of lucid intervals when people sustained a head injury, then appeared to be fine, and then died afterward. He said that the reason he looked at this aspect of the injury was because the retinal hemorrhage was only a secondary process to that injury. He already knew that children could die from a fall, but he didn't know if a lucid interval was possible.

The hypothesis he wanted to disprove was that of the pediatricians and pathologists who said that it was not possible for a child to be killed by a low level fall and that any child who sustained a fatal head injury could not have a lucid interval. What he was attempting to show was that a child might not immediately collapse after a short fall and that the last person standing may not be the one who caused it.

He also wanted to disprove what I think is an error of the courts, not the medical field: that retinal hemorrhaging is only found in abusive head trauma in infants and children. It is already known that difficult births can cause these types of eye injuries to babies. And some injuries, such as vehicle accidents, can also cause retinal hemorrhaging. A hard enough fall, perhaps with a skull fracture, can present with retinal hemorrhaging. What isn't stated here is what type of retinal hemorrhaging is being considered. Is it due to an immediate tear in the retina causing bleeding inside the eyeball from an impact or trauma, or is it a secondary response to edema on the brain? The situation itself can possibly indicate which one. In the case of SBS, or more accurately, shaken impact syndrome in Maria's case, does it really matter whether the shaking or the brain edema caused her eyes to bleed if either one originally stemmed from abuse?

Dr. Suzanne Starling, mentioned earlier, and her colleagues analyzed eighty-one cases in which an adult confessed to shaking and/or battering a child. They found that in cases where only shaking was admitted, the children were 2.39 times more likely to have retinal hemorrhages than victims of impact alone, "suggesting that shaking is more likely to cause retinal hemorrhages than impact" alone. As I will discuss later, however, I don't think children are shaken and then the abuse suddenly stops. The shaking likely culminates in a slamming or throwing event.

"I think that's about the best proof I'm going to get that this actually occurs," Starling says, who notes that she's also testified for the defense in such cases. "The truth is the truth, and science doesn't take a side."[3]

Plunkett, in the same article, claims that Starling's analysis is tainted by false (wrongful) confessions in the courtroom. Really? People would actually consistently perjure themselves by confessing to a crime they did not do in order to be sentenced to prison for many years if not life? Eighty-one people? That is hard to fathom.

Plunkett, in his study, used medical records that he was able to obtain with permission from the families in the study and other information based on the US Consumer Product Safety Commission Database for head and neck injuries involving falls. He used it because of the information it contained regarding playground equipment and because generally, on a playground there are observers other than family members present.

Remember, his ultimate goal was to disprove the theory of pediatricians and pathologists who believed that a lucid interval was impossible after a fall resulting in a subdural hematoma. There were 600 reported injuries during the eleven-and-a-half-year period. (Actually, there were over 75,000, but they were not pertinent to his study because they were not head injuries and/or they were not reported in a timely matter). The age range of the injured was from one to thirteen years old. Six hundred lowers the sampling significantly. Even more so, there were, according to Dr. Plunkett, 114 deaths. Of these 114, most occurred when a piece of equipment collapsed and struck the child in the head, ruling out a fall. The second most common cause of injuries was from accidental suffocation or asphyxiation when a jacket or drawstring became caught up in the playground equipment and smothered or choked the child. Last was the category of children who fell from equipment. There were eighteen fatalities out of the six hundred injuries actually reported in a timely matter in this study.

Of the eighteen fatalities, twelve had lucid intervals. I pulled up his study, which I was easily able to locate online. Yes, there were twelve with lucid intervals. Two children had lucid intervals of only ten minutes. These two fell from a swing. (More on these later.)

In his television interview, Dr. Plunkett indicates that the twelve children who had lucid intervals had experienced falls that were witnessed by one, two, three, or four people who were not caretakers and not family members. But when I looked at the actual study, six children who fell with resulting lucid intervals had fallen without being witnessed by anyone. Also, nowhere is it indicated how many witnesses there were to the other falls and if they were family members or caretakers or neither.[5]

His study shows that only six children out of the eighteen had retinal exams at the hospital, and of those, four had extensive bilateral retinal hemorrhaging. (In the study, one of these with retinal hemorrhaging had a severe skull fracture, and one had a venous malformation, which made it difficult to compare to a normal brain. Other clinicians who have downplayed this study have indicated that a child with this type of malformation was more susceptible to death from a head injury than one without it, so this child should have been eliminated from the study.)

From his small sampling of results, Dr. Plunkett concluded: "I was able to disprove the hypothesis offered by these pediatricians and pathologists. First, short falls can kill. Second, retinal hemorrhages can occur with characteristics said to be for inflicted trauma. Third, there may be a period of time in which somebody with an ultimately fatal head injury appears to be okay."

Oddly, I don't think any of his conclusions were in dispute. There are plenty of examples of people who sustained fatal head injuries who first had lucid intervals. It is the degree and severity of the injury that would determine whether a lucid interval would in fact be possible. If a child sustains a blow to the head so hard as to knock him out and cause immediate brain swelling and bleeding, it is not likely that he will wake up and act like nothing is wrong. But if someone gets knocked out, say as in a concussion on a football field, he may pop up and seem okay, only to have an oozing brain bleed and lead to swelling and unconsciousness within hours, then perhaps death, if no immediate intervention is attempted. As for retinal hemorrhaging, the professionals were not saying that in and of themselves they are not present in cases outside of abuse, but that they are often seen as part of the whole gamut of head injuries that include subdural hematomas and brain swelling and can include external injuries, but do not necessarily have to. It is also well established that retinal hemorrhaging is very uncommon in non-abuse cases in very young children. My conclusion is that this study contained not nearly large enough a sample, and it was conducted with variables that were too wide in scope.

For instance, let's examine the difference between a child falling from a height of five feet from a monkey bar set that is stationary, to a child falling from a height of five feet off a swing that is in motion. To his credit, Dr. Plunkett has included a referenced discussion on the laws of motion and acceleration of swings, but he does not separate these events out of his actual database study for purposes of injury evaluation. A child falling from a swing that is in motion will not just drop to the ground, but will accelerate forward with momentum and will hit the ground with a much greater amount of force than a gravitational drop to the ground from a stationary object. A child falling three feet off of a couch into the carpet at home will not be injured as badly as he would be if he is thrown three feet into the carpet by an angry boyfriend of the mother. Rapid acceleration/deceleration. Momentum. These things all play scientific roles in abuse (and swing accidents) that cannot be compared with a straight fall from a height. Another visualization would be to imagine being pushed down the stairs with a hard shove from behind as opposed to falling down the stairs. The degree of force will play a part in the severity of the injuries that result. There is no doubt about that. It's common sense.

In the playground equipment study, seven of the eighteen children who died fell from swings. Of these seven, five never regained consciousness after impact. The two that did regain consciousness had a "lucid interval" of ten minutes. It is difficult to say if they acted totally normal or if they were visibly upset and crying or just awake. They would obviously have been in some pain. These were the children who had momentum behind their accidental injury. They were not only less likely to ever wake up, but the two that did were only awake for ten minutes. This response coincides with abusive head trauma. It is the momentum behind the injury that makes the difference. This is where accidents and abuse can retain a commonality. But how many accidents outside of automotive crashes, falls from a swing, or flying off a high slide or a diving board onto dry land involve momentum? Of those, how many are mistakenly considered abuse? Close to zero, I would venture to guess.

One more thought that comes to mind is, how many of these children had an epidural (external) hematoma as opposed to a subdural one? This differentiation is not delved into in the study. Epidural hematomas are much more likely to present with lucid intervals before death. Maria Harris did not have an epidural hematoma, and of course, she had no lucid interval.

Before proceeding with Dr. Plunkett's testimony in the trial itself, let's examine where we are so far. The defense has put forth a myriad of experts who focus on different potential diagnoses for Maria Harris. There are only so many reasons why a baby could suddenly become sick in this way, because nothing is 100 percent certain. What are some of those reasons?

Well, breathing problems for one. Could she have been experiencing a heart attack at the Spurgeon home? Is that possible? It was never presented by either side. Can a child get an acute subdural hematoma as a result of a heart attack? No. How about as a result of a lung clot? That is unlikely, but if so, how would she even get a lung clot? These are almost unheard of in a healthy child. But together with retinal hemorrhaging and brain swelling, a heart attack is just not feasible.

We looked at diabetes and ruled it out because she had no history. The elevated blood glucose levels were from stress, and different doctors indicated that this is very common. The levels quickly dropped in the hospital with proper treatment. When a diabetic child slips into a coma, it is usually very difficult to bring his sugar levels down because it is like a switch has shut down and it is often too late. Not so with Maria. Her blood glucose levels fell because she was not diabetic. Also, can diabetes cause subdural hematomas? Yes. In toddlers? I only found one case in the US, and the child was a known diabetic, and it was a chronic subdural hematoma with no retinal hemorrhaging. Bridging veins do not tear either because there is no shearing effect.

Could it have been caused by her vaccinations? There appears to be no death on record of a one-year -old child resulting from vaccinations of the same type that he or she has had in the past coincident with the brain conditions in Maria Harris. Other conditions, such as autism, are questionable and even highly suspect in some rare cases. However, deaths from vaccines that a child has had in the past and suffered no adverse effects from are just not an option to consider. Even if they were, would those vaccines cause subdural hematomas, torn bridging veins, and retinal hemorrhaging? No. The diagnoses shown here don't add up when all the pieces of the puzzle are examined together.

Now, for the blame that many Spurgeon supporters would like to cast: Did one of the Harrises do it? Well, Maria spent the first year and two weeks of her life with or within a few yards of someone in her immediate family. They all loved her to pieces. She was never taken to the doctor for an injury. She never had any injuries or suspicious marks indicating abuse at her well-baby checkups and her first physical. She was well adjusted and happy, and her height and weight were always comfortably within the normal margins.

Then, on the very next day of her life, she went to spend less than eight hours away from home and away from all her family members for the very first time. Less than eight hours. It led to her death. Let's do the math here. If her mother or her grandparents were going to harm her in any way, they had a year and two weeks in which to do it. Maria surely had periods of screaming and crying during that time. But the very first time she is away from home and family for a short period of time, which would of course, lead her to panic and scream and cry, she is picked up limp and unresponsive by her grandmother. If this were your child, what would you think? Add to this, a caretaker who uses a cuss word to describe your child's behavior on her very first day there.

Then later, you find out this additional information:

1. That the caretaker was licensed, but not bonded or properly insured, and had not taken child care or child safety classes in the recent past

2. That she spent a lot of time on the phone that day with at least one person who admitted this at the bond hearing. How can you talk on the phone and watch young children entrusted to your care at the same time?

3. That there had been a prior complaint against her for abuse

4. That the defense would, after the trial was over, try to say that there was evidence not provided to them by the state, that a *child* could have caused these injuries to Maria as another ploy to detract from the guilt of their client, after it called an expert physicist who testified under oath during the trial that no adult was possibly strong enough to do it (More on this later.)

5. That her first team of lawyers had been fired. Why? They are among the best defense attorneys in the county.

6. That one of her new attorneys would resign after doing the case pro bono, on the day of sentencing

An inverse way of looking at a criminal trial is: What is the probability that these events could have happened any other way? This is how reasonable doubt can also be examined. Where is the reasonable doubt here? The only day Maria is away from home or her family *ever*, events happen that lead to her ultimate demise. That alone is cause for looking outside the family for blame. The odds are just too ridiculous.

Maria left Pat's arms sometime between 7:15 and 7:30 a.m. on August 21, 2008. She came back into them without knowing she was in them. Inside her head, her brain was bleeding without stopping. Her retinas were torn and bleeding inside her eyes. Her brain had begun to swell. She vomited on her shirt on the way home, a very common occurrence after an abusive head trauma. What happened to Maria Harris in the Spurgeon home that day? The odds show beyond a reasonable doubt that whatever occurred happened at that location in that space of time between 7:30 a.m. and 2:45 p.m., or more likely, between 11:00 and 1:00 p.m. Stephanie Spurgeon was the only adult there during that time. This is what she told her attorneys. There was no other day in Maria's life that she was in any jeopardy. I had seen her myself only the evening before along with many other people, and she was a normal, active, and happy little girl. All doubt is unreasonable.

Dr. John Plunkett is the defense's final witness in the courtroom trial. After taking the stand, he is asked if he has reviewed a number of records and formed an opinion on Maria Harris, including her medical records and those of Dr. Thogmartin, the medical examiner. He says that he has. He agrees that he also reviewed the records of neuropathologist, Dr. Nelson.

Ron Kurpiers asks Plunkett to "take us through what you did and what you saw."

"I looked at Maria's records exactly as if she died in my jurisdiction, and I did the autopsy."

"How many autopsies have you done?"

"Two thousand to three thousand," Plunkett responds, painting a wide range. "The day Maria collapsed, there was no striking abnormality, no external indications, no internal organ damage other than the brain. None to the neck or skull."

Dr. Plunkett attributes this information to the records he has reviewed since he never actually laid eyes on Maria at any point. He also fails to note that she did have damage to her lungs, which Dr. Thogmartin had established in his testimony, ruling them out for organ donation as well.

Plunkett notes that there was a marked increase in her blood glucose level of four hundred milligrams. He is the only expert to point out that cortisol can occasionally cause increased glucose levels, but he doesn't specifically say that Maria's was attributed to cortisol. He stresses that Maria also had acetone in her urine at her first evaluation, which he says indicates that there was incomplete utilization of sugar as an energy source. He explains that if it interferes with the oxidative breakdown of glucose or without enough insulin, it stops with the ketones. In layman's terms, this means there is a metabolic abnormality that cannot be explained based on prior history, and, he goes on to say, it is a significant finding.

In light of this analysis, one must again consider the entire constellation of Maria's injuries: acute subdural hematoma, retinal hemorrhaging, tearing of bridging veins, vomiting, difficulty breathing, unresponsiveness, and so on. Separately, or even taking a few into consideration together, might lead to the improbable conclusion that she spontaneously leapt into a diabetic coma after never having any outward manifestation or positive test for diabetes in her life. But if these symptoms are considered in totality, it is impossible to justify this diagnosis. Subdural hematomas and torn bridging veins do not present together in children who lapse into diabetic comas. But rapid shallow breathing (panting) does. This was not one of her symptoms. The horse cannot have the stripes of a zebra.

Dr. Plunkett continues with his evaluation of Maria's medical records. "Bleeding on the surface of the brain is seen on the CT scan and the MRI. It predates the collapse, and she has clots you can see on the initial MRI scan." He says that these are findings usually not seen with trauma and that it had been going on for some time prior to the collapse! He continues by clarifying that he is not a radiologist. He has just made the claim that the bleeding predated Maria's "collapse" and had been going on "for some time" but he has no way to verify this and is not asked to do so!

Plunkett obviously had not heard the prior testimony of Dr. Thogmartin regarding the clot formation. First of all, the MRI was not taken until hours after EMS arrived at the Harrises' home. She had that scan done at All Children's Hospital. The CT scan was done first at Mease hospital within an hour after Maria's arrival, but Plunkett does not mention any clots noted on that CT scan. He should have seen them if they were there. He looked at that scan and saw the bleeding on the surface of the brain. But he only saw the clots on the MRI scan, which leads one to believe that they formed sometime after the first scan was taken, lining up with the testimony of Thogmartin. This negates his statement that the trauma had been going on for some time. There is no evidence to lend credence to that possibility, medically or otherwise.

Ron Kurpiers asks Dr. Plunkett if reviewing radiology studies as a pathologist is part of his review, and he responds that it is, but he would contact a radiologist if he needed to. He does not mention one here, so there apparently was no radiology consultation to confirm that clots were visible on the MRI but not on the CT scan. It must have been obvious.

Plunkett goes against the majority of witnesses again as he states that Maria's subdural hematoma was chronic and not acute (fresh). He is able to discern this by looking at the CT scan, the MRI scan, and the autopsy information, even though Dr. Thogmartin had actually looked at Maria's brain itself at autopsy and noted an acute subdural hematoma. Plunkett reasons that she had an acute bleed which preceded her collapse by *ten days to two weeks prior* to that time. "I don't know if it was from a subdural effusion. The dura may react by pouring fluid and go on to form a chronic process from one that began as a bleeding. It can go on for years unless it gets large. It may go completely unrecognized."

He says that the cause could be due to a number of conditions in a toddler or a child that is a little older. He names these conditions: impact trauma which could be inadvertent, effusion, a viral process, an increase in extra-axial fluid, cortical vein thrombosis (which he says that she had, but once on a respirator, "you can have it"), and vascular malformations. (Maria had no evidence of these or they would have been discovered at autopsy.) I note here that the diabetes that Plunkett stressed earlier is not mentioned as one of the conditions. And of course, he does not mention abusive head trauma within hours of her scans because that would rule out a chronic bleed. He does not discuss how he knows that the bleed is chronic rather than acute and recall from his immediately earlier testimony that he has not consulted with a radiologist since he is not one himself. And of course, it just happened to throw her into a coma the only day she is ever away from her loved ones for a few hours.

Plunkett deduces that this bleed is a chronic subdural hematoma, which has new bleeding as part of its natural history. It is why it persisted and it is not rebleeding, but actually new bleeding. He notes that one can see new bleeding specifically in infants, and this appears to be related to unique clotting characteristics. This testimony is vague and doesn't really tell the jury anything it can use, and besides, Maria is over a year old and technically is not an infant. No other witness has mentioned anything about unique clotting characteristics including the other pathologists.

Maria presented her symptoms on August 21, 2008. Plunkett states this to the court. He states that there is only a small volume of blood.

Kurpiers asks him if there is any way to tell how fast the bleeding is occurring. Plunkett responds that there is an experimental technique of MRI venography used to measure this, but it was not used. The volume of bleeding was very small unless it excluded her compensatory mechanisms. Here he is saying that Maria could have absorbed a good portion of the bleeding as a natural way of coping with the injury to her body, but there is no way to tell.

Plunkett tells the court that Maria responded to her injury with a "dural compartment seizure." He says that the brain center that controls breathing also controls wakefulness, and there was interference with her wakefulness. This is what he believes caused her to be semicomatose. When asked whether her death was due to brain swelling or the subdural hematoma, Plunkett says that the brain swelling was the reason she did not wake up and that the subdural hematoma led to the edema. He is the first person to draw this conclusion. Other witnesses stated that they could not tell which happened first.

Kurpiers asks the doctor if he knows what caused the subdural hematoma, and he responds that he cannot tell.

"You see no external or internal injuries to the body?"

"That's correct."

Of course, Plunkett couldn't tell whether or not there were any internal injuries based on just looking at the scans since they referenced her brain and not her body. And obviously he could not note any external injuries for the same reason. We already know that her lungs showed significant damage from being on the ventilator, but this was technically not an injury.

Plunkett goes on to say that subdural hematomas can be caused by any number of natural conditions. He purposefully avoids mentioning accidental or abusive head trauma, both of which are a fairly common cause of subdurals in children.

Kurpiers asks him if the swelling was throughout the entire brain. "Global massive edema, did you see that?"

"Yes."

"Throughout the brain?"

"Yes."

Dr. Plunkett then describes the progression of Maria's retinal hemorrhaging based on the studies that he reviewed. She had, according to All Children's Hospital records, bilateral hemorrhaging to the base of her retinas the second day she was there. The time frame here is likely twenty-four hours or less since the event, since it was the second calendar day and this exam may have been done in the morning. By the time she was taken off the respirator five days later (it was actually six days), according to Dr. Plunkett, she had developed detached retinas due to the increase in pressure in her brain.

Kurpiers asks him if the increase in pressure would have to have been considerable in order to see retinal hemorrhaging, and Plunkett agrees.

"Do you know what happened to Maria Harris?"

"No."

Kurpiers encourages him to hypothesize about what could have happened in spite of his negative response. "Would you have expected her to become immediately incapacitated?"

"Well, she wasn't. You don't develop signs or symptoms unless your head gets larger. "Someone who hasn't seen you may notice it." (What? Notice a larger head?) Then, in contradiction to *all* of the state's witnesses, Plunkett continues by saying there was "no acute bleeding to cause signs or symptoms by itself. As far as anyone could tell, she was normal."

This statement in itself seemed to be quite a fantastic leap of diagnosis. Plunkett believed she had this subdural hematoma, which, unlike other witnesses that included numerous radiologists, he believed to be chronic, not acute. He also believed that she would have not exhibited any noticeable symptoms until she reached the point of brain and head swelling where she ultimately collapsed. No one else has indicated this possibility, especially head swelling. And the fact that this would have coincidentally occurred when she was not within reach of her family for the first time ever seems rather odd.

When asked if inflicted trauma caused Maria to collapse, Plunkett emphatically says it did not, but yet just a minute earlier he stated that he did not know what happened to her. How could he rule out abuse if he didn't know the cause? At this point, I conclude that his statements are pure bias for the defense and not something that the jury should seriously consider as truth. A paid witness needs to have his testimony scrutinized very carefully to see if it fits in with testimonies of other witnesses or merely supports the defense's stance even if the testimony is not plausible.

Kurpiers asks about encephalopathy, a type of brain swelling. "Did she have that?"

"Yes. I know she had cortical vein thrombosis [clotting] and a chronic subdural hematoma. That process is related to her encephalopathy." Plunkett is the only witness who is asked about encephalopathy and makes this conclusion alone, again stating that Maria had a chronic and not acute bleed.

I also found information indicating that encephalopathy can accompany inflicted trauma (emphasis mine):

> Shaken Baby syndrome is a form of physical non-accidental injury to infants, *characterized by acute encephalopathy* with subdural and retinal hemorrhages, occurring in a context of inappropriate or inconsistent history and commonly accompanied by other apparently inflicted injuries.
>
> Injuries to the neck and spinal cord may also be present. Controversy surrounds the precise causation of the brain injury, the retinal and subdural hemorrhages, as well as the degree of force required and whether impact in addition to whiplash forces is needed.[6]

Plunkett then makes a quantifying statement about her glucose levels based on his experience with other cases. "[She had] marked elevation of her glucose to a marked degree. I haven't seen it to this extent [in this type of trauma]." This is a flawed conclusion because one first has to surmise that her subdural hematoma was not acute and then conclude that just because Plunkett had not seen this sort of glucose elevation, it could then be generalized that it was not typical in a stressed patient. Maria's glucose level responded rapidly to treatment at Mease Countryside Hospital, dropping almost two hundred points.

Plunkett is then asked by Kurpiers if brain removal for additional analysis is a common procedure, and he responds affirmatively, also stating that it is done through a neuropathology department and not through him.

"In this case I would have asked a neuropathologist to look at her brain, first for dating and second to confirm an infarct—a distinctly unusual finding. I would want a neurologist to confirm that finding."

Earlier in the trial, medical examiner Jon Thogmartin stated that there were clots present at autopsy that were not unusual for someone undergoing brain death and on a ventilator. For Maria to have had a stroke, which was what Plunkett was alluding to when he used the word *infarct*, would indeed have been very unusual. There was no evidence that she did so. The clots were not present on the first CT scan. Plunkett had mentioned this clotting (thrombosis), apparently trying to show that it was something that led to her collapse, and not something that happened after she went on the ventilator, as Thogmartin points out. My feeling is that he introduced this rare and strange possibility to create doubt in the minds of the jurors. I didn't know if or how the state would deal with it on cross-examination, but I was about to find out.

CHAPTER 22

HOLLY GRISSINGER APPROACHES Dr. Plunkett prepared with questions to discredit his background. He admits readily that he is not a pediatrician, a neurologist, or a radiologist. He says that he has done or attended approximately two hundred autopsies involving children.

When asked how many of them had head trauma, he indicates that there were ten and that the last time was twenty-five years ago, and that it was an exhumation autopsy. A second one was done in Minnesota. This happens when a body is dug up after being buried and another autopsy is performed due to misdiagnosis of cause of death and/or new evidence has been introduced and needs to be verified by examination of the exhumed body. It is unclear whether this exhumation was of a child.

Dr. Plunkett says that there are approximately 1,500 death investigations at the Minnesota Medical Examiner's Office every year. He says he has done about fifteen thousand total, or about five hundred a year.

Grissinger asks him if he determined cause and manner of death in these five hundred investigations a year, and he says that he did not do all of them himself, but he had two other trained pathologists working with him.

"You appeared in over a dozen [court] cases with Dr. Leetsma?"

"Yes."

"For the defense?"

"Yes."

He explains that he receives a $2,000 flat fee for documents and a consulting letter and $4,000 plus expenses, assuming he is being paid—for court and travel.

Grissinger introduces to the court that Plunkett had recently spoken at a conference on head trauma.

Then they get to the brunt of Maria's injuries where he again avoids nonaccidental trauma in his responses.

Plunkett states that retinal hemorrhaging in this case is the common denominator with other such cases resulting from intracranial pressure. He says that other reasons such as clotting, cortical brain thrombosis as in the case with Maria, and diabetes can also case retinal hemorrhaging. There was increased cranial pressure. This is what he believes lead to her retinal hemorrhaging. He says that there was no evidence that anything else caused it.

He is asked about blunt force trauma and rapid acceleration/deceleration causing the brain and skull to move separately. When asked to define this mechanism, he says it is "not humanly achievable." (What about the tearing of the bridging veins that was evident? Is he really saying that it is not possible for Maria to have received a blunt force trauma to the head? Again, remember earlier that he stated that he did not know what had happened to her.)

Holly then asks him that if there is rapid acceleration/deceleration with impact, whether it can cause retinal hemorrhaging.

"Well, yes, but the pure impact motion doesn't matter. It's not the fall that kills you, it's the impact."

This statement really throws me for a loop! Is he saying it's not what happens before the actual impact, but only the impact itself? If he is, then several issues become obvious. First, he is contradicting his own study of playground injuries where the children on swings—the ones who would have had motion accelerating them into a higher degree of impact into the ground—were the ones that had very short or no lucid interval at all. Next, he is denying that a back-and-forth shaking can lead to any form of death, when there are recorded cases cases on record of people admitting guilt to shaking a child to death, consistent with internal injuries attributable to acceleration/deceleration. So, according to Dr. Plunkett, a slower fall without momentum behind it is no different than one where a child is pushed harder into a surface, whether it be accidental or not, because it's the impact itself and not the force behind it that causes the death. The best analogy that I think of again is someone falling down stairs as opposed to being pushed aggressively down stairs. Which person would be more likely to sustain worse injuries and/or to die? I wonder if the physicist, Dr. Ipser, would argue Plunkett's hypothesis.

Dr. Plunkett tells the court that bilateral retinal hemorrhaging would deteriorate vision in children, but that "rotation" has nothing to do with retinal hemorrhaging. Plunkett states next that brain swelling is the determining factor in retinal hemorrhaging. He must have meant this in the context of an injury or abuse, because it is common for the birthing process to cause retinal hemorrhages in a child.

He notes again, this time for the state, that Maria had no internal injuries or neck damage.

Grissinger asks him how he would determine evidence of an impact and he responds with "scalp impact at autopsy." But Dr. Thogmartin had said that after a week's time, it was very possible for scalp bruises to have faded if they had been present soon after the injuries. He had also said that they could have been missed by the doctors in the ER since Maria had such a full head of hair. Plunkett admits that he would accept a history of an impact event as evidence.

Next, he reviews the glucose elevation prior to the IV used to bring it down. He says that ketones were also evident with acetone, which would be unusual in a stress response. It turns out, however, that the release of ketones happens with traumatic brain injury as mentioned in this abstract from the Critical Care Forum (emphasis mine):

> There is evidence that other conditions including TBI (traumatic brain injury), ischemia, hemorrhagic shock and hypoxia induce rapid changes in both vascular and cellular transporters *that favor ketone uptake and metabolism*. In addition, ketone-metabolizing enzymes demonstrate the ability to change in response to neuropathologic conditions.[1]

So, in contrast to Dr. Plunkett's suggestions that Maria had an underlying metabolic abnormality, we find that these imbalances that he suggests are often present with traumatic head injuries in children. He tells Grissinger that he doesn't know whether brain swelling precipitated these results. Obviously, knowing that would help a great deal because if she had these conditions prior to the injury, she would have been diabetic. But if that were the case, it could not result in tearing of the bridging veins in the brain.

Grissinger asks if glutico steriods could have resulted from a stress reaction from Maria's injury.

"Well, she was certainly stressed, mediated by adrenal glands—epinephrine in her case—but the degree was greater than what I would expect. I don't know what caused it. Diabetes? Fasting? Acetone in the urine? But not glucose elevation."

I carefully weighed this contradictive response by Plunkett. He states that glucose elevation could not have resulted from her stress reaction. Maybe he misspoke. There are boatloads of evi-

dence that head trauma produces increased glucose levels, especially in children. Second, we know she had breakfast and apparently vomited some of her lunch. So fasting is easily ruled out.
Acetone is usually present in conjunction with ketones, and, as
the article above points out, they do occur in abnormal levels in
a TBI in a child. Dr. Plunkett also mentions that her epinephrine levels were a higher degree than what he would expect. The
meaning of this comment is left hanging for the jury to wade
through. What levels *would* he expect and where does he draw
this evidence from?

"Severe stress could have caused it?" Holly reiterates.

"Yes," Plunkett admits.

"Does the fact that they were able to stabilize her have
any bearing?"

"No, they used insulin."

"Have you seen this in children with trauma?"

"Not to this degree in my experience."

Actually, as previously mentioned, children in diabetic comas
are often unable to stabilize with insulin, and subsequently die
from their high glucose content due to diabetes. The same is true
with adults. There comes a point of no return where stabilization
of the blood sugar is not possible because there has been too
much damage to the endocrine system. I have a friend who lost
her nine-year-old godson in this very way. It was too late for the
insulin to bring him around and he died.

Grissinger gets to the heart of Plunkett's comments under
direct questioning regarding how he knew that Maria's subdural
hematoma was chronic and not a new bleed (acute).

He responds that it is an inflammatory response with white
blood cells (scavenger cells) causing the inflammation. He goes
on to say that she had a subdural hematoma with the exception
of acute bleeding, and it occurred days if not weeks prior to her
collapse. Remember, he had stated that he did not know what
happened to Maria, so it would seem confusing in the least that

he could be certain that she had bleeding that occurred days or weeks earlier in her brain. He also says he saw cortical brain thrombosis (those clots), and it came from the sagittal sinus at the top of the brain and ran from front to back. He gleaned this information from having viewed a scan. Remember that he is not a radiologist. Then he states, "I did not personally see evidence of sagittal sinus thrombosis in Maria, just cortical vein thrombosis." (Thogmartin had seen the SSST in Maria's brain at autopsy, but Plunkett was not aware of this at the time).

Grissinger ties up her questioning with, "Is it common for a brain-dead person to have cortical vein thrombosis?"

"Yes," Plunkett admits.

There is no redirect by the defense, but instead a dramatic conclusion to the questioning aspect of the trial is introduced: the 911 tape.

The call is very emotional, and one can hear a very hysterical woman calling for help to come. Esther gives the address and says something is wrong with her baby. The reason why the tape is played is so that the defense can point out that there is crying in the background of the tape. It is very difficult to tell whether this is Pat crying, (she does have a voice in the higher ranges of speaking), or if it is Maria. There is no definitive way to determine by listening to this tape, who is crying.

In my opinion, if the defense is absolutely sure that it was Maria who is crying on the tape, they would have introduced it after putting it through some voice analysis testing to eliminate Pat as the one who is crying. Maybe they had done this and did not introduce the results because they were not conclusive or they were contradictory to what they are trying to achieve. In any event, the defense assumes they can get away with just stating that there is a child crying on the 911 tape. I also wonder if it is even relevant. If it was Maria who was crying, then so what? She was still fatally injured, which would give her all the more reason to cry if she was awake, since she would have been in tremendous pain. But I have my doubts as to it being her.

During the playing of this tape, I notice that Stephanie Spurgeon is in a highly agitated state. The tape is being broadcast to the entire courtroom from a computer in an inconvenient location right in front of where she is seated. She is wiping tears from her eyes, and she cannot keep her hands still. They move up and down her arms and up to hold her head in her hands. The dire reality of her situation is no longer something she can escape. The death of a child who was in her care has come back to haunt her after four years. Will it ever go away?

Judge Newton speaks to Spurgeon at this point, and she indicates that she has chosen not to testify. The judge tells her that she does have the right to remain silent. She has chosen to do so. She asks Spurgeon if she needs more time to decide, and she says no. Even though her attorneys have advised her that it is best not to testify, I somehow do not think she would have chosen to do so. Her demeanor throughout the trial except for the playing of the 911 call has been very detached. Spurgeon will keep her secrets, believing that her chances are better if she does not have to face Grissinger or Daniels on a cross-examination. It is, as Judge Newton advised her, her right to remain silent. She need not take the stand in her own defense. Will she regret that later? How many people second-guess that decision, playing out what they would have said on the stand like an old movie cycling over and over in their minds in the dark and lonely hours of prison cells?

Spurgeon is asked some of the rote questions that are asked of everyone who is sworn in for a trial or a hearing. Her age? (Forty-one.) Was she nervous? (Yes.) Her education? (High school diploma.) Was she under the influence of alcohol or drugs? (No.) Was she taking any prescriptions? (No.)

This is the only time that Stephanie would speak out in court for the entire trial.

CHAPTER 23

BEFORE CLOSING ARGUMENTS begin, Judge Newton reviews a couple of cases involving aggravated child abuse. One case involved multiple injuries sustained by a child due to repeated motion of pushing the child into a soft object. The state says that it is allowed to use aggravated child abuse as the underlying felony charge due to its similarities to this case. Judge Newton says that more than one act of violence constitutes separate charges, and there were numerous witnesses in this case.

The defense does not argue this stance.

The other case concerned a single stab wound and is not applicable to Maria's case.

It is at this point that manslaughter is added by the judge as another possible verdict. Judge Newton describes to the jury what a verdict of manslaughter means. I realize that Spurgeon and her attorneys have agreed to add this option and it is most likely a wise one for both her and the jury.

The defense again asks for a judgment of acquittal in the *State v. Spurgeon* case. This is an expected motion.

Judge Newton responds by saying that in light of the arguments offered, the case is most favorable to the state. She says that, "Again, (as before), we have had the testimony of numerous witnesses saying in the case of the deceased." She goes on to say that these witnesses presented information that on August 21, 2008, Maria Harris died due to homicide, blunt head trauma, accelerated stopping, and rapid starting with impact to the head, as per medical examiner Thogmartin. According to Dr. Rodriguez, these injuries only come from a rapid acceleration and shearing. It was nonaccidental trauma. Maria acted like a normal child earlier that morning.

The pediatric ophthalmologist showed that Maria's injuries were fresh and consistent with acceleration/deceleration, and it was nonaccidental. She had bilateral retinal hemorrhaging separate from a subdural hematoma.

Dr. Potthast, a pediatric radiologist, said that there was an acute subdural hematoma resulting from a nonaccidental trauma. Maria was comatose and on life support. She had no prior brain injuries and no diseases. Judge Newton concludes by saying that all this is "just a fraction of the state testimony for a prima facie case (information presumed to be true unless it is disproved). The court will deny the motion for judgment of acquittal."

Brian Daniels begins what would be a very brief closing argument for his part of the state's conclusion. He summarizes Maria's background as a child who had passed her first birthday and was happy but spoiled, demanding to be held and was always accommodated by her family. At the YWCA, Pat would assist with her care when necessary. She appeared happy and healthy at her regular wellness doctor appointments.

Next, he dictates back summaries of what the state's witnesses each said on the stand, in particular that Maria's injuries were consistent with nonaccidental trauma. Her brain had moved and then stopped very quickly inside of her skull.

He suddenly stops and looks up with a fierce intensity as if he is seeing the individuals in the jury box for the first time, his face reddening in an angry manner that I had not witnessed during the entire trial. With heated passion he shouts out that Maria was not the one who had gotten p——d off. "The person who got 'p——d off' in this case was the defendant, Stephanie Spurgeon, when she could not get her to settle down! *That's* what caused the injury to Maria Harris!"

Daniels pauses for several long seconds. The air seems to have gone out of the courtroom, and everyone is holding a collective breath. This was a new side of the quiet and composed state's attorney, and the people on Spurgeon's side of the courtroom did not like what they were seeing.

The female bailiff is wiping away tears now. Daniels finally continues, saying that Maria's injury would not have been caused by any vaccination, but instead by rapid acceleration/deceleration with impact. The retinal hemorrhaging could have occurred at the same time as the subdural hematoma. He emphasizes that Dr. Sally Smith had stated that there was severe enough repetition to cause abrupt nonaccidental trauma.

Again, his voice builds in anger and indignation at what he has heard from the defense. "Live doctors say there was no other cause but abuse! Forensic doctors didn't see her!" He speaks of the defense expert witnesses here.

"Let me point out to you—the doctors of the defense want to point out to you—it occurred prior to August 21, she was accidentally injured. They would not take their daughter to a day care with a stranger!" How would Maria react to going to a new babysitter after being with her grandma? After being placed in a playpen by herself?" Daniels wants to drive home the point that Maria, a spoiled child, is suddenly for the first time, in an environment unfamiliar to her, without any family members around, and no one is holding her.

He mentions that Ronald Chola saw Maria standing in the playpen. Maria reached toward his son, and she showed no sign of being injured.

With the extent of her injuries, she should have exhibited immediate physical problems. The state's doctors agree—she would not act the same nor be able to function. "She would be unconscious shortly after that," Daniels pointedly summarizes.

As Brian approaches the end of his closing argument, he tells the jury that the defense will tell them that there was not one witness who saw it happen. But he says that it is not the type of crime that would have witnesses present. It happened in Spurgeon's own home. She had the opportunity. There should be no surprise that there are no witnesses.

Daniels starkly contrasts the state's doctor witnesses with the defense's expert ones. He says that the state's doctors have spent five days a week over a period of several years working directly with children, while the defense's experts, from places like Chicago and Minnesota, only have the job of consulting with defense attorneys and get paid handsomely for their work.

He explains to the jury that the state does not have to prove a premeditated murder, but only that there was aggravated child abuse. The abuse would have caused Maria's death. "You can choose manslaughter, and it doesn't require that the defendant intended death to occur but only intended that the act happen."

This comment, though awkwardly phrased, really does get to the heart of the matter. The jury needs to already know that in order for Stephanie Spurgeon to be charged with a felony in this case—the charge of manslaughter, not the charge of first-degree murder—all she would have needed to do was demonstrate the intent to harm Maria and to have that harm be severe enough to lead to her death. Taking premeditation out of the equation removes the charge that could sentence her to life in prison for murder in the first degree, but the state seems to be trying to reach a compromise here because it knows that without witnesses, that charge has a possibility of not sticking.

Judge Newton's decision to add manslaughter to murder one as a choice of convictions for the jury to consider left the door wide open for this compromise. She had already seen the turn of events in the Casey Anthony case and possibly considered that a guilty defendant might walk if the jury doesn't have a lesser charge to fall back on.

As I mentioned earlier, Spurgeon obviously did not set out with the intent to murder Maria Harris. She was possibly charged with first-degree murder simply because the system allows it. But with the option of manslaughter, if the jury decides upon it, who would be satisfied? The Harrises and friends would be disappointed because they would likely feel that Spurgeon should have gotten life in prison in exchange for taking their daughter's/granddaughter's life. The Spurgeons and friends would also be upset because they would have wanted nothing less than an acquittal, as they would stand behind the words of Ron Kurpiers when he stated that no one saw Stephanie Spurgeon commit the crime. Like many crimes, it's not cut-and-dry. Everything hinges upon reasonable doubt.

As I write this, about ten months after the trial, new information has come to light on the Casey Anthony case showing that there was a search for foolproof methods of suffocation on Anthony's computer. The search was done after both of Caylee's grandparents had gone to work. It was done the day before she went missing. Somehow, this very crucial bit of information was not discovered on Anthony's computer until now, over a year after the trial. No one saw Casey Anthony do this computer search. But I have no doubt that the result of that trial would have been different had this been known and revealed at that time. It reasonably rules out an accidental death prior to Caylee being stuffed in a garbage bag.

This is not to say that Stephanie Spurgeon killed Maria Harris, just because I believe that Casey Anthony murdered her daughter so she could party. They are two separate cases. The common bond is that they both do not have room for reasonable doubt. I will delve into this logic a little later.

Brain Daniels wraps up his closing argument by saying, "We have proved to you beyond a reasonable doubt that Stephanie Spurgeon is guilty of the murder of Maria Harris."

He has spent less than half an hour trying to persuade the jury of Spurgeon's guilt. Although he had some powerful points, I am certain that Ron Kurpiers is more than eager and prepared to respond.

CHAPTER 24

RON KURPIERS FAIRLY leaps off his chair. "'The *only* person who got p——d off was Stephanie Spurgeon'? I say to you folks, where did which come from? His mouth!" Kurpiers points vindictively at Daniels. For the next forty-six minutes, he would be on the attack against the state and its witnesses.

"Not one person indicated that she had problems—had difficulties with the child that day. Not one!" Kurpiers shouts. (Hold on, didn't Stephanie admit to Patricia Harris that she had problems getting Maria to take a nap? That her child was spoiled rotten, even cussing about Maria's behavior?)

Kurpiers is again pointing at the state's table and saying that what the jury has heard regarding problems "comes out of the mouth [*sic*] of these two people. Not one witness can testify that Stephanie Spurgeon committed a single violent act against Maria Harris."

Kurpiers has got out in the open and up front what would likely be the contention in the deliberation room. The jury would have to consider that just because there were no witnesses; does that mean that this crime cannot be proven to be committed by Spurgeon? Is there reasonable doubt? This means that: does the doubt created by the defense outweigh the likelihood that she fatally injured Maria?

Continuing on in his choppy and fragmented style, Kurpiers says, "First-degree murder. That's not our problem. That's their problem. The most serious charge, the most serious penalty, the most serious crime. That she murdered a child. Okay. So we don't have a witness. Every doctor testified that they could not say what happened to Maria Harris."

He is distracting the jury from the lesser charge of manslaughter so that they focus on the defense's logic against murder. Because Kurpiers is such a passionate speaker, his voice has reached high volume, and I notice that some of the jurors are not very happy, looking at him with furrowed brows or from heads dropped downward and eyes riveted upward.

Kurpiers veers to his next topic by asking the state in front of the jury, "Can you date for us in hours when the injury you see at 4:21 occurred? You get a complete divergent [*sic*] from every one of the witnesses."

He reviews the times of the CT scan on August 21 at 4:21 p.m. and the MRI study on August 22 at 8 a.m. "Would you expect to see a child with the type of injuries on the CT scan be able to walk, talk, interact? No!" Here he readily agrees with the state. But then he says, "The real issue is, what was the CT scan at 1:00, 3:00, and at 8:00 a.m. the day before?" (Did he mean in the middle of the night, or the previous afternoon times and then the morning mentioned in reverse?)

Of course, he was posing a hypothetical question because the first CT scan was the one at the hospital at 4:21 p.m. Later on, when I was free to reread his testimony, I thought there was some contradiction there. First, he is saying that as a result of the injuries, which were reported to be fresh by more than one doctor who had examined these X-ray films, Maria would have been unable to function normally. Remember, these are the CT scans, and the defense witnesses primarily testified about the MRI scans that were done at All Children's Hospital the next day. I wondered why they didn't spend time testifying about the original CT scans taken right after Maria was rushed to the ER. They couldn't! The injuries were too fresh on that scan and would have harmed the defense's arguments. They had to focus on the MRI that was taken the next day in order to make their testimony work.

Kurpiers wonders what the scans would have shown had they been taken the day *before* she arrived at the Spurgeon home day care. Well, based on his argument that she would not have been able to function with the injuries presented, a CT scan taken the day before would not have shown those injuries. They were fresh. That was not disputed with regard to the CT scan. Arguments only occurred regarding the MRI, taken after necrosis was spreading in her brain, killing cells at a rapidly increasing pace about twenty hours after the injury.

He further confuses the jury by mentioning that Dr. Rodriguez had stated that the injury was six to twelve hours old, but that Dr. Thogmartin, the ME, said that the subdural hematoma occurred at least seven days in advance of death.

Examining these statements made it easy to determine that they were both correct. The problem was that Kurpiers was mixing apples and oranges. It would be true that the injury was approximately six to twelve hours old by the time the CT scan was taken at Mease Hospital. It would also be true that the subdural hematoma occurred approximately seven days before Maria actually passed away, since she was on life support for seven days at All Children's Hospital. I didn't know which was worse: that Kurpiers himself was confused by this data, or that he knew what he was doing and was simply trying to confound the jury.

Kurpiers goes on to mention what the other state's witnesses had testified to regarding the injury's timing. Dr. Hess had said it happened either immediately prior to hospitalization or was weeks old. Dr. Potthast had said that it happened an hour to twenty-four hours prior. And Dr. Sally Smith had said, "*I don't know what to tell you.*" Kurpiers recalls to the jury that when he asked Dr. Smith to date the injury that she had said she was dating it based on the child being unresponsive immediately prior to the reporting of the injury. He goes on to lambaste Dr. Smith by rattling off a string of attacks, most of which seem personal. He questions whether or not she was "intellectually honest"; decries her attitude; and reminds the jury that when she was deposed, she was asked what caused the injuries and she replied, "*I don't know.*" He says that "she had a fit" and said he was taking her out of context. (This appeared to be the case, though.) He haughtily mentions the "animosity that she carried into the courtroom." Kurpiers next tells the jury to remember that Sally Smith works "hand in hand with the police and the state's attorney's office."

Having never seen her before this trial, I did not see her as a rude or aggressive witness, especially at first. She seemed protective, yet nervous in demeanor, and if anything, on the defense quickly from Kurpiers' rapid and forceful questioning. I believe he spent so much time trying to discredit her because she was a good and honest witness and she had the most hands-on experience with child abuse cases out of any witness presented by either side.

Kurpiers diverts to reviewing his team's witnesses now, prefacing this by stating that "Stephanie Spurgeon wasn't required to hire experts but made a choice to present some doctors." He then mentions Dr. Ipser, the biomechanical physicist who said that Maria's injuries could not have occurred by shaking and that there was no indication of impact. Kurpiers recalls Ipser's testimony that one thousand pounds of impact at fifty Gs would have been required and how he diagrammed various equations and no one contradicted him. (This witness's viewpoint in particular becomes critical later on when the defense itself actually contradicts him to the extreme in a posttrial hearing).

Next, Ron talks about Dr. Herbst and his testimony about the injury being twelve to twenty-four hours old but how he became "surprised" by the MRI study (during his actual testimony), and decided that because of the color of the blood, "I believe it is at least three days old, I don't know."

His arguments, like many defense team arguments, focus on time. Time was an important issue in this case, but more important was what witnesses noted about Maria's behavior prior to the injury and how believable they were. More important as well, is opportunity. Who else could have done this to her, had a reason to harm her, was with her when no one else was present that lines up with Maria going from awake, alert, and focused to limp and nonresponsive? The issue of time comes into question here too, because it is a rather narrow window of time that allowed for this opportunity, however sudden and unplanned, to unfold.

Kurpiers decides that the time element is so critical that he rehashes what his own side's witnesses said about the timing of the injuries. It is interesting to note that although they are all expert witnesses, mostly paid ones, they contradicted each other, so the defense in fact, punched holes in its own argument that the injuries could not have happened as recently as noted by the state's witnesses. The state's witnesses agreed that the injury was recent, occurring within a few hours prior to hospitalization, or approximately a week before death according to Thogmartin, which does not contradict the others. But the defense witnesses were all over the board.

The reader may recall that Dr. Plunkett stated that the subdural hematoma was a couple of weeks old, and he was the only one who said that it was chronic and had become acute. Other witnesses said that this does not happen. Dr. Leetsma said that the injury was a week old, but the neomembrane thickness was "about" fourteen days old. Dr. Herbst, well, he even contradicted his own timeline, and his testimony was inconclusive. These expert witnesses, specialists in their field, none of whom had seen Maria at any time, all contradicted each other as to when Maria's injury happened. I wonder whether the jury will note this in deliberations.

Ron Kurpiers continues with his summation by mentioning why the paramedics were important. I think he did this because they were the only witnesses for the defense who actually did see Maria. He discusses how the paramedics related that Maria was unresponsive at the scene, the family was very upset, and that there was crying heard from Maria in the ER. One was concerned that the family might interfere with the situation. (Kurpiers used the word *case* here). I noted nothing untoward in this summary that would introduce reasonable doubt. We had already been told that people with subdural hematomas can be semiconscious enough to emit cries.

But Kurpiers now starts to shift to the Harris family, and things begin to get interesting. He mentions that Patricia Harris heard a cough and a gurgle coming from the back of the car, but kept on driving. She had noticed froth and vomit, and took the child inside. (Pat had a short distance to go, there was no safe place to pull over, and of course she would take Maria into the house before calling for help. It was August and very hot in Florida. It would have made no sense to leave her in the car).

He hones in on Maria's family to try and create that elusive reasonable doubt. "At no time are we pointing the finger at anyone else. To point the finger at them is no different than the state pointing the finger at Stephanie Spurgeon." Ron Kurpiers has opened a very big window here because a defense attorney has to come from some position of strength to direct the blame at the victim's family when his client was the one who last saw the child awake and alert. He even goes on to pose this question: "Are there some things that are a little strange?" Then, "You're going to have to deal with *them*." Really? Where is this evidence? And is this not finger-pointing?

Kurpiers tries to shift the jury's attention to Pat Harris by telling them that she was the first witness "up and down," that she didn't pull over when Maria made noises in the car but just wanted to get her home to see her mom. He recalls that Maria hated the playpen, that she hadn't napped, and that Patricia "wasn't surprised she was sleeping so hard."

In talking to Pat later about this comment, she revealed that she was quite surprised but was not ever expecting anything to be so very wrong that Maria would not be asleep, but unconscious instead. After all, what grandmother would pick up her grandchild at a day care or from a babysitter and hold her while she appeared to be sleeping soundly and carry on a conversation with the caretaker and suspect something was wrong? The situation, for all appearances sake, didn't seem way out of the ordinary, even if Maria was lying rather oddly in the Pack 'n Play. After all, Stephanie Spurgeon stood there talking to Pat. If anything was wrong, she surely would have said something, wouldn't she?

Kurpiers tells the jury that Esther had made both 911 calls. This information was never relevant as the second call was placed to see why it seemed to be taking so long for the ambulance to arrive. Whether Esther or Pat made that call, whoever made it hung up, because she heard the ambulance sirens wailing in the distance. It is easy to understand why Pat and Esther could not recall, almost four years later, who had actually placed the second call.

When Pat carried Maria from the car, "she had no bones." Kurpiers tells this to the jury, saying that he doesn't know what that means. I think the jury understood what she meant. Earlier Pat had described Maria as feeling "like a bag of rice." Both descriptions depict Maria as being limp and unresponsive. Remember, when she was placed in her car seat, she did not cooperate with Pat at all, which was when Pat began to get very concerned.

Kurpiers mentions that Maria was always rocked to sleep for twenty to forty-five minutes and that sometimes Pat would hold her the entire night. He also reminds the jury that she had fallen "a few weeks before," and the doctor had been called. (But the defense never got the records from the doctor as to the timing of this fall and phone call and the extent of the injury, or if they did, it was not used and therefore wasn't advantageous to their case).

Next, Esther's behavior is questioned. Esther had said that she had done everything she could to wake Maria. "*I called her, talked to her, that's all I did...touched her cheeks, opened her eyes.*" Out of context, he tells the jury that Esther had said on the stand that the situation was not stressful. I believe her recounting of the situation showed just how much stress she had undergone and that she misinterpreted his meaning of the word *stress* as an understatement for how she felt. She meant to say that it was way beyond merely stressful, as a day filled with stress on the job would be, for instance.

To repeat Kurpier's own words, "*A mother who was hysterical, a grandmother who was hysterical...*"

The distressing tape of the 911 call is mentioned again. "In the background," Kurpiers says loudly, "the baby is crying in the background! Listen to it again!"

Pain causes semiconscious people to cry out. Was that Maria crying, or was it Patricia Harris crying is her high-pitched voice? If it was Maria, does it matter to the case?

Kurpiers says that Maria had no seizures at Mease Hospital, but they were "all over the place at ACH." So? Then he mentions the parent, Ronald Chola, who testified earlier and said that he saw no other adult including Patricia who said she was sitting in the driveway, at the Spurgeon home on the morning of the twenty-first. This was another question that I asked Pat about. She said she was not in the driveway, but on the side of the house in her car, crying, and Mr. Chola would not have seen her there if he wasn't paying attention.

Without adding "beyond a reasonable doubt" to the end of his statement, Kurpiers says, "The state has to prove that Stephanie Spurgeon was the person who actually killed Maria Harris." He points out that they have to show that she was capable of doing something so sinister as to kill a twelve-month-old baby, but there has been no proof. "They haven't done it."

Kurpiers gives the jury the standard spiel regarding reasonable doubt, telling them that "the court will instruct you as to the definition of reasonable doubt. Speculative, imaginary, or forced doubt? In this case, the government wants you to speculate on the cause of this case, on the motive." He mentions that not one person ever told what the manner of death was.

This part is not true. Thogmartin did say in his testimony that the manner of death was homicide and that was his conclusion as a medical examiner. That is pretty blatant.

"If you start guessing," Kurpiers goes on to say, "then the reasonable doubt bell should be ringing off the hook." (But if the medical examiner has reached the conclusion that this death was indeed a homicide, and he is the most qualified person to do so, then there should be no guessing at this stage as to the manner of death).

"This process is about finding the truth. Stephanie Spurgeon did not testify." (I find it fascinating that Kurpiers has put these two statements together. If we are seeking the truth, it certainly would have been easier to discover had she testified!) But he goes on to tell the jury, and rightly so under our justice system, that it cannot use it against her. "The state must prove her guilty." (Again, he leaves out "beyond a reasonable doubt.") "You must not view this [Spurgeon's not taking the stand] as an admission of guilt. Burden of proof is with the state. It never leaves them. It goes with you back to deliberation. It would be another tragedy if you held Stephanie Spurgeon responsible for this."

Ron Kurpiers ends his summation here. He has spent a great deal of time attempting to convince the jury that the state has not proven its case. As with most defense attorneys, he has con-centrated on the witnesses and information which would benefit and back his client's situation to keep her from being sentenced to prison time. Now it will be up to the state to show that they do have a case against Spurgeon and that she did fatally harm Maria Harris beyond a reasonable doubt.

CHAPTER 25

"WHO MURDERS A twelve-month-old child in front of wit-nesses?" Holly Grissinger asks as she stands and approaches the jury. She lets the query hang in the air for a moment.

Then she tells the jurors that the medical doctors are the ones who are left; that they were the ones who were "hands-on with Maria, who looked at her, read her actual charts. I'm not asking you to speculate on anything."

Grissinger states that it "proves beyond a reasonable doubt that when she sustained violent head trauma that it was Stephanie Spurgeon." She explains that although nobody can agree on dates, they give ranges. The injuries show that up until approximately noon on August 21, 2008, Maria became unresponsive, and that the doctors said that this would be consistent with the injuries that they saw.

She reviews that the subdural hematoma was acute and "that child's brain had such force upon it again and again and again, the bridging veins actually tore, the brain was bleeding, her eyes were bleeding."

Grissinger responds to Kurpiers' demand for a motive. "You can speculate about a motive. Nowhere do we have to prove a motive. She did not have to have a motive. We don't have to prove premeditation. She caused blunt head trauma. It led to her death. The chief medical examiner, Thogmartin, was not speculating. He said the cause of death was blunt force trauma. The manner was homicide."

This response was powerful because, as I had mentioned earlier, it negates what Kurpiers had stated about no one ever mentioning a manner of death. The jury would no doubt remember this. Nowhere was an accident mentioned in this entire trial. This fact is critical too, because later on in a hearing, when the defense tries to raise another way Maria could have died based on information they claim they had no access to during the trial, the manner of death must stick.

Grissinger states that the defense's own experts cannot even agree as to exactly what caused her death. "I disagree. It was abusive blunt force trauma. Head trauma." She says that no one knows exactly what happened in that house to that child. It is the medical evidence that must be relied upon. The doctors have to be relied upon. "Those who come in here and tell you what happened to that child."

She then tells the jury that people take kids to pediatricians because they specialize in kids. "She was fine. She was interacting with her mom. There were no injuries, no medical history or problems with this child. Nowhere in the records was there a metabolic disorder. Nowhere in the family."

Grissinger reminds the jurors that Dr. Thogmartin had stated that Maria's metabolic disorder (high glucose reading) was a result of the blunt head trauma. The other doctors also indicated that this trauma can cause such disorders.

Next, highlights of the tragic day at the Spurgeon home are reviewed. Holly says that there is a conversation with the grandmother (between Patricia Harris and Stephanie Spurgeon) in the morning, and then when mom (Esther) calls at lunchtime, Maria is miraculously asleep. For twelve months, every day of her life, Maria is rocked asleep, and "miraculously, the one day she goes to the defendant's residence, she goes to sleep on her stomach without her pacy. We are creatures of habit."

"Was she outside of her comfort zone? Yes. Did she have a fit? Yes. Did it cause the defendant to snap? It did. That child did not come out of the house." Grissinger's voice has a slight quiver now. "The injury to that child occurred in her house. That makes her guilty of murder. The defense wants to talk about how Sally Smith was argumentative. She was being misrepresented. She cleared it up on redirect. Someone attacks your credibility. She had a right to be argumentative."

Grissinger goes on to argue that Dr. Ipser, the physicist, admitted that almost nothing is known about children in his studies. His studies were from the 1970s and were based on conclusions drawn from experiments on primates. He also used crash test dummies. These are not reliable representations of children. His equation was based on a "*single episode.*" He also admitted that repetitive force could generate fifty Gs.

She discusses defense witness Dr. Herbst next, telling the jury that his emphasis on timing concerning Maria's injuries is irrelevant. "What is relevant are the neurological changes to the child. If these were old injuries, she would have been comatose [when the injuries occurred]."

All the doctors who examined Maria hands-on said that the injuries were not old injuries. If the time factor is what the defense appears to have focused on in their summation, then Grissinger has just let the air out of their balloon since none of their experts could agree on a time, none of their witnesses examined Maria firsthand except for the paramedics, and none of their witnesses could adamantly conclude that Maria would act completely normal for an extended period of time after sustaining such severe injuries.

Holly reminds the jury once again that Maria was "happy and healthy until she went to the defendant's house. There was a ticking time bomb?"

With all the strength and emotion she could muster, Grissinger speaks with her body language, almost as if in anguish. "Don't you just know? She goes to the defendant's house. She won't take her nap! There is this ticking time bomb. Just randomly, this subdural hematoma that she's been walking around with for months? All of a sudden, she just has a meltdown?"

Grissinger tells the jury to use common sense. Drs. Rodriguez, Potthast, and Smith all told the court that it was nonaccidental trauma. "Just because we don't want to believe someone would kill a twelve-month-old child doesn't mean it would not happen. She used enough force to tear her brain and make her eyes bleed!

"The state has met its burden beyond a reasonable doubt… She walked in healthy and happy. She never walked out."

As Holly Grissinger slowly walks away from her position in front of the jury box, the air in the room is heavy. People can hear each other breathing. A reporter at the end of my bench whom I had not seen during the entire trial rapidly types on a tablet. The seated jury members are all stone-faced, each one. The clichéd stereotype holds true. No one can read a jury and certainly not this one.

After a brief approach to the bench by the attorneys, the jurors are given their instructions.

Initially, the jurors are told by Judge Newton that they cannot go home; that once deliberations begin, they cannot stop until they are done. But then, in the same delivery, the judge tells them that "it can be now or you can come in tomorrow."

The jury decides to come in the following day to begin deliberating. They get to go home. Do any of them disobey court orders to not watch any television reports about the case, not look online for information, not read the newspapers? No one will ever know.

CHAPTER 26

FEBRUARY 16, 2012

I ARRIVE BACK at court the next morning for what would turn out to be a long and boring day. The Harrises are in the building waiting for a verdict, and the victim's advocate, Bobbie Hodson, is with them, lending her tireless support. Spurgeon's family is at the courthouse as well, although there are far fewer of her supporters present than during the trial. It is likely that they had to go back to jobs. Those that are here gather in the cafeteria by the vending machines and make sure that they take note of everyone, including myself, who wanders in from time to time for a coffee or a snack. Spurgeon is with them, laughing and talking, but there is a deep-rooted tension present, and it seems that everyone around her is trying to keep her from dwelling on the possibility of a conviction. I speculate that there are some thoughts spoken aloud that begin with, "When you come home..." Or, "when this is over, we are going to have a big party." Or even, "Pretty soon you will be home, and this will all just seem like a bad dream." Of course, none of that may have been said, but similar expressions of hope were likely voiced—not only to lift Stephanie's spirits, but to keep despair from tapping at the hearts of those who love her as well.

At 10:00 a.m., Spurgeon is called back in to the courtroom. Is this the verdict? It seems way too early for that. It turns out that Judge Newton has received some questions from the jury. The jury wants to know if the depositions are included in the evidence, and if so, the jurors would like to read them. Judge Newton says that "you have received all the evidence in this case, you may continue with deliberations."

This wouldn't be the only time this jury wants more information from the judge. At one point later on, they ask for the transcript of some of Patricia Harris's testimony. This is denied as well. The denial of information to the jury would become a bone of contention to some of Spurgeon's supporters because they felt that it was an injustice to not supply the jury with information that it requested. Having been a juror myself, I recall that we asked for four pieces of information in a criminal case and were denied all of them by a judge who would have made a perfect drill sergeant. He reprimanded us for requesting information that we had the opportunity to take notes on and that we should have paid more attention to the testimony. He also told us that the very idea of deliberating was to discuss and review testimony based on what we heard and could agree on so that we could reach conclusions. Hearing it again should not be necessary.

I mention this personal embarrassment here because I wanted to note that it is not typical for a judge to give a jury any transcripts, and never any depositions, unless they are introduced as actual pieces of evidence. What a judge can do for a jury is clarify definitions and allow examination of certain evidence that was introduced to the court, such as diagrams or recordings, like the 911 call. There was neither side-taking nor wrongdoing on Judge Newton's part by refusing to give the jury transcripts from the trial (which weren't even digitally transcribed yet), or depositions (which were not even part of the trial itself).

Thirteen hours after deliberations begin, the jury is called back into the courtroom. The Harrises are seated in front of me, looking exhausted from doing nothing but sitting and pacing all day long. I can see traces of Maria in Esther's young face. We are told that there is no verdict yet. The jury is to return tomorrow at 8:30 a.m.

When I get home that night, I pull up "jury deliberations" online and try to glean some meaning from prolonged debates. Did longer deliberations indicate acquittal or guilt? After a couple of hours of mindless Google searches, I come up empty-handed. The answers were fairly equally divided, and I know no more than when I started. Needless to say, I end up having a sleepless night, imagining myself in that deliberation room and trying to get a grasp on what could possibly be going on in there that was taking so long.

February 17, 2012

It is 9:10 a.m. when I arrive the next morning, and I feel slightly apprehensive that I may have missed the verdict, even though I know that is nigh impossible. However, I do know that it certainly would be the last day of deliberations. I could feel it.

I had done a very informal straw poll of some of the folks I had gotten to know from hanging around the courthouse throughout the trial and the deliberation drag-out. The consensus appeared to be that the jury is battling between a manslaughter charge and the murder one charge. The defendant waived murder in the second degree and all lesser charges. Murder in the second degree carries a mandatory twenty-five-year sentence. Judge Newton was very adamant in asserting that Spurgeon consider the lesser charges, even to the extent of making certain that it was Spurgeon's own decision to do so and not that of her attorneys. Lesser charges could have included aggravated child abuse and negligence. I don't know what sort of sentence these would have carried, but if Spurgeon turned down lesser charges, thus ruling them out as an option for the jury, how would that come into play if she receives a severe sentence and then fights for an appeal? Could the state then say that, "Hey, you had your chance to personally choose a lesser charge as an option, but decided that you could take the chance that you would not get a harsh sentence. You denied yourself that option." Would it lessen her chance of obtaining an appeal? Stephanie Spurgeon had self-limited the jury's options to murder in the first degree, manslaughter, or not guilty. These choices would seem to place some pressure on the jurors to compromise to choose a manslaughter conviction if they did not want to let her go free, and on the other hand if they thought that the ramifications of murder one went too far.

Aggravated child abuse is the underlying felony to these charges. It would attach to both murder one and to manslaughter as part of a conviction. Could it stand alone as a charge? It has been done before. If it was left on the table as a conviction option, the jury may have ruled that Spurgeon never meant to fatally injure Maria but did abuse her enough to cause injury. The very fact that it was a fatal injury though should have eliminated this possibility. Judge Newton wanted Spurgeon to know that she had choices and that she needed to consider them due to the possible grave implications for her future.

Could we see a hung jury? The thought became more plausible with each passing hour even though it is not a common occurrence. A hung jury could benefit the state since they would be entitled to retry the case. Brain Daniels is retiring in March so the Harrises would pick up a new attorney to be paired with the ambitious and talented Holly Grissinger. They would not have the huge costs associated with hiring a private attorney since it is the state's case. They would, however, have the prolonged anguish of having to relive the dreadful and tragic last days of their beloved little daughter and granddaughter's life.

Stephanie Spurgeon, who has already put up $35,000 in bond backed by $350,000 in collateral assets, would have a problem coming up with the funds for another trial. Retirement funds have been liquidated. She would soon lose her home to foreclosure. Even though Bjorn Brunvand is now offering his talents as a high-profile defense attorney pro bono, he is unlikely to do so again in the event of a new trial. He has spent countless hours of his own time and his staff's time on this case, all unpaid. Ron Kurpiers is an unknown in this scenario, but my guess is that unless he feels that he has a slam dunk win on a retrial, he will be out of the picture as well. A court-appointed public defender is not someone whom anyone that is being tried for murder wants in her corner.

If Spurgeon does get a conviction of murder in the first degree, there would no doubt be an appeal, and it would be likely to gain a new trial. This is because there were no witnesses and the evidence is circumstantial, even though it is incriminating. Again, the issue would be the cost. She would best be served by a high-profile attorney team willing to try the case pro bono because she could never afford it. And even with help from her supporters, there does not seem to be any strong outpouring of funds available. After all, they left her in jail over Christmas in 2008 instead of posting bail by chipping in funds together to get her out.

If Spurgeon gets a manslaughter conviction, it is certain an appeal will be filed as well, but the likelihood of an appeal overturning the case diminishes dramatically. First of all, the importance of the entire matter is lessened because she would be sentenced to much less time in prison. In Florida, murder one is life without parole, or the death penalty in severe cases. Manslaughter carries a maximum of fifteen years, with time off for good behavior. There is no parole however. The time off could be up to 15 percent of the sentence. The appellate process can drag out for months, if not years. Attorneys on both sides will often ask for time extensions to file and answer legal briefs. These extensions alone can add up to a year of time to the appeal process. Usually, the defense attorney must document in his or her initial brief that something was done improperly or ineffectively in the original trial to the extent that an appeal is warranted, or that new evidence has come to light that could overturn the conviction on appeal. Perhaps the defense will want to prove that they discovered a leak in the jury, or that the judge brazenly favored one side by only ruling in its favor on any matter. But an appellate judge may still find these to be weak arguments and will want very strong evidence to show that the trial was prejudicial against the defendant. It takes a pretty blatant flaw in the courtroom to overturn a verdict on appeal when someone is imprisoned for a violent crime. This is not to say it doesn't happen, but it is not very common.

In Spurgeon's case, a potential appeal would likely point to a poor defense. I find this ironic when her first legal team was "relieved of its duties" so that she could get this super-team combo of Brunvand and Kurpiers, from two separate law offices. They were highly touted, and they seemed to present fair arguments on Spurgeon's behalf. In other words, they will only have presented a poor case to the jury if they lose the case. That is Monday morning quarterbacking, and I find it reprehensible. Blaming the defense for losing a case is pretty weak, unless it was a really bad defense that did not do its job or its homework. Their witnesses may have not been remarkable, but they were the best that could be found to refute what Maria's hands-on doctors had to say. To go to appeal based on an ineffective defense nowadays means that the defense would practically have to have slept through the case. Spurgeon's attorneys are not wimps. They are bulldogs and they fought hard for her, presenting a tough battle for the state to overcome.

Also, the possibility of Judge Newton's sentencing decision needs to be considered prior to any appeal. If Spurgeon gets a manslaughter conviction, the judge could sentence her to less than the maximum of fifteen years. If she sentences her to ten years, for example, and Stephanie receives 15 percent time off for good behavior, she would only serve eight and a half years in prison. An appeal would easily take a year to reach the appellate court and maybe two or three more years to even get on the docket. Then, if a trial is warranted, more years could go by so that by the time she is going to trial, and her sentence would be almost finished. And the attorney involved would probably have to do all the work pro bono, unless someone or some group comes up with a generous sum to fight for her appeal. It is my belief that this money will not come forth on her behalf, unless there is an overwhelming faith in her innocence by the donator(s). Even if that is the case, there is a huge difference between backing someone with your words and backing her with your money.

Of course, if she does get the maximum of fifteen years under manslaughter, working for an appeal makes more sense because of the length of time involved. It certainly makes sense for a murder one conviction. I mull and speculate as I alternate pacing about the four floors of the courthouse and sit on various window benches. Either way, I can't shake off the eerie sensation that the jury is getting down to the wire, and the very things I consider are being hashed out in some form in that windowless room where they are gathered.

All week long we have been in courtroom number 7. Now I am a person who does not believe in luck, but the number 7 carries significance way back to biblical times. What that significance implies is yet to be seen. Knowing that the Harrises are faithful church members doesn't make them better people than the Spurgeon family, but because the Harrises have each admitted to being sinners and needing the saving grace of Christ, they have been forgiven for their sins and have been granted the peace to endure through this tragedy, which has dragged on interminably. To have received this forgiveness through God's grace and mercy leads them to pray and ask their church family to pray for them. They also have comfort in knowing that Maria is in heaven with the Savior at this moment and forever. This comfort has given them the ability to pray for the Spurgeon family. Admittedly, Pat has told me this has been very difficult for her to do, but she knows it is what God expects of her, so she prays for them.

Many people in this type of situation who do not know this peace that passes all understanding will try other methods of numbing the pain, such as drinking or drugs. All that these activities do is make the tragedy worse when the effects wear off, not to mention the harm that is done to the body by continually taking in these toxins. But as a Christian, I find it not only extremely sad but also ironic that the very people who try to avoid emotional pain by drinking heavily or doing drugs are the ones who bash my faith, one based on love and the truths of God, which help me walk through emotional pain, since, as we all know, once it calls on us, there is no avoiding it. People who abuse alcohol and drugs are often full of vengeance and have a mean spirit and use foul language because they have no peace. I'm not talking about addiction here. That is a sickness that needs intervention. I am talking about everyday lifestyles of people that we know, people who hold jobs during the day and spend their money on their bad habits instead of paying off credit cards and helping others in need. Yet, when the chips are down, these same people claim to pray and call on God to help them, and they expect him to answer them, like some genii in a bottle who responds to their whim. God hears all prayers. He answers the prayers of the faithful, not the vengeful. Not the ones who do not place their trust in him. To pray to God means to agree with him. How can a person who sits in a bar drinking and cursing others ever be in agreement with the Lord of heaven and earth?

Hollywood is full of examples of what alcohol and drugs can do to people who become "depressed" over the most trivial matters. They pay big money to their "therapists" when all they really need is the Lord. Personally, for these depressed elite I would also prescribe a month-long trip in a third world country or in a very poor town here in the US without any of the comforts they are used to, where their only jobs are to assist the people around them in any way they can that does not involve giving them money and walking away. I guess I have a lot of time on my hands to spend on such tangents while I wait and wait for the jury, but it feels good to put my thoughts down on paper.

The Harrises are here somewhere, in a hidden but comfortable area of the building. There is a victim's advocate area where they could likely be. They certainly do not want to cross paths with the defendant at this stage. There is only the one cafeteria in the entire building, and it becomes very crowded at lunchtime. Then it is hard for the Harrises to avoid the defendant and her supporters as the narrow hallways are conducive to frequent encounters.

Everyone has been civil, yet hush-hush. It is Spurgeon's legal team that the Harrises avoid like the plague since they seem to have eyes and ears everywhere. They are bold and intimidating in appearance. Brunvand is a well-known defense attorney who has had mixed success in his cases. However, a win/loss ratio of better than 50/50 for a defense attorney is commendable. Kurpiers was able to stay on board with the case, putting his own charges on hold until this trial is over. Spurgeon was even encouraged by Judge Newton to seek other counsel when these charges came to light against Kurpiers, but she chose to stand her ground and keep him. At first glance, who would want to be represented in such a serious case by an attorney who was being brought up on felony charges? But in retrospect, I don't know that it would have helped her at all to start over with a third attorney, and lack of money would have been a major issue.

Once the verdict is rendered, this case will be over in the courtroom, but for the families, not really. One side or both sides are going to leave the building unsatisfied, and there is always the chance that a family member or a supporter will run into someone from "the other side" somewhere. After all, the parties involved are all from Palm Harbor, and it's not that big of a town.

Later, while seated in the cafeteria by the windows, I take in my surroundings. I notice that someone with the Spurgeon group has brought in a baby slightly younger than the age Maria would have been at her death. Is this Spurgeon's granddaughter? Very possibly. Is there some irony in the fact that Spurgeon's daughter is also a single young mother just like Esther? Yes, I believe so. (Just as there is a sad irony in Stephanie's middle name: Marie). It would seem that this baby and the circumstances should keep people from pointing fingers at Esther and accusing her of promiscuity when the defendant's own daughter ended up in the same predicament. However, Esther, the victim in this case who lost her baby, is viewed as the enemy because she seeks justice for her own child, whom she will never see on this earth again. Fortunately for Spurgeon's daughter, her own daughter is still alive. The silver lining in these months of sorrow is that both girls chose life instead of having an abortion.

It must be difficult for the Harrises to see this baby and hear it cry and make baby noises, because I notice that they are also sitting in the cafeteria, on the other side. I wonder if the baby will be brought into the courtroom when the verdict is read. Even though it would be unintentional, that action could be very hurtful to the Harrises if Spurgeon gains an acquittal. On the other hand, if Spurgeon is not allowed to go free, but is taken out of the courtroom by a bailiff and led down the long corridor to the county jail, it may be the last look she has at her little granddaughter for a long, long time.

This case has been broadcast over every local news channel, Internet news, and various sites about child abuse online—some accurate, some not very much so. Detailed and accurate reports have been published daily during the trial by Curtis Krueger, the court journalist for the *Tampa Bay Times*, who outlines the facts along with unbiased analysis. His articles are also available in the online versions of the newspaper, with added comments from readers posted in a blog afterward. Other blog commentaries after online news and editorials relate similar posts. These comments are often not only derogatory toward the Harrises, but frightening in their viciousness. I could not understand how people could say such terrible things, many obvious outright lies, and then turn around on Facebook sites and post that they are praying to God to help Stephanie go free. This behavior of course is not true for all of Spurgeon's supporters and family, but it seems to be for a good many of them.

When I consider all of this media attention, I again think about the jury sequestration. The jurors get to go home every night, unlike during the Casey Anthony trial. Both cases involved a baby's life. Is it not possible, truly, that one juror would hear or read these articles, or the unfortunate commentaries? Wouldn't one or two sneak a peek and violate the judge's formidable instructions? Wouldn't there be pillow talk with a spouse who happened to catch a snippet on the news about the case? Sadly, although we hope for the best in people's integrity, that there is always a group of people in society, that when they are told that they cannot do something, such as in instructions given to a jury by a judge, that it gives them a strong desire to do it more, even if it would have never crossed their minds in the first place. Should every jury in a murder trial come under strict sequestration? Maybe. But sequestered jurors in the Casey Anthony case and in the OJ Simpson case both came in with a verdict of acquittal. Too much time on their hands? Private conversations between jurors outside of the deliberations room? Or just lack of enough evidence to convict?

We all have our feelings on those two cases, and we remain quite polarized one way or the other.

Jurors will tell you that they feel privileged to serve on a jury until the time starts to drag out. Then many start thinking about all the chores and activities and work that needs to get done. And they can't get to it until their jobs as jurors are finished. I'm certain that the three or four jurors who are teachers in this case are anxious to get back to their classrooms. Others may have family members to care for and have had to make arrangements that have stretched beyond the time frame that they had expected. It has come to light that a person on the jury was supposed to fly out to California this morning and obviously had to postpone those plans. This juror had been told along with the others that this trial would conclude by Wednesday, but it was certainly not expected that deliberations would continue beyond that first day of thirteen hours. What impact does this change of plans have on this person? Is he/she angry, anxious, distracted, or just impatient to get this part of the job done?

In my own life, I am fortunate to have a career that allows me the flexibility to take the time away to sit through this trial. However, with the myriad of other projects I am currently pursuing, the timing could hardly have been worse.

My career requires major responsibilities, and I am on the phone and in meetings constantly, as well as on airplanes and in hotels around the country. Suffice it to say, there was no *good* time for the *State v. Spurgeon* trial to finally go to court after Maria's death in August 2008.

I feel that without the grace of God, I would have been unable to write this book. You see, there is something that I have not revealed up to this point. Way back when the Harrises were first going through the information gathering stage about this trial, they were frustrated with the slowness of the state's progress on the case. Why weren't character witnesses being interviewed on their behalf? Why wasn't Brian Daniels taking a more active role in pursuing evidence against Stephanie Spurgeon, and about what happened that day in that house?

Before I met with Patricia Harris and Esther to interview them as I began to take notes for this book, Pat warned me specifically that we could not talk at all about what happened at Stephanie Spurgeon's house. I agreed. We would discuss Pat's growing up years, how she met and married Clyde, and then Christopher and Esther's younger days, right up to the point where Esther gave birth and then started the day care search. I knew it would take more than one meeting to cover all those topics, and it did. But the Harrises did express to me that they were not happy with how the state was handling the prosecution. They felt that not enough was being done. I told them that I had a contact and I couldn't promise anything, but I would see what I could do.

I reached my contact who called his friend who, at the time, worked at the state's attorney's office in Tallahassee. My contact filled his friend in briefly about the situation. The person told my contact to have me call. I called and provided more details, including expressing the Harrises' dissatisfaction with how a child abuse and subsequent murder case was being handled by the state. So the person told me specifically to send an email referencing the case number and what I knew. I did so.

I knew that the Harrises at best might get another state attorney assigned. I did not know Brian Daniels, and I certainly did not know that he was retiring within a few years. I could not make my own judgment call on how he was handling the case since I only knew that the Harrises felt that not enough action was being taken. I wanted to voice this to the person in Tallahassee so that somehow maybe he/she could get this case moving along at the clip that the defense seemed to be moving. Obviously, the state is bogged down with a load of cases and does not have the money or the manpower to do what a private defense attorney can with all his staff to back him, but this case was not typical. It involved the charge of murdering a helpless twelve-month-old girl. I felt that I had done all I could do by bringing the Harrises' concerns to the attention of one of the higher-ups in the state's attorney's office. This person admitted to me that this sort of case is taken very seriously by the state, and he/she would personally look into it.

Emails are evidence. They require full disclosure to the defense in a case. This is what I was told when I received a phone call from the person in Tallahassee as I left a meeting in Michigan where I was working the following week. "But," I insisted, "you *told* me to email you the information!"

Had I realized this (and I should have), I would not have done it. The person then told me that the email had to be turned over to the defense—Olney's legal team—and that I may be deposed regarding its contents. There was concern because in the email I mentioned the "guilt" of Spurgeon. I knew though that I would not have done that on my own. I had been following the hearings in person and in the media, and derived the language in the email from somewhere. I would dig for that information as soon as I got home.

CHAPTER 27

IT WAS A good thing that I didn't believe in luck, whether it be good or bad, because it was on a Friday the 13th in November 2009 that I received a call from Brian Daniels, who told me that I would have to take my notes from the Harris interviews to a court hearing and give them to him. I wouldn't have to actually be present at the hearing itself, but I wanted to be. I wasn't concerned. I hadn't even started outlining the notes yet, and there was nothing incriminating in them.

On November 19, I went to the hearing. I waited for Mr. Daniels outside the courtroom with my notes since I didn't know what he looked like. He had told me the hearing was at 8:00 a.m., but I when I got there, I found out it was at 8:30. No hearings were scheduled before 8:30. The courtroom had been moved to number 7, the room that would be used many times throughout the trial. When the bailiff unlocked the door, I still waited outside for Mr. Daniels, as instructed. He entered the courtroom in a hurry without looking for me or at me at around 8:25, but I didn't know it was him at the time.

I went in at 8:30, since I didn't know what else to do, and sat down on the side that was opposite the defendant. Spurgeon was sitting with two or three other women. They were rather loud for a courtroom setting. At one point, one of her attorneys nonchalantly asked her if she had been working on her "diagram" in front of everyone sitting in the room. She laughed and said, "Oh yes, yes, I'm working on it."

When the judge started the hearings at approximately 8:40 (it was Judge Newton), she called Spurgeon's case first. It was surreal as I heard my name mentioned, and her young defense attorney from Olney's team, who I would describe as a rookie with a shaved head in his late twenties, proceeded to bash my email. He said that I had presumed Stephanie guilty from the start and had mentioned incriminating things in the email.

Then he tore into my interviews, which he knew nothing about whatsoever, saying that I was conducting interviews with the Harrises regarding the case, which I was not. It became blatantly obvious that Spurgeon's legal team knew nothing about what I was doing, because the interviews only concerned family history and Esther's pregnancy. All the same, my heart beat too rapidly in my chest. The young man arrogantly rambled on about my yet unrevealed interview notes and requested a subpoena. Interesting. So they couldn't touch them without a subpoena. Mr. Daniels must have known this, but he had not told me so on the phone.

But then Brian Daniels bolted up like a rocket and said that my email was not sent to an attorney, as the defense had mistakenly said, but to an administrator in his office, and that he had no problem with the email being subpoenaed.

Now I was confused. I thought the defense already had the email. Otherwise, how could they know what it even contained if they didn't have it? Wasn't it part of discovery? That's what the "administrator" in Tallahassee had told me. What about my interview notes? Maybe I missed them being mentioned, but I didn't recall Mr. Daniels tying them to any subpoena.

Judge Newton asked if I was present in the courtroom. I stood and said, "Yes, Your Honor," notebook very visible in my left hand. I really thought that I would leave the courtroom without it that morning, and had made copies of every page.

Judge Newton stated, "Subpeona so ordered," or something to that effect. Then everything happened in a blur, very fast. Daniels jettisoned out of the courtroom. I stood up quickly, still bearing my notes and wondering if I should follow him, and at the same time trying to avoid Spurgeon and the women who were with her. I managed to elude Spurgeon and her entourage, avoiding eye contact as well. By the time I had exited the twin sets of double doors, Brian Daniels was at least thirty yards down the corridor and moving rapidly away. I decided that he was not interested in obtaining my notes, and that was fine with me. So I simply turned around and left to await whatever came next. I didn't know.

What was apparent was that Mr. Daniels did not want to speak with me. I don't think I could have possibly damaged his career as he was closing in on retirement. I don't know what his caseload was at the time, probably too heavy to be singlehandedly working on a murder one prosecution where the victim was a one-year-old child. My heart and soul lay with getting the Harris family the best representation from the state of Florida possible because they only had one shot at this.

Now, I had been made known to Spurgeon. Whether she would remember me and know that I was writing a book about the case is not known, and it really doesn't matter. Many people say they are writing or are going to write a book. Some do. Most don't. Over three years have passed since that hearing as I write this now. Some things take time, and I have to trust that this work will be completed according to God's timing as I am past my own deadline now.

A couple of weeks after that hearing—these defense attorneys don't waste any time—I received an in-person visit from a subpoena deliverer. Yes, I was to appear for a deposition regarding my email to the Office of the State Attorney General. *Now*, I thought derisively, *I really was inserting myself quite unintentionally into my own book—if I get to write it at all!*

It was Christmastime in December 2009. Knowing that I had nothing personal to worry about, but feeling slightly nervous nonetheless, I sat in a stark lobby containing several rows of government-issue vinyl chairs with metal arms, waiting to be called in for my deposition. I had never been deposed before, and unlike most people, I had no one who was going to be "friendly" to me in this meeting. After all, I had criticized Brian Daniel's lack of attention to the case to his superior and he would be in attendance, and I would be questioned by the defense's representative attorney for the content of the email, and other details yet unknown. Usually, a person being deposed has someone who is on her side. This was weird, and I was in the process of writing about it to boot.

No one had told me that I could not discuss my deposition after it was finished. So I decided—now that the trial was over and because my deposition was immaterial to the case—that it was public information. After all, I am certain that transcripts exist if anyone bothers to hunt them down and pay for them. Here are some of the questions that I was asked by the very young Olney defense attorney.

I was first asked how long I knew the Harrises. I didn't write down my answer, but at the time of the deposition, I would have known them about four years.

I responded yes, when asked if I knew Esther.

This rookie attorney, edgy to get at the meat of the deposition questions, asked me if I had ever seen Maria running back and forth, screaming. I answered no, and I went on to say that I had never even seen her running at all and didn't even know she was able to run—that she was barely a year old and had just learned how to walk.

I was asked in several different ways why the Harrises told me that they could not tell me anything about what happened at the day care. I kept responding that the Harrises did not want to jeopardize the case, so they did not want to discuss it. (Pat and I had agreed not to tread in these waters specifically even before we met for the first interview.)

I had mentioned in the email that Maria was a "mild and gentle child," and I was asked how I knew that, and I told them that I often sat with her and watched her in our church nursery.

The lawyer wanted to know what my connection was to the state's attorney's office in Tallahassee, particularly the person to whom I had sent the email. I explained that it was through a mutual contact, and that the two were merely acquaintances.

There was some back-and-forth discussion about whether I was aware that pending their divorce—at the time Stephanie Spurgeon and her husband were going through a divorce, which has now been completed—her husband could not be called as a hostile witness. I said that I was not aware that this could not be done, and that was why I had asked about it in the first place in the email. (It was just something that I was wondering about, not knowing the legal ramifications of the issue at the time. Since Spurgeon's now ex-husband was possibly on the property when Maria was dropped off, he may have witnessed something about Maria's or his wife's behavior, and I did not understand why the either side would not or could not call him as a witness. I guess I still don't).

When I was asked about the divorce itself and how I was aware of it, I mentioned that it came up in a hearing. They did not pursue this angle, and I think it was probably because they were aware that the Spurgeon divorce was brought to light in a hearing by their own legal team earlier in the year.

The lawyer wanted to know if I had recorded any of the interviews. I had not. (I don't believe in using this technique, as I think that it makes the person being interviewed nervous). I then had to describe how the interviews took place and who was present. I explained that there were three interviews with different members of the Harris family present at each one, with Clyde being present only briefly at two of them.

Then, flipping back to trying to get information about the Harrises, he wanted to know about Esther's disposition and if she hung out with the "wrong crowd," particularly in Clearwater. (This information had to have come from somewhere, and it would be interesting to know where it came from. Esther, at the time, could not drive, and did not live anywhere near Clearwater). I responded that, no, I never saw her with or knew her to be with the wrong crowd. She was a "home" person, and she spent most of her time with her mother. She was also at church every Wednesday night, and Sunday morning and evening. But it was apparent that the attorney was using my deposition to pry for information that he thought might be helpful at trial.

Now for the disparaging part...Since my original notes from the interviews were written in my trademark illegible script with my own personal shorthand, and I had annotated them after the various meetings with the Harrises so that I could recall details, they were not very legible to anyone but me. I had not typed them out or outlined them yet. The attorneys certainly could not read them. So I was asked to read them aloud from the beginning, which I proceeded to do, so that they could understand them. This oral recitation on my part took some time, but in the end, I guess it paid off, because they did not keep my notes, not that they would have been of any value. The notes just contained the Harris family history summary up to the point of when Esther had placed Maria in the day care at the YWCA where she attended high school.

I had scribbled a note partway down the first page underlined in red that said "kill him." That stood out to the attorneys, and they were very concerned about it. I explained it was simply a remark made in jest by Pat's mother referring to when her father decided to retire; her mother went back to work because she said that if she stayed home with him she would end up killing him. They would have gotten under each other's feet, and she didn't want to be home with a retired husband all day long. She wasn't ready for that yet.

After or before this narrative, I cannot recall which, there came a point when I felt that the defense attorneys were attempting to turn me against Brian Daniels right there in the room by persistently asking me why I did not contact him at first instead of contacting the person in Tallahassee. As I thought about this later, like many people do, I wished I would have responded with a stronger statement, such as that I realized that the state's attorney's office does not have the money to work with that private attorneys do, and I was only trying to get more expedient help for the Harrises in this case. Unfortunately, I was not so clear at the deposition. My purpose was not to harm Mr. Daniels, but to help the Harrises. Sometimes, by doing one thing, it starts a chain reaction that was never intended. But if my actions in any way brought Holly Grissinger on board to assist in the case, then I am extremely grateful. If she would have joined the case regardless, this still strengthened the case for the state by spreading the workload that Brian Daniels had originally been dealing with mostly by himself. I just responded at the time though that I only knew the Harrises side of the story and that they were very frustrated with the slowness of the case, and so I told them that I had a contact who knew someone at the state attorney's office in Tallahassee and I would see what I could do.

Then, in what struck me as a humorous query, one of the attorneys asked if I had ever contacted the state attorney's office before to get things done in a "trial that was not working properly." Of course, I had not, but I hoped that they felt this case had been strengthened against them by my actions. I wisely did not say this aloud though.

The attorneys wanted to know about how I knew about some of the "abuse" that supposedly occurred at Spurgeon's day care I told them in responses to two separate sets of questions that it came from what people said at Spurgeon's bond hearing and what was printed in the media. I did not have the transcripts to that bond hearing. This was a crucial hearing that occurred in December 2008, and I was unable to attend. They wanted to know if I had attempted to get the transcripts. I had not at that time, and I told them that they were digitally inscribed and that I was also told by Mr. Daniels that I could not get them because they would have to be transcribed and that it would be too expensive. He denied telling me this there at the deposition, but he had told me this very thing on the phone several days before the deposition: "No you cannot get them because they would be too expensive."

When I finally did get the transcripts in 2012, I found that yes, they were expensive, but not too expensive—the cost of a good dinner for two at Ruth's Chris Steakhouse. And they were worth it, but not for the reasons in the deposition, so I really did not need them at that point. But I did need them posttrial, and you shall see why later on.

I was finally asked a question though that I felt confident and prepared to answer, and I think I caught them off guard, if even only slightly. The question was about child abuse and involved how I knew what happened at the day care. I pulled out a copy of an article from tbo.com, the website of the *Tampa Tribune* newspaper and quoted from it the police blotter: "The authorities say that Stephanie Spurgeon was arrested on account of shaking a child causing abuse (alternately—death)." Then I said, "Note, it did not say "allegedly." I also read another part of the article that mentions that she (Spurgeon) and Mrs. Harris said that the child arrived alert and healthy at the day care, and later on that Stephanie Spurgeon changed her story and said, "That's not how she arrived at the day care." (Thank you, tbo.com.)

The Olney team thought it of import to ask me if I knew the difference between a plea bargain and going to trial, and why, in some cases, a trial would not be necessary. This seemed like an odd question to ask me, but I knew, and so did Mr. Daniels, that the Harrises wanted the case to go to trial because a plea bargain would allow Spurgeon to possibly get a greatly reduced sentence instead of the great unknown result of a jury verdict and subsequent sentencing by a judge. I told them that if a person goes to trial and there is one inkling of reasonable doubt in the minds of the jurors, then the person can go free, but in a plea bargain, then there is some justification for imprisonment or some other form of punishment, or something like that. It would be out of the hands of a jury at any rate. What seemed to have occurred here is that Spurgeon felt so strongly that she would be acquitted that she refused to plea bargain. But I could be wrong. Her attorneys are not supposed to tell her what choice to make. It is a decision of great consequence, and it needs to be made by the defendant. I also did not know if Brian Daniels was hoping for a plea bargain and was willing to accept one if offered, even if the Harrises wanted to go to trial.

One question that reoccurred throughout the deposition was why the Harrises might have thought they were worried that they did something wrong. Now, not only was that hearsay to ask me such a thing, but I never got the sense from them that they personally thought they did anything wrong. I was asked though, why they thought they were on the defense, and why the defense might go after them for doing something to the child (and why they were worried about that), because it was in the email. I simply told them that I had told the Harris's not to worry because they were not the ones on trial, and in response to the attorney's question I directly said that it was just something the Harrises were concerned about—not that there was worry that they had done anything to Maria. They were concerned that the case would be turned against them, but not regarding anything specifically. They just did not know how the court system worked.

A very important question from the young attorney caused my heart to skip a beat or two, because I realized that in spite of my response, it might not happen. They could put me on the witness list and block me from the courtroom during the trial. I was asked if I was going to continue writing the book, and I said yes.

At that moment, I felt defeated. It would be a small victory for the defense and Spurgeon to keep a book about her case from going to print in any way possible. Putting me on the witness list, even if I was never called to testify, would make this writing extremely difficult because I could not document the case with my own eyes and ears and I needed to do so. All I could do at that point was pray and wait.

Somehow, I must have slipped through the cracks, probably when Olney was "dismissed" by Spurgeon from the case, because I was not on the witness list, which meant I was allowed in that courtroom. Otherwise, I would have missed the entire trial and would not be writing this now. Thank you, Lord, for seeing this through!

CHAPTER 28

AS THE JURY is in what I believe to be the final stages of deliberation, my thoughts are free to wander back over the trial. I start to think about how much weight some of the witnesses' testimonies carried with this jury. I wonder about the past records of these doctors in court.

How many times has Dr. Sally Smith testified for the state in an abuse case where she personally examined the child, only to have her testimony outweighed by a strong enough defense case to gain an acquittal? How many times has Dr. Plunkett or the physicist, Dr. Ipser, testified for the defense using analysis of case evidence provided to them, only to have enough proverbial grains of salt planted in the minds of the jury to cause them to convict the defendant anyway? These are questions that may be pondered but I believe are not really important in the grand scheme of things, since each trial is unique and brings to the table its own special set of circumstances and victim. I realize that this case must be looked at through the eyes of a jury that has heard arguments for and against the conviction of Stephanie Spurgeon for the very first time, not jaded by what friends and family of either the Harrises or Spurgeon already thought they knew. Neither side had all the information that was presented in court. The jury, like all juries, will need to analyze and debate this case until it is satisfied that it has done the right thing, in spite of what emotions may be pulling at each one of its member's hearts.

In so doing, each circumstance and each bit of information needs to be turned over and over and examined from every angle so that the jurors can ask themselves, what is logical and what defies logic? What is reasonable and what produces doubt that is reasonable doubt and is not just grasping at any straw to save someone from prison? What has truth written upon its appearance?

Maria, I consider, "What did your one-year-old eyes see after Pat left you at the day care at Stephanie Spurgeon's on August 21, 2008?" (If not for the infinite grace of God, Pat would have never been able to rise above the guilt of blaming herself for leaving Maria that day, and falling into the depths of a deep depression. Her faith and his strength pulled her through, and for that I am so thankful). "The fear that you felt, Maria, must have been unimaginable. When did your fear become based on something real and terrifying? What did you see that changed you from a scared and screaming child to one who felt pain?" Sadly, Maria cannot speak now, and even if she could have before she died, she would have been too young to understand. So her body must speak for her.

Could it really be that the answers to these questions would all come down to some medical films of Maria's brain shown in a courtroom almost exactly four years later? I hoped that the nuances of the case would help the jury see that there was something to this situation that was evident: yes, there was doubt here. There is always doubt when there is no witness to the crime, or at least not one who is willing to testify. But what kind of doubt is it? The defense introduced other possible causes that could have led to Maria's death throughout this trial, so let's take a look at them.

The list of alternate causes of Maria's death by the defense is a long one, but what is important is that each possibility suggested was never followed up on or given any credence by more than one witness testifying for the defense. Here are some of the causes that they introduced:

- Maria was diabetic and went into a diabetic coma.

- Maria had a preexisting condition that caused her to become unconscious. (Her very first day that she is more than just a few yards from any members of her family)

- Something happened to her the day before she came to the day care.

- Something happened to her on the way home from the day care.

- Someone who had the strength of a super hero had to be the culprit.

- Esther dropped Maria several days before. (There is no evidence that this happened.)

- Maria fell and hit her head hard against a wall about ten weeks before with no external injuries, and it led to these sudden and severe and fresh head and eye injuries and no symptoms until she was at the day care.

- Her last round of vaccinations caused her to have a subdural hematoma, tearing of bridging veins in her brain, and retinal hemorrhaging, eventually causing cell death in the brain and leading to her death. (This is basically unheard of.)

Valid arguments against each of these improbabilities were already given earlier and some will be discussed again later, so suffice it to say that if there were scenarios at all that could detract from the apparent truth, that Stephanie Spurgeon fatally harmed Maria Harris, the defense would try to keep pushing them into the red zone. It was, after all, their job.

In place of all of these wild conjectures, I would like to "take license" here and present a scenario that plays out in my mind as to what happened at the Spurgeon home that day, August 21, 2008. I believe it to be far more plausible than the multitude of trial balloons floated by the defense. There is factual information here regarding the room and its condition that was, for whatever reason, not made public at the trial.

After Pat has dropped off Maria, and Maria's curiosity about Stephanie's cat has worn off or she has chased it away, she becomes gradually more agitated and anxious. She realizes she is in a strange place and her Grammy and Mommy are not there. She starts to fret and cry. Even though she has already had breakfast, Spurgeon attempts to feed her again. She does not eat much. More children arrive, and Maria becomes apprehensive and frightened and continues to fuss and cry. Spurgeon tries unsuccessfully to get her to take a nap in the spare room. It is an unusual room, rather small for a bedroom. There is a computer in there on a desk and a chair at the desk; presumably this is where Stephanie Spurgeon goes online to post on her own Facebook page. There is a high three-quarter bed. Pat described it to me as too large to be a twin bed but not quite a full bed. There is a window and a closet, but Pat remembers that there were no pictures on the wall to indicate that it is a boy's or a girl's room. It just appears to be a spare room. The bed sits rather high up off the floor. And at the base of the bed is a Pack 'n Play portable playpen. This playpen is where Spurgeon attempts to place Maria for her nap, but I think that she screams in the Pack 'n Play, so it is my conjecture that

Spurgeon gets her out and carries her around at first, while at the same time trying to care for the other children.

Spurgeon is on the phone. I believe this to be true because a friend had indicated at the bond hearing on December 23, 2008, that she had been on the phone many times with Stephanie that day. I certainly would like to know the times and lengths of those conversations and those with other people too. If she was trying to take care of children, console Maria, and talk on the phone, the tension would certainly increase. The person that she is on the phone with most of the day is self-described as being just like her sister. This is what the woman told the Harrises on the first day of the trial. She had peeked into the side room where the Harrises awaited the outcome each day since they were not allowed in the courtroom. She had asked a question about whether she was allowed to go in the courtroom. Then she said, "Ya'll look funny." One of the Harrises asked her if she knew Spurgeon, and she said, "She's just like my sister," in her thick drawl.

Continuing with my hypothetical scenario, eventually it is lunchtime at the Spurgeon day care. She feeds Maria first so she can put her down to nap while the other children are eating. Maria eats lunch and is put back into the Pack 'n Play. Spurgeon hopes that she will just lie down soon and fall asleep, but she does not. The other children eat lunch. Maybe one has to go to the potty or needs a diaper changed. Maybe a couple of toddlers are whining about both wanting the same toy. The tension escalates.

In the Pack 'n Play, Maria is screaming at the top of her lungs now. She has been deserted. Her crying upsets the other children. She is exhausted. Where is her Grammy or her Mommy? What is she doing in this strange place where she is not used to anything at all? Is Spurgeon on the phone again? The following information comes from the bond hearing held on December 23, 2008, taken from the transcripts that I obtained after the trial.

At the bond hearing, the friend mentioned above stated under oath that she spoke with Spurgeon four or five times a day, and it was during when Spurgeon was providing child care services. The first call between the two friends on August 21, 2008, happened at around 9:00 a.m., before Stephanie's son went to school. She also specifically said that she spoke with Stephanie around noon on that day, and talked in general about the day. What does that mean? How could they talk in general and not discuss Maria? Another call is referenced at 1:00 p.m. What happened in between? The phone call at 1:00 p.m. lasted forty to forty-five minutes. It was supposed to show that Spurgeon was not angry or upset, but that sure is a long phone call for a day care provider who is alone watching multiple children, all very young. Are the children all napping now except Maria, who is already unconscious in the playpen? Another call is referenced at 3:00 or 3:15 p.m. I will mention in detail other aspects of this bond hearing later, because some of it does not line up at all with what was stated on the witness stand in the trial by Patricia Harris, and it was never disputed by any defense witness. Now, back to what may have happened that day...

Spurgeon tells her friend on the phone that she will call her back. She has reached her breaking point with Maria. She doesn't want to call Pat and wait the twenty or so minutes for her to come and get Maria and endure all this screaming in the meantime, or she forgets about that option entirely in her lapse of rationality. Or maybe she doesn't want Pat to think she failed in caring for Maria on the very first day.

She goes to Maria and roughly pulls her out of the Pack 'n Play and throws her down on the bed that is in this strange spare room. Maria is now more frightened than ever. Barely able to catch her breath because the wind has been knocked out of her, she struggles to her knees and tries to crawl away from the angry woman who grabs at her and pulls her toward her by her ankles, lifting her, shaking her, and shoving her down repeatedly, yelling, "You are going to sleep!" She slams Maria's head, forehead first, into the mattress. Each time Maria, who is strong and stubborn, gets up on her little knees and tries to crawl away, still screaming. But Spurgeon does it again, harder this time while yelling and screaming herself and shoving Maria with an additional surge of strength that adrenaline provides when a person is angry. The covers and sheets on this bed become a massive tangle of fabric, like someone has wrestled with nightmares during the night, tossing and turning. Another possibility is that as Maria attempts to get away again, she falls head first, off this high bed and onto the carpeted floor.

At any rate, this time, this final time, Maria can barely move. Maria does not cry anymore. Spurgeon stares at her in anger for a few seconds, and then roughly picks her up and places her in the Pack 'n Play on her stomach. Maria tries to lift her head. Spurgeon pushes her head down into the Pack 'n Play mattress. Twice. She walks out of the room, thinking, *Finally!* Maria weakly tries to get up, but cannot, her breathing coming in short and raspy inhalations. She is in pain. She maneuvers sideways until her head pushes up against the netting on one side of the playpen, and her feet push against the other side. Then, with hiccup-like gasps, she closes her eyes and no longer moves. The bridging veins inside her skull have now torn, and the irreversible bleeding process and cell death have begun.

Hence, there were no "two pats on the back," but instead two shoves into the thin mattress. It was Spurgeon's grand finale of abuse.

At some point, Spurgeon goes back into the room where Maria is "sleeping" and checks on her. She notes that she is breathing, so she feels that nothing has happened to implicate her in harming the child. She may have even checked to see if there were any bruises on Maria's forehead. As in many similar cases, Spurgeon hopes that, although Maria does not appear to be sleeping normally, she will wake up soon and all will be well. Perhaps this is why she didn't call EMS herself when she knew that Maria was obviously not in a normal state. She just wanted it to all go away, as if it never happened. At 1:00 p.m. Spurgeon phones her friend because she needs someone to talk to. No one but those two women knows what was said on that call.

From this point in the narrative, the information I will relate comes directly from what Patricia Harris told me and is no longer conjecture. When Pat returns to pick up her granddaughter over two and a half hours later, several things are very *wrong*. First, Stephanie Spurgeon appears almost shocked when she answers the door. Her hands fly to her mouth. She says to Pat, *"My goodness, you're here! I didn't know what time you'd get here!"* (Spurgeon knew Pat had to be there by 3:00 p.m. because Maria had to be picked up before the other little girl arrived at 3:30 p.m. on a bus. Pat had arrived at 2:45.) She told Pat that Maria was sleeping and that she "didn't have the heart to wake her up."

Second, when Pat accompanies Spurgeon into the computer/guest room, Maria is sideways in the Pack 'n Play; her head and feet are poking at the webbing on each horizontal side because she is too long to fit that way.

Third, her pacifier is not in her open mouth.

Fourth, and most telling, she is sleeping on her stomach, which she has never done in her entire life. These things tug at the back of Pat's mind, but she gives Spurgeon the benefit of the doubt because she is told that Maria played hard that day and was tuckered out. But Spurgeon also uses a cuss word when describing Maria's behavior, which is something that a day care provider would not say to a parent or grandparent under any circumstances, let alone on the very first day the child was left in her care, unless the person had deep-rooted anger.

Fifth, while Pat and Spurgeon are in the room conversing about the day's events, Pat's eyes roam about the room. She notices the bed, and this also bothers her at the back of her mind. Why would someone leave such a terribly messed up bed in a room that obviously wasn't someone's bedroom? She thinks that the covers looked all torn up like a tornado hit them. They are all twisted up and out of place, way messier than if someone had merely slept there. Then, she glances out of the door and into the open doorway of a room across the hall. She recognizes a little girl lying on the bed in her line of vision. She also sees a little boy who is squirming around. Neither child makes any noise, but the girl is motionless and looks very frightened. Her hands are curled around and in her mouth, and her eyes are like round saucers. She has a pitiful look as if she is afraid to make a sound. Pat remembers the three-year-old girl from when she visited Spurgeon's day care with Esther and Maria a week or so earlier to interview her. This little one had crawled up in Pat's lap and promptly curled up there and fell asleep. She knows there are other children resting in that room, but she cannot see them beyond the doorway.

Spurgeon did not know, or acted as if she did not know, that Maria would not be back the next day since they had discussed leaving a bottle there for her. She hoped with all her heart that this incident would not have any lasting consequences for Maria, and at this point she has no idea of the severity of the injuries she has caused. After all, when she had allegedly done a similar throwing/slamming of Gabrielle Anderson in 2002, Gabby had experienced no lasting injuries. Maybe she hoped that by using a cuss word to describe Maria's behavior, Pat would not bring her back again. Little did she know that Maria would not be back, but not because Pat would choose not to bring her.

As I mentioned before, up to the point of Pat's arrival at the Spurgeon home and the bond hearing transcript information, the previous account is just speculation, a possibility of what could have very well happened that day. The problem is that there is nothing to refute it. It would be nice to have Stephanie Spurgeon read it and tell me the parts that I got wrong. But she will remain silent. She or her attorneys have not given any satisfactory explanation as to what could have happened otherwise in that house on that day. We didn't even see a diagram of the inside of the Spurgeon day care at the trial. She had a chance to speak at sentencing and tell everyone present that she did not do anything to harm Maria, that it was an accident. Even though there was nothing introduced during the trial to suggest it was an accident, it was not too late to explain something that may have happened—that she kept quiet because she didn't want to appear negligent. Then she could explain what happened. But I know it wasn't an accident. I also know that all the conjectures of her supporters are not believable, because when all of her injuries are considered together, each of the alternative scenarios suggested for what could have happened to Maria is impossible.

Esther loved Maria far too much to ever harm her, yet commenters of articles written about this case indicate that Esther probably hurt Maria because Esther was on medication. If she was on medication, and it is only speculation, it certainly does not mean that it would cause her to harm her baby daughter. If it did, then there would be thousands upon thousands of young children harmed every year by parents simply because they were on medication. And it would not explain the multitudes of children who are harmed by parents who are not on medication. The very thought is despicable. The idea that Esther, who loved that baby dearly, would harm her with or without medicine is not believable at all. Maria had lived an entire year and two weeks without having to go to the doctor for any injuries, and none were ever detected at her well-baby checkups. Patricia Harris even went so far as to admit that her granddaughter was very spoiled, and they held her almost all the time.

Some bloggers accuse Pat of harming the granddaughter that she would have died for. Again, that is ridiculous. To be fair, these scenarios are as far-fetched as saying that Spurgeon's son did it. But let's examine that possibility for the sake of a similar stretch of the imagination. When did he leave for school that day? He was likely in middle school at the time, which doesn't start until 9:30 a.m. in this county. Pat didn't see him when she dropped Maria off, but he was possibly elsewhere in the house. We already know that Spurgeon received a phone call from her friend that day at 9:00 a.m. before her son left for school, according to her friend's own testimony at the bond hearing. Did her son injure Maria and then it took a couple of hours for her to become semi-comatose? When did he get home from school that day? Did he tell his mother that he would take care of the screaming baby and, not knowing his own strength, shake her, throw her, and slam her around—making a disaster of the covers on that bed? Did his mother take the fall for him, which is why she is being so silent and not rebelling against the charge openly? Is this why she claims, "I didn't do it"? Is it because she really didn't, but her son did? Spurgeon would not have been thinking straight to cover up for her son if he did it. Ironically, because this case dragged on so long, he would have been released already from juvenile detention, having reached the age of eighteen, unless he was tried as an adult at the young age of fourteen. Brunvand and Kurpiers, Spurgeon's second legal team, if not Olney, her first attorney, certainly would not have known about it or their legal ethics would not have, in good conscience, let them to continue to defend her. But on the other hand, wouldn't she, like any mother, vigorously protect her son from going to prison, regardless of how long the risk of her own sentence might be instead? She would have, out of necessity, lied to her attorneys in a backhanded way. By saying she didn't do it, she would have told the truth. By withholding evidence, she would have been an accessory to the crime.

Spurgeon's family and supporters would be outraged that I even hint at such an absurd possibility, but it is more outrageous to speculate that Maria's family who loved her deeply and cared for her daily for over a year harmed her, timing it so that it lined up with the very first day that she was more than a few yards away from them and for less than eight hours.

Did Spurgeon's former husband come home for lunch from work or from wherever he was and go into the room and hurt Maria because she wouldn't stop crying? This, of course, is extremely unlikely as well, but if the defense and Spurgeon's supporters are going to throw improbabilities out there for the media and others who weren't in the courtroom and at every hearing to ponder, then I have every right to do the same from the other side of the fence. These bases were apparently all covered by the police because we heard nothing about them. This case is against Stephanie Spurgeon, and no one else. If there is a possibility that someone else in her family is involved, or even if someone unrelated stopped by that day and hurt Maria, Spurgeon's lips are sealed. She is the only one who would know whoever else would have been there. You can be certain all persons of interest were investigated thoroughly. The bloggers suggest that only Spurgeon was. Should the police have checked out her family more thoroughly? We already know the results of the other distractions that the defense introduced.

Maria had no diseases or conditions that would warrant her lapse into semiconsciousness on the very first day in a new environment where she was very frightened and no doubt cried unceasingly once she became overexhausted. And the EMS was called within minutes after Pat arrived home with her. Not only was that recorded in court records, but the times are memorialized on the EMS reports as well. There was no delay of several hours, as some commenters posted.

Occam's razor is a well-known philosophy that basically says that when you have more than one competing theory as to what happened in a situation, the more obvious one is the best one to go with because it will be the correct one. That's what I see here. It is not a stretch to see why my supposition could have very well played out, with minor adjustments. But anything else pointing away from the defendant or strange suppositions proposed online are wild speculations, with nothing to back them. Especially since this is not the first time Stephanie Spurgeon was accused of harming a child, if you recall the Williams Rule discussed earlier.

CHAPTER 29

AS I CONTINUED working on the details surrounding this tragedy, I found myself inextricably interwoven in its fabric. The seeming randomness of a child who died because of a head trauma was obliterated by the facts of the case. Long after my own deposition, more information became available to me, and it appeared providential that these details were not coincidental. I knew people who knew people who knew things that I needed to know. And they told me. The information that I gleaned was valuable in that these were not facts that would have normally reached my ear. These details were of such import that Spurgeon's family would not have wanted them known, but some people had a hard time keeping that grapevine shut down and said things to people who liked to talk.

For the sake of those people, I will not mention them here or even what they knew, but I can say that it led me back to a revelation that I had early on in this case. I wanted the transcripts of that bond hearing that I was unable to attend in person. Not only had numerous friends and family members supporting Spurgeon spoke at this hearing, but law enforcement testified for the state as well. There were some statements made that were not admissible in a jury trial, but were memorialized in the transcript. No one can ever say that these statements were never made in a public forum. And so, with that in mind, let's revisit what was said on the day of Stephanie Spurgeon's bond hearing on December 23, 2008.

There were a multitude of issues covered at this hearing. The most relevant ones will be addressed here. First, several people testified as to the high integrity of Spurgeon's character as a caregiver because she had cared for their children in previous years. Then, Spurgeon's sister-in-law (at the time) took the stand and expounded on Stephanie's husband's health issues, which included diabetes and a kidney problem for which he was seeking a transplant. It is unknown to the author whether he received a transplant or not. But the transcripts did indicate that he was employed at the post office at the time of Maria's injury. His sister was living with and caring for Spurgeon's children while she was in jail prior to this bond hearing on charges of first-degree murder. The hearing itself was being held to determine if bond should be lowered or eliminated. The sister-in-law indicated that she had never seen Spurgeon lose her temper with a child. Then another woman, who was pregnant and had Spurgeon care for her children in the past, indicated that the first person she thought of to care for her new baby would be Stephanie. There were five testimonies in all as to the credibility of her character in addition to "dozens of affidavits...of other day care parents who have had their children with Stephanie," a statement made by Mr. Olney, her lead attorney at the time.

Brian Daniels responded by saying, "They are strictly for a character nature, and there's nothing as far as evidentiary-wise in this case. With that Mr. Olney's indication and I do not object." (I copied this word-for-word from the transcripts, and it does sound awkward, so it is probably not quite what Mr. Daniels really said, and there is some transcription error here. But the gist of the response is clear. There were a lot of niceties stated about Spurgeon, but nothing to indicate that she did not commit the crime, and Mr. Olney was aware that these were strictly character reference statements.

In fact, Mr. Olney responded, "None of these affidavits are testimonial in character or would—well, they're all testimonial in character, but none of them would address any of the issues that are present in the charges that are currently pending. These go to whether she'd be a danger to the community, whether or not she's appropriate for release, whether or not she'd be a flight risk."

After this, there was some discussion of how, after Spurgeon had been released on a $50,000 bond for aggravated child abuse (before Maria died), she voluntarily gave up her day care provider license because she didn't want other families whose children she was caring for to have any concerns. The attorneys wrote a letter surrendering it with a request reserving the right to ask for the license back "when these charges were resolved."

The $50,000 bond meant that $5,000 would have needed to have been raised, ten percent of the bond, in order to secure her release.

Spurgeon was not arrested for "two or three weeks" after Maria died, and Olney explained that she did not attempt to flee or avoid arrest. He elaborated on Raymond Spurgeon's illness and how he was unable to run the household and care for their two children, ages sixteen and thirteen at the time.

Olney indicated that Stephanie would cooperate with any form of release, and would not contact the victim and has not had any contact with them. Then he asked for a $50,000 bond to hold her because he believed it to be appropriate, since it was the original bond amount and he said that "it's been demonstrated to work."

This completed Olney's part of the hearing on Spurgeon's behalf, and then Mr. Daniels called two witnesses and reviewed the case.

First, Detective Greene from the Pinellas County Sheriff's Office was called, and he stepped up to the podium. I was excited to read this, having obtained this information long after the completion of the trial, since no law enforcement had testified at the trial itself. Detective Greene at the time worked for the Crimes against Children Unit. He testified at this bond hearing that he had met Mr. Ronald Chola and had gone to this man's residence and interviewed him about what he had observed at Spurgeon's day care when he dropped his son off on Maria's first day there. That interview, Detective Greene believed, was the day after Maria's injuries, August 22, 2008, and it lasted about forty-five minutes to an hour. During that entire time, according to the detective, Mr. Chola never indicated that there was anything wrong with Maria, nor did she have any trouble standing, focusing, or balancing.

Three days later, Detective Greene spoke with Chola on the phone. Then, Brian Daniels said to Detective Greene, "He's testified here today that he [Ronald Chola] spoke with you and told you that there was something wrong with the child's focus or balance. Did you hear that here today?"

"I heard that, yes. I heard what he said."

"Was there any discussion of that during your phone conversation with him?"

"No, sir."

"Did he tell you any of these things?"

"No, sir."

"Did you talk to him on any other occasions besides the one at the residence in person and the phone call?"

"No, sir."

So Mr. Chola lied in court or to the police. At the time, it wasn't known for sure what was true, but there was no indication from him that anything was wrong with Maria in his actual testimony during the trial.

Seeing the potential damage this had caused, Mr. Olney asked for permission to redirect questioning to Detective Greene. He inquired if the detective notified Mr. Chola that he was coming to his house to interview him, and Greene said that he believed he did, but he did not know how much time elapsed between the call and the visit. However, he remembered that it was the same day. And he did remember that he called him because that's how he knew that Chola would be home.

Olney clarified, "And he was not pretty clear with you throughout that initial discussion that, as far as he's concerned, what may be normal for one child may not necessarily be normal for another?"

"We never went into anything that deeply," Greene answered. "[We] just discussed the behavior of the child then; the victim child then."

Olney then distracted the questioning from Detective Greene's visit to Ronald Chola's house. "Are you aware as you stand here today of a single witness that saw her put her hands on Maria and hurt her?"

"No, sir."

Is this why Detective Greene was not called to testify as a witness in the trial? To avoid this question? He did no harm in his questioning of Chola, but it seems that he really had nothing fruitful to add to the state's evidence, and they did handle Chola by themselves when he took the stand. But what about Detective Kelly Lyons who was key to the entire investigation?

Detective Lyons, also with the sheriff's office, stepped up to the podium as the state's final witness in the bond hearing. She also was with the Crimes against Children Unit, but as of this writing, she no longer works in Pinellas County. She is the one who revealed the information regarding the other allegations against Spurgeon by the family of another child, while she was also investigating the death of Maria Harris.

She interviewed Carl Dorr,* who at the time was one of the paramedics. Mr. Dorr had made a comment to another deputy at the fire station that he wanted to talk to Detective Lyons' unit.

The deputy notified Detective Lyons who called Mr. Dorr and arranged for him to come in with his cohorts at the fire station for an interview.

Detective Lyons interviewed both other men that were on the truck with Dorr the day of Maria Harris's emergency, going to the Harris home to provide treatment.

"Can you briefly tell the court the results of your interview with those three?" Mr. Daniels asked.

Lyons explained that Dorr gave a lengthy statement, lasting about three hours, but at the end, he recanted everything he had said and "admitted that he was under a lot of personal stress." He felt that "his personal feelings had come in on his judgment of the case involving Maria."

Lyons also explained that the other two men on the truck indicated in their interviews that Dorr's observations "were inaccurate and incorrect," and they did not see anything that he saw. Dorr had said that there had been a torrential downpour, but the other men said that there had not been one.

Mr. Dorr is no longer employed at the fire department as a paramedic.

But Mr. Olney, in spite of hearing what Dorr's coworkers had stated in the interview, asked Detective Lyons on cross, "Did Mr. Dorr ever tell you that he, in fact, observed the victim's mother showing signs of remorse?"

"Yes, he did." (This was not the expected answer.)

So Olney repeated the question. "He said she showed signs of remorse?"

"Later on, he did, yes."

"Okay. And was he specific?"

"Semispecific."

"Okay. What did he tell you?"

Lyons was given permission to refer to her report. "Specifically, what he told me is that his observations of her may have been inaccurate, and that it was very common for parents to act the way that she was acting when this type of thing...as for remorse, I don't know if he ever used that word."

When Olney told Lyons that she is not sure whether Dorr told her that Esther was actually exhibiting signs of remorse, she responded by telling him that her report is nine pages long and she would be happy to read it to him.

He asked if the statement was recorded and she told him it was not. However, the next question was asked and quickly dropped by Olney:

"Did you recover any physical evidence whatsoever from Stephanie's house that would suggest that a child was injured there?"

"Possibly."

Mr. Olney took his questioning into what he hoped was a safer direction, but Detective Lyons was prepared. "Are you aware of any witnesses as you stand here today that observed her harm Maria?" Now Detective Greene had just said no to this very question, so Mr. Olney was assuming her answer would follow suit.

Instead, Detective Lyons simply said, "I am."

Oh, to have actually been in the courtroom at that moment instead of just reading the transcripts!

"Okay...who?"

"There was another child there that observed Mrs. Spurgeon strike Maria."

"Okay. On that day?"

"Yes, sir."

"And what was that child's name?"

Here, Detective Lyons provided the name of the child, which is withheld here for identity protection. She is then asked how old the child is, and she answered that she believed the child to be three years old.

She continued to answer questions regarding this remarkable discovery, stating that the child was interviewed within a day or two of the event by Detective Sherman* and Detective

Kline.* The child gave specifics as to how Maria was struck, but Detective Lyons could not recall these specifics. (It had to have been in the police report, but of course this information was never admitted into evidence in the trial itself.)

Next, the transcript has an oddly phrased question from Mr. Olney. "Did [?] exhibit any physical signs of injury?"

Here, he might have been referring to Maria and mistakenly referenced the other child, or he could have been referring to the child, or it could have been a typo, but there is no way to know.

Detective Lyons responded to the judge here, not Mr. Olney. "I don't have his report in front of me, Judge, so I'm not sure what actually...I can tell you that [the child] said that she struck Maria."

"Okay." Olney answered. "But as you stand here today, are you aware as to whether or not [?] suffered any physical signs of injury that would corroborate being hit?"

I thought this particular question was a little strange because the child had never indicated that he/she was struck by Spurgeon at any point and had only apparently told the detectives that he/she had witnessed Spurgeon strike Maria. Was Olney trying to distract from what had been seen, or water it down, or discount it from being true, if, in fact, it was true?

Lyons responded, "[The child] did not, Maria did. [The child] witnessed Mrs. Spurgeon hitting Maria."

Next, there was some discussion between Mr. Olney and Detective Lyons about the credibility of the child as a witness. When asked if she had concerns regarding the child's credibility, she responded that she did not complete the interview. There was apparently a concern by the detective who interviewed the child as to his/her credibility, but there is no indication in the transcript as to why.

From my outside view looking in, and knowing the huge variation in the ability to discern fantasy from reality in three-year-old children, it would have been a very difficult decision to make for the state as to whether to enter this child's interview into evidence in the trial. Even if a conviction is the result, the grounds for appeal may be much stronger with this interview, if it becomes the mitigating factor in a jury's ruling. It was probably wise for the state to leave this one alone. Had the child been age five or six, the case for admission would have been stronger. However, all that reasoning aside, the very idea that a child would talk to police detectives about it adds to the likelihood that Maria was abused by Spurgeon in that house on that day.

Next, as per the bond hearing transcript, Mr. Daniels gave a brief synopsis of what happened on August 21. One statement he made in these transcripts that I do not recall being mentioned in the trial was something told to him by Patricia Harris. She told him that Spurgeon had said this about Maria: "I can't carry her around all day with these other children that I have to watch."

I thought about that statement for a while. Maria weighed about twenty pounds. It would have been very difficult to carry her around on a hip for too long with one arm. A person would frequently have needed to shift her and use her other arm to do so. If Spurgeon carted Maria around for a while, did she use a Bluetooth or some similar headset to make and receive her many phone calls? Did she use the speaker button on her phone? Was it a cell phone? Cell phones are very small and difficult to tuck between an ear and shoulder while talking. Even without carrying Maria, how did Spurgeon manage to care for the other children and be on the phone so often at the same time? I am trying to envision how this works. Personally, I can't even begin to imagine being on the phone with the same person for multiple times every day while I am trying to watch a handful of children under five years old who are not mine. Even without the children to watch, I couldn't do that. Besides, what can be so important to talk about since the last phone call?

Brian Daniels made a very important statement in his summary at the bond hearing. It may have saved the state of Florida some time and money if Detective Lyons had been able to make this statement herself at the trial, but she was not called as a witness. What Mr. Daniels said was, "Ms. Spurgeon related to Detective Lyons that there were no incidents from any of the other small children that were at the residence with Maria." Because the word *from* is used here, it implies no child caused any incident. If that is what is meant, you will see the significance of this statement later on. She also could have meant that no other child there suffered any injury that day. If so, then the sentence is very vague and easily misconstrued.

Mr. Daniels, at the very end of his summation, revealed the situation referenced earlier in this book involving Gabrielle Anderson, whose sister Lindsay had witnessed Spurgeon yank her out of a walker and shake her violently in 2002.

"[Lindsay] told me that it was of such violence that she thought her sister's head was going to come off...She told me that after a few seconds or a few moments of this, Ms. Spurgeon took the child, went over to a playpen, and without bending over, dropped the child into the playpen, this three-month-old. She said that her sister was hit on her rear end, her butt. She flew back. Her head hit in the playpen."

Mr. Daniels continued by saying that he was able to interview Lindsay because Detective Lyons had uncovered a complaint to the Department of Children and Families (DCF) during an investigation. That complaint had been made by the parents of Gabby and Lindsay on the same day as the incident.

As was shown earlier from the hearing on the Williams Rule, Gabrielle sustained no known or lasting injuries from this incident, but Mr. Daniels wanted it known to the judge in this bond hearing that there had been a prior complaint made against Spurgeon for child abuse.

As a result, he asked that no contact be made with other children besides her own, and upon release on bond, that she have to wear an ankle monitor or a GPS monitor and surrender her passport. Daniels asked for a bond in the amount of $500,000.

The judge ruled. Bond was set at $350,000. She would be fitted with a GPS monitoring system so that her whereabouts would be known. Her passport would be surrendered to the clerk of the court. She would have absolutely no contact with any child under the age of ten, unless under adult supervision.

A $350,000 bond meant that a good faith monetary amount of $35,000 would need to be raised to obtain her release from jail. The date of the bond hearing was December 23. Stephanie Spurgeon was released from jail on January 27, 2009. The significance of these two dates did not escape me. It took over a month for her staunch supporters who stood up for her so strongly at the bond hearing, speaking to her high integrity and lack of bad temperament, to raise this money, if they did at all. Perhaps someone in her family had to raise the entire amount via a home equity loan or something of that nature. It had to have been money that was not easily accessible since it took over a month to secure the funds for her release. Needless to say, Spurgeon spent Christmas and New Year's in jail.

CHAPTER 30

IN BETWEEN THE interminable waiting for the jury to wrap up its deliberations over these last two days, I have been praying for God's perfect will. He alone knows what the future holds for Stephanie Spurgeon and for the Harris family in this terrible tragedy. Some good has already come out of the death of little Maria, because her liver, heart, and kidneys have been donated and transplanted into others who were much in need of them. But what other good can possibly come out of this situation?

Already, Esther and her family have been bashed in unbelievable ways on the Internet, with someone even posting that the Harris family had a beer party on Maria's grave. If it wasn't so ridiculous in its incredulity, it could certainly be considered as a case for libel. Beautiful flowers and balloons are often present at Maria's gravesite, brought by the Harrises on some of their frequent visits. Flowers dedicated to her memory were present at the front of our church sanctuary on what would have been Maria's fifth birthday.

The Harrises are prepared to hear whatever the judge rules. They feel that this situation is out of their hands now, and that God will provide wisdom to the judge. But they are also very anxious because they fear that they will break down uncontrollably if Spurgeon is acquitted, since Maria's murderer would have gone unpunished. The Harrises just want to put this behind them and get some sense of closure after nearly three and a half years of struggling with Maria's death. They will never be free from the loss and the void that remains in their lives, but to put the reason for it in the past would make the future a little easier to face.

The defense attorneys have gone into the courtroom, which is diagonally across from where I am seated on a window bench. Why just them? The jury has been deliberating now for twenty-one hours. The same two bailiffs have stayed with this case almost the entire time. The Harrises are so grateful to the staff at the courthouse. They have been treated like family. On Valentine's Day, the kitchen staff brought Pat and Esther red carnations and candy to their table. Everyone was so accommodating and respectful to them, especially when escorting them in and out of the building so that they would not have to see or hear anyone that they did not want to from the media or otherwise.

Suddenly, a camera crew enters into the courtroom, and my stomach knots up. Then I see the Harrises coming down the long hallway. Of course, there have been several false alarms up to this point where all were called in because the jury needed clarification on some issues, but because the camera crew is now in there, I know that this has to be the verdict. The woman bailiff comes out the door, whispers to another employee, and nods. I hear her say, "Yes, they have decided." I realize that it has not taken twenty-one hours to get to this point. It has taken three years and five months. Over 1200 days.

The bailiff props open the door to the courtroom, and everyone around enters. I go in and sit right behind the Harris family. As other people file in around and behind me, I tap Esther on the shoulder and whisper, "This is the verdict."

"It is? Are you *sure*?" She asks, eyes wide with astonishment. After all the false alarms, she can hardly believe it is happening. We had sat earlier, speculating on what the verdict might be, and then on what the sentencing might be and why. And now that the time is here, well, we have no idea. The waiting is over. It is almost as if we are not ready for this.

She leans over and tells her mother, who then turns around and looks at me, eyebrows raised. I nod. Clyde sits looking straight forward, shoulders rigid, jaw clenched. No one wants this moment to be over with more than he does. Since he lost his granddaughter, he has never been the same man, even though he knows he will see her one day in heaven. He misses her now, every day.

Stephanie Spurgeon is seated. She does not seem outwardly anxious. Her face is a mask. Her hands rest loosely in front of her as she stares ahead, shoulders slightly hunched. Judge Newton walks in, straight and somber, and we all rise and are seated. The jury comes in. My mind reels with all kinds of thoughts and emotions, so I don't write. I don't really hear. But from this moment, things start happening too rapidly. Suddenly, the judge is asking the jury foreman if the jury has reached a verdict. Contrary to what I expect, Spurgeon is not asked to stand. She remains seated and clasps her hands in front of her, raising them off the table.

On the count of murder in the first degree: not guilty. There is no pause as the foreman continues.

On the count of manslaughter: guilty.

It feels as if all the air has gone out of the room.

Stephanie Spurgeon's head falls forward into her hands, and her face contorts in agony. It is the only real emotion she has shown in the courtroom outside of silently crying during the playing of the 911 call. She would not walk out of the courtroom with her friends and family today, but instead be fingerprinted, handcuffed, and led back to the county jail where she had been held on bond back in December 2008. Now she would await sentencing, which, under a manslaughter conviction, could be as much as fifteen years. The moment is surreal, and it almost seems like time has stopped just for that few seconds while everyone absorbed the word. Guilty.

At the moment of the verdict announcement, some of Spurgeon's supporters and family, against Judge Newton's instructions, but with understandable inability to hold back extreme emotions, cry out, some with anger, some in tears. Most in disbelief. They had hoped and prayed and imagined their friend and relative walking out free that day, surrounded by them, and rejoicing that it was over. It is not over though, and they would actually be able to come to court again, and not for sentencing!

The Harrises succumb to a quiet and tearful sort of relief. They stand, each embracing Holly Grissinger in turn. I believe Clyde shakes her hand. Then they are quickly escorted from the courtroom through another exit and not with the rest of us. Pat told me afterward that it was for their protection, in case they were heckled or threatened. Later on, they did receive threats, but I will not go into detail about those for the family's protection. Those threats are in the hands of the sheriff's department.

According to the Tampabay.com article posted by Curtis Krueger on the day of the verdict, several of the jurors were reached by phone, but did not wish to comment about it, including the foreman. Mr. Krueger stressed how, although Kurpiers argued that no one saw Spurgeon harm Maria and that none of the doctors who testified knew exactly what had caused her injuries, the prosecution had "built a powerful circumstantial case against Spurgeon." Krueger also stated that "the case relied heavily on medical evidence...This evidence was crucial for attorneys on both sides."

Krueger talks about the different doctors in the article, and I want to highlight what he says about Dr. Ipser, because it will come into play yet later.

A professor emeritus of physics at the University of Florida said a human could not muster the force to shake a 20-pound child with enough force to cause the type of physical damage that Maria suffered."[1]

Judge Newton schedules sentencing for May 7. Little did anyone know at the time of this verdict what would take place prior to that sentencing date that would keep hope alive for Stephanie Spurgeon.

CHAPTER 31

OVER THE ENTIRE three days of the *State v. Spurgeon* trial, the basis of the defense's argument had been that Spurgeon was innocent because nobody saw her commit the crime. That was it. That seemed to be a weak position when there is plenty of circumstantial evidence, both inclusive and external to the trial, that point to her as the perpetrator.

Here is that circumstantial evidence:

1. Maria arrived at the day care alert, aware, walking, talking, and able to eat. She left limp and unresponsive. She had eaten breakfast that morning—oatmeal and juice at around 5:30 a.m., which would have been digested in full by 2:45 p.m. when she was picked up. However, she vomited up a solid substance in the car on the way home, which meant she ate again at Spurgeon's house, probably lunch.

2. Spurgeon was the only adult at the day care that day. This point was never disputed by either side.

3. Spurgeon, according to Patricia Harris, used a cuss word to describe Maria's temperament and told her that she was spoiled. This was never disputed by the defense. This comment is not a remark that would typically be made to a grandmother who has left her grandchild at a home day care for the very first day. It is insulting and far from proper business etiquette. It goes to the feelings that Spurgeon had toward Maria.

4. All the expert witnesses for the state came to agreement that the cause of death was not accidental and that there had been abuse. Only one doctor, Dr. Luis Rodriguez, said that the cause was shaken baby syndrome. The other witnesses all agreed, without knowing each other, that it was blunt trauma to the head. There was a strong consensus. None could admit how it was done, but all could agree it was done in that way.

5. Spurgeon had a prior incident in 2002 that was similar, and it was reported to the DCF by the parents that she had thrown and/or shaken a three-month-old child into a crib/playpen when the child would not stop crying. This situation was argued at a prior hearing, but the state chose not to introduce it during the trial. It was a good decision because including it at trial would have been a likely cause for appeal and reversal since it would have biased the jury as to Spurgeon's character and kept them from isolating their decision on the basis of what happened to Maria Harris alone. It was fragile ground and best kept out of trial, although it can be mentioned here and now since she is already imprisoned without the information being needed. Including it here after her imprisonment only strengthens the proof that they chose the right verdict.

Now, here are the holes in the defense's case:

- They deduce that just because no one saw Spurgeon commit the crime, she is innocent. This reasoning would be like saying that if there is a missing iPad off the counter in a home and the pest control guy was the only guy in the house that day, but no one saw him take it that he *definitely* did not do so. It is a flawed argument. It doesn't mean that he took it, but the evidence would point to him over anyone else. Someone else would have had to break in and take it without showing evidence of being there. Or some illogical reason for it being missing would have to exist. It did not get up and walk away on its own. The owner left it there that morning, and it was gone when he returned. The pest control guy was the only guy in the house that day.

- The defense runs through, on its own volition, a whole mixed bag of wild conjectures as to what could have caused Maria to become comatose, have a subdural hematoma, have torn bridging veins in her head, have retinal hemorrhaging, become worse, and then eventually die after her first day out of sight from her family. They didn't have to do this to deflect from the truth. It wasn't required to go off on rabbit trails to show other scenarios as to what could have happened instead, but it opened these issues up for inspection, and in so doing weakened the case for their client considerably. The defense never stuck to one variance as an alternate cause of Maria's tragedy and ran with it. They could not, as there were significant defects with each surrogate possibility.

As the case progressed, I have responded in detail to each of these alternate causes for Maria's injuries, so I will just summarize what the defense has put forth here:

1. She had diabetes due to high blood glucose levels after the injury. This was disproven due to the glucose levels ris-

ing, especially in children, after a head trauma. It is documented to be very common and easily stabilized.

2. She had a reaction to her vaccinations from her well-baby exam a week before her visit to the day care. A week before. At worst, it is suspect, but far from proven, that vaccines have a possible link to autism, but not death from the combination of an acute subdural hematoma, retinal hemorrhaging, and torn bridging veins. Those veins just don't tear by themselves. An overt violent action is necessary.

3. Maria was injured prior to coming to the day care, the week or the day before. It was not the day before because numerous witnesses, including myself who was not called, saw her active and happily playing in the church lobby after 8:00 p.m. the prior evening. There was no evidence of any odd or lethargic behavior; no red flags. These indicators would also have appeared the week before, and no witnesses noted them, especially the Harris family who would have been quick to call her pediatrician.

4. Maria was injured on the way home from the Spurgeon home. This argument is the least plausible because by this time she had already been injured and was unresponsive. The fact that Patricia Harris did not pull over to check on her would have made little difference since she was close to home, and the two lane-road would have made pulling over dangerous anyway. At this point she was concerned but did not truly realize the grim nature of Maria's injuries.

5. Spurgeon could not have done it because, according to Dr. Ipser, she could have not exerted 1,000 pounds of force on Maria. No adult, according to Dr. Ipser, could have exerted the kind of force necessary to cause the injuries that Maria incurred. However, the defense introduces a new tactic after the verdict, which follows this summary!

As an observer, here are the missing pieces of the puzzle that I would have liked to see in this case, particularly if I were on the jury. I realize that in a trial such as this, some of these questions would never be admissible, but I would be curious to know the answers, just the same.

1. Where are the phone records of incoming and outgoing calls for Stephanie Spurgeon that day? Who they were from, what were the times of the calls, and how long were they?

2. Where are the police reports and/or testimony from the investigating detectives?

3. Let's see a schematic layout of the inside of the Spurgeon day care. Where was the kitchen located relative to the Pack 'n Play? What was the layout of the room that contained the Pack 'n Play?

4. How many cats did she have?

5. How many children was she caring for that day? What were their ages, arrival times, and departure times?

6. Did they all eat lunch at the same time? Did Maria go to "bed" while others were being fed? What was nap time and how long did it last? Did all the children nap at the same time?

7. Were any children outside playing that day? All at the same time?

8. Were any children left alone in any part of the house at all at any time? How about during a diaper change or potty assistance?

9. Were there any disabled children there that needed special attention? If so, what kind of attention?

10. Was Spurgeon licensed? Bonded? Insured? By whom and for how much?

11. Had Spurgeon taken any safety courses that were not, at the time, required for home day care providers, but were available?

12. What other injuries/accidents had ever occurred at the Spurgeon home? Were any insurance claims ever filed against the day care? (Keeping the names anonymous)

13. Did Spurgeon keep a logbook of all that went on at her day care? Was it current? Did she fill it in as the day went on or at the end of the day? Why wasn't it admitted into evidence? If it was, why didn't the jury hear about it?

14. Was her day care ever inspected by the Department of Children and Families? If so, was it given a grade? What were the findings?

15. Were the police ever called to the premises for any other situation, even one disconnected from the day care itself? Was there any charge of domestic violence ever brought against Spurgeon or her husband?

These are questions that I would have in my mind as a juror, and I'm sure there would be many more. But since it seemed to be a truncated trial in spite of the fact that a death occurred, they remain unanswered and only a few people know the real truth.

The following are statements that appeared on various Internet blog sites, libeling the Harrises, and I do know the answers to them beyond any doubt, reasonable or otherwise. (Many of these sites or the posts in them have disappeared, but I have preserved them and the posters' names or usernames via the simple copy-and-paste method, and I retain these on backup hard drives and a flash drive in a safe deposit box.)

1. *The Harris family had a beer party on Maria's grave.* This is a despicable post, and the poster has out-and-out lied about this good-hearted and deeply religious family. They are not party animals. They are a loving and close-knit family.

2. *Maria's father was in town and dropped her.* Well, Maria's father had been out of state and out of her life for many months, so this was impossible.

3. *"Look to the grandmother."* About what? Patricia doted on that baby as if she were her own child. She sacrificed many days from work to stay home and take care of her until they could get situated at the day care at Esther's school. She loved that baby with all her heart. Like she said at the sentencing, she would have died in her place, but she couldn't.

4. *The family is white trash and is out for money.* Far from it. Not only do they live comfortably, with both grandparents holding decent employment, but a civil trial would be held merely to verify any insurance that should have been in place at the day care and that the Harris family had a right to seek it due to the death of their daughter/granddaughter. Also, it could verify if Spurgeon was properly bonded by the state of Florida even though she told the Harrises that she was. So there may be no financial gain for the Harrises, and whether they needed it or not is immaterial. Their purpose in seeking civil justice is to make sure that Spurgeon cannot profit from her circumstances since Maria cannot enjoy life now or ever again.

5. *The Harris family has a prison record.* This is libel, pure and simple. Put the facts behind the allegations.

6. *Esther is full of tattoos and piercings.* Well, unless you count pierced ears, there are no other such markings or holes.

She respects her body and doesn't believe in such damage. However, Spurgeon does have a tattoo above her left breast, and several of her cohorts have tattoos and piercings. Her own daughter has a newer large tattoo that is visible in her Facebook photos on her chest.

There are numerous blogs posting other ways in which Maria could have sustained an acute subdural hematoma in conjunction with retinal hemorrhaging. However, every medical journal article and site that I perused indicates that these two injuries together normally ring true in a non-accidental event. In other words—abuse. All the hopeful grasping at straws will not change the fact that the circumstantial evidence strongly points to Stephanie Spurgeon in this crime. Some have said that Brunvand may have suggested to her that she should not speak at her sentencing. He was leaving the case and really had no vested interest in her situation any longer. He has bigger fish to keep from getting fried. If she were sincere, it may have been in her best interest to speak with true remorse, even if she insisted upon her innocence. But no one in the courtroom would hear the voice of Stephanie Spurgeon. Maybe one day she will honor an interview from prison. I know that she won't do so with this author.

CHAPTER 32

I HAVE READ many novels involving court drama, and you may have as well. John Grisham comes to mind, and he has delved into nonfiction too, and quite successfully. But the phrase "stranger than fiction" definitely fits this case more than any book I have ever read. It is like a suspense movie: just when you think it's over and your heart rate begins to slow down and you begin to subconsciously breathe that sigh of relief, you realize that the bad guy is not dead; that his hand is inching toward the semiautomatic, and you stop breathing and your eyes widen in horror. Well, not to be overdramatic, but this case was not over either, not by a long shot.

Medical examiner Jon Thogmartin often gives lectures to medical and law students concerning autopsies. But because he just happened to be giving such a talk the first week in May at Stetson University College of Law and he referenced Maria Harris's case, it caused the impending sentencing scheduled for May 7 to be delayed. Thogmartin commented to the class of law students that he believed that Maria's type of injuries that led to her death could have been caused by a three-and-a-half or four-year-old child. One of the students in attendance told Ron Kurpiers what he heard in the classroom, and this report triggered a chain of events ending with both legal teams and the defendant back in court before Judge Newton.

Thogmartin told the *Tampa Bay Times* that his information in the lecture was misrepresented to Kurpiers and that he said, quoting from the *Tampa Bay Times* article, "It is 'anatomically possible' for a child of that age to cause the type of injuries that killed Maria. However, he said that he also added that 'it does not fit the circumstances' *of this case*."[1] (Emphasis mine.)

He told the reporter that the defense attorneys had decided not to consult him prior to the trial and that he found it "somewhat disgusting that the defense is now trying to pin this on a three-and-a-half or four-year-old kid when there is no evidence that is what happened."[1]

Kurpiers responded that the decision not to sit down with Thogmartin for a pretrial interview was a tactical decision made for legal reasons, not an oversight.[1]

This response first came up when Kurpiers was interviewed by reporter Yolanda Fernandez on a local NBC affiliate, and she did not ask Kurpiers what those legal reasons were. Kurpiers may not have told her if she had asked.

Judge Newton scheduled a hearing for June 25, 2012, to address the issues the defense had in their new and amazing discovery.

I was totally taken aback, and several thoughts immediately came to mind. First, Spurgeon herself had reported to the police that no child had done anything to Maria that day. I will quote again what Brian Daniels had said at the bond hearing, *"Ms. Spurgeon related to Detective Lyons that there were no incidents from any of the other small children that were at the residence with Maria."* This statement goes against any implication that a child harmed Maria at the day care. If she meant that no other child was injured that day, then this point does not apply. But it would be obvious that no other child was injured, or it would have been reported by the parent because they all knew about what happened to Maria. (The word *from* implies that there were no reports *from* any child regarding harm, not of harm *to* any other child).

Second, why would the defense act so surprised that Thogmartin had indicated that this was a possibility, even if not in this case? It didn't make any sense. They would have thought of it themselves because they had to consider every individual in the day care as a "suspect" and then rule each one out on the basis of police records or obvious circumstances in the attempt to help rule out their client. Even though they did not have to prove Spurgeon's innocence, it certainly would be to their benefit to plant reasonable doubt by placing the blame on someone else that was there if there was reason to believe it to be true.

Third, and very telling, as Kurpiers himself admitted, the defense chose not to consult with Thogmartin prior to the case because they had a different strategy. That strategy, by my deduction, was the testimony of Dr. Ipser, whether intentional or not. The physicist, as you recall, indicated that not even an adult would have been strong enough to cause Maria's injuries. The defense chose to go with this expert witness, instead of using the testimony of the ME who had performed the actual autopsy on the victim. Dr. Thogmartin is not a witness who favors either the prosecution or the defense. He will, by the very nature of his career, testify for either side or both in the same trial. But now, the defense is denying their own witness's testimony, Dr. Ipser's, by saying that they did not have access to information that was kept from them by the state; that supposedly the ME told them a child at Spurgeon's home day care could have fatally injured Maria! Nowhere is this mentioned by Thogmartin or the state. So which person does the defense want the jury to believe, Thogmartin, or its own witness, Ipser? And what do they think Dr. Thogmartin actually said?

When the state keeps discovery information from the defense when it is supposed to be available to them, it falls under something called Brady Disclosure. But this rule is very specific, and it must apply to the case in such a way so that not only is new evidence introduced, but the evidence is such that it would have altered the verdict. The term for this type of evidence is *exculpatory*. The smoking gun that the defense now claims to have from Thogmartin, who says he is misrepresented, not only seems to be evidence that is not new, but isn't evidence at all. Not only is there no proof that the state withheld exculpatory evidence from the defense, but there is no proof that a child did anything to Maria. What hidden exculpatory evidence did the defense not have?

So where are they going with this? In that videotaped interview with Yolanda Fernandez, Kurpiers said, "We think if the jury would have been presented this evidence...which is critical, the jury would have [returned] a finding of not guilty." He also relayed to Fernandez that Thogmartin told the state "on multiple occasions" that a child at the day care could have harmed Maria. But where did he get his information from? The person in the law class went to Kurpiers and told him that Thogmartin had suggested another small child and not an adult could have caused the injuries that killed Maria. Did Kurpiers verify the information with Thogmartin? Thogmartin says that he never gave such information to the state. So where did Kurpiers get the information that Thogmartin told the state on "multiple occasions" that a child could have done it? Thogmartin states that he also never said that a child at the day care could have harmed Maria in the law class lecture, but that the student in the law class took him out of context. There were other people in that class who could back up what Thogmartin actually said, including adjunct instructor and Pasco-Pinellas County State Attorney Bernie McCabe and another senior prosecutor. Neither heard Thogmartin mention any new evidence, or they would have reported it to the court. Maybe Kurpiers should have consulted one of them. Maybe he did. Unfortunately the video which was viewable online was taken down in March 2013, but there is a link in the bibliography to a brief summary of that interview.[2] Another unbiased source for the above information is in the *American Bar Association Journal*.[3]

June 25, 2012

Today is the day that the evidentiary hearing is being held on the *State v. Spurgeon* case with respect to the Brady Disclosure. I am bringing my friend Carole with me to court to get a fresh perspective on the case since I have become so wrapped up in the semantics of the Brady Ruling that I don't quite know what to expect and what the results would mean for the Harris family.

Carole was quick to point out afterward that it was obvious to her that things did not look good for Spurgeon at all based on what was presented in court today. Because it is a hearing, the questioning of the lone witness is more relaxed and his freedom to respond is given more leeway than would be the case in front of a jury. That witness, Dr. Jon Thogmartin, has much to say about what the defense considers new evidence. The tone of the questioning is established when Ron Kurpiers asks a confrontational question to lead off the testimony. The animated and quick-witted medical examiner is quite prepared with his response.

Kurpiers calls Dr. Thogmartin to the stand as a witness for the defense. After a few preliminary questions regarding his testimony at the trial and review of Maria's autopsy and the trial transcripts, Kurpiers asks Thogmartin a question that will steer the testimony in an unusual direction for the duration of the hearing.

"Is it your opinion, Doctor, that the defense screwed up because we didn't take your deposition?"

"I don't think I've ever had a child abuse case where the ME is not deposed [by the defense]." Thogmartin goes into detail, saying that he, at least in the past, would have received a phone call to prepare for a deposition.

Kurpiers asks him if it is his opinion that he may have said something (in a deposition) that was not in the autopsy report. Thogmartin curtly explains that opinions are forbidden in autopsy reports. They are for anatomical findings only.

Kurpiers gets right to the heart of the Brady Disclosure and asks Thogmartin if he believes that the defense screwed up because "we didn't ask you if another child caused this."

"Not exactly."

Kurpiers and Thogmartin are interrupting each other at this point, and I hear, "Three defenses." "Someone besides my client did it." "Ninjas at back door?" "Family members?"

"Would that have made a difference?" Kurpiers asks. (In other words, if the defense had asked him this question about whether another child could have harmed Maria prior to the actual trial, would that have made a difference?)

"Not in these circumstances," Thogmartin responds. "It is anatomically possible for a child at the right age to induce these injuries. Not a specific child. Not one to two-and-a-half years old." Thogmartin explains that is his opinion to use to anyone who had bothered to ask.

Kurpiers redirects the questioning to the lecture at Stetson University. "You spoke to a class—"

Thogmartin interrupts. He explains that it was a prosecution class taught by state attorney Bernie McCabe, without naming this particular case. He said that he explained that a medical examiner is a witness for the decedent. "Any attorney has access to us! If you want reports and information, you can get it from your ME."

He answers questions regarding the lecture, responding that yes, he was the only speaker and no, the Maria Harris case was not mentioned specifically. He explained that he had a slide about "what your medical examiner is." He told the class he had a case where the defense didn't prepare and didn't probe him. He explained that he said in his lecture: "'It's appropriate to ask if someone else did it. There was a three-and-a-half or a four-year-old who could have done it. Could someone else have come in the house later?' It doesn't fit these circumstances. I told *you* that!"

Kurpiers asks him if he used a PowerPoint presentation in the classroom.

"PowerPoint referring to this case? No way!" Thogmartin continues on, saying, "You decide yourself what you need to bring up. The defense should have asked me."

Kurpiers asks a few more repeat questions, then, "Do you recall meeting with Mr. Brunvand and myself [*sic*] at your office?"

"Yes."

"During this discussion, you brought up that another child could have done this to Maria Harris—"

"I never said specifically, "*This* child!"

"Why did you feel it was important to bring up in the discussion?"

"You asked. You can call me. You can talk to me. In future cases, it would be a good idea," Thogmartin responds, not able to withhold the rancor in his voice.

Kurpiers goes back to blaming himself and Brunvand. I thought this was a risky way to go about obtaining success for Spurgeon in the hearing, but success seemed improbable anyway, so why not go for it? "I thought the meeting was about what we did wrong. Why would you tell a room full of students that we screwed up?" Maybe Ron is hoping for a retrial based upon blaming themselves for a major miscalculation in Spurgeon's defense. It seemed quite a stretch considering the circumstances surrounding the case.

Thogmartin explains that the key is preparation, that the medical examiner will "talk to you."

"Nobody prompted you to discuss Maria Harris," Kurpiers retorts.

"It was a case fresh in my mind, the freshest and most recent case on my mind."

Kurpiers wants clarification from Thogmartin, asking him to confirm that he believes it was a "bad strategy" for the defense not to have asked him if someone else could have done it.

Thogmartin tells him that he wasn't asked, skirting a direct response to the bad strategy query.

Kurpiers asks him how many times he had met with the prosecutor, Brian Daniels.

Thogmartin says that there were eight phone calls with Mr. Daniels and "one female but I don't know her name."

Kurpiers then asks the key question to the hearing: "How many times with Mr. Daniels did you express that another child could have done it?"

"I didn't bring this up." Thogmartin continues on to explain that he discussed diabetes, organ donation, and natural causes. "What I would have done with you if you were prepared. It's still gonna be blunt homicide. It doesn't matter." Thogmartin has become very standoffish toward Kurpiers at this point, his body language portraying that he is quite busy and would like this questioning to wrap up.

Here, as I had mentioned twice earlier, he says something that underscored that I had been right about this hearing being a waste of time: "[There were] no incidents reported between the kids." (Detective Lyons was the one who took that report, and she took it directly from Stephanie Spurgeon.)

Then Thogmartin says something that doesn't escape a single ear in the courtroom: "The four-year-old I have at home could do this to a kid under the right circumstances. [But] *you would be picking a comatose kid off the floor and putting her in a playpen.*"

I thought about this statement later and realized how powerful it was. Thogmartin, among other doctors, had testified in the trial that Maria's injuries were fatal and would have caused almost immediate unconsciousness. So if another child injured Maria, Spurgeon would have recognized that something was wrong shortly after. She would have had to call emergency or at least called Patricia Harris. She would not have just picked up a very obviously injured child and put her in the playpen!

Thogmartin repeats that it is anatomically possible for a child to do it, but it would have had to have been under the right circumstances. He explains that in his lecture, he said, "a kid that's three-and-a-half to four years old could have done this under the right circumstances."

Kurpiers confers with Brunvand and then asks more questions, trying to trip up Thogmartin. "Do you recall that every time you met with the prosecution, you said another child could have caused these injuries?"

"Boy, I don't think I said that. I said it to Mr. Daniels at least once. We discussed lots of things that didn't fit the circumstances." He explains they reviewed other possibilities such as Maria's injuries being self-induced or that she fell off a picnic table and hit her head, but [they didn't] fit the circumstances.

He responds to a question about a medical examiner's role in death investigations.

"I would never write anything in a report that implicates a person." Then Thogmartin paraphrases a statute: "Under 406.12, anyone in a county where a death occurred must notify the medical examiner and give all records. False statements would be criminal behavior...If there was a different manner [of death], I would have put it."

There are some wrap-up questions that are not relevant. Thogmartin says condescendingly to Kurpiers at one point that he needs to know what his medical examiner is going to say; he needs to be better prepared.

The questioning ends on a poor note for the defense with Thogmartin explaining that in the pretrial period, the prosecutor meets with him a lot, and he likes this. They look at things like thrombosis, ketones, etc. "This is what you are gonna hear," he tells the prosecutor. "Prepare."

When Holly Grissinger stands to question Dr. Thogmartin, he does not change his countenance in any way. She asks him if he is allowed to give opinions in his [autopsy] reports, and he answers with a resounding, "No!" Then, more calmly, "Only the objective findings of the autopsy."

He explains that he must report any and all circumstances such as child abuse. He tells the court that it applies to every person, and that failing to provide such information is a crime. Also, altering the scene is a crime.

Grissinger confirms that there were no recent falls and no incidents that occurred in Spurgeon's house.

Thogmartin talks about how a four-year-old could have "clotheslined this child," meaning running with an arm outstretched, so that Maria would have been knocked over by the older child's arm. He details this behavior a little later on in his testimony, explaining that Maria could walk and talk so it was anatomically possible.

He goes on to say that "[it was] also possible she could have killed herself by pulling a TV on her head, or climbed up on a bookshelf and did a 'header.' None of this was reported. There were no indications it was a fall, or we wouldn't be sitting here."

He had also stated earlier that there was not enough room in the Pack 'n Play for another child to have climbed in there when Maria was sleeping in it and to have killed her.

Thogmartin repeats his conclusion that he still would have determined that the cause and manner of death was blunt force trauma—homicide.

Grissinger clarifies that the defense had erred in not asking Thogmartin his opinion.

He agrees, "Hindsight is 20/20."

"What are the most common defenses in child abuse cases?"

"I didn't do it. Somebody else did," Thogmartin responds. "In any case an ME telling a lawyer what they [*sic*] should do is Monday morning quarterbacking. Defense attorneys tend to think the ME wasn't approachable, but that's not true. If they skipped over something—thrombosis, glucose levels—I would have said they should have brought it up."

Grissenger asks him pointedly, "You never told Brian Daniels that the three-and-a-half-year-old did this?"

"No. Never."

Then Thogmartin makes an odd statement. "It's one of the main defenses. The Apollo 11 capsule alone with baby. Not the case here. Multiple people around become important. Getting your ME to say what 'homicide' means and was this a fall—is a better approach."

"Your position (Grissinger references the trial transcripts here), you go through other anatomic possibilities. Does the fact that a three-and-a-half or a four-year-old could have done it change your testimony?"

"No!"

"Change the cause and manner of death?"

"No!"

Holly Grissinger finishes on this note, and Kurpiers stands to redirect, looking more than slightly agitated.

He asks Thogmartin who the investigator was and Thogmartin doesn't remember.

"Look!"

Thogmartin reads the investigator's name from the report.

Kurpiers asks him to read the report, and Thogmartin asks him why. Kurpiers wants him to read the second page, which says there was no confirmation of an interaction, and he says, "Are you familiar with the report that there was an interaction [at the day care]?"

"Was there a fight?"

Judge Newton asks for a bench approach, and she is given a copy of the report.

After this, a discussion ensues back and forth between Kurpiers and Thogmartin about whether this report indicated an altercation or not. Kupiers tells Thogmartin that he said under oath that he had no evidence of an interaction.

Her responds that a strike in the head with a plastic toy wouldn't do, and that there may have been an escalation to this disagreement, but no injury. But if there was some huge incident, then someone would have lied to the court or the police."

"How do you know?" Kurpiers inquires.

"According to your own client telling you?" Thogmartin replies sardonically.

Then he adds that doesn't change things for him.

Kurpiers continues to hammer on this incident. "You've testified. Why didn't you bring it up in front of a jury?"

"Holly never asked. You never asked. You gotta ask. I'm not going to volunteer that. Picnic tables, tree roots, climbing up stuff, we didn't just talk about that."

It seems that Kurpiers doesn't want to hear any more about not asking the right questions, so he stops his redirect at this point and Grissinger has more to ask of Thogmartin.

In front of the courtroom of supporters of Spurgeon and those who sit on the Harrises' side of the courtroom, as well as the television camera, Grissinger asks a question regarding an issue that had not surfaced since the bond hearing nearly four years earlier.

In spite of Thogmartin skirting the issue in his response, she asks a question that he does not deny.

"Didn't another minor say decedent was hit many times by the caregiver?"

"[If she] climbed a bookcase, [this would have been] anatomically correct. Most concerning for me would be one that would alter the manner of death, but it was never reported." (Meaning that no other incident was reported that would have changed Thogmartin's entry on the autopsy findings on manner of death from homicide to something else).

Grissinger confirms with Thogmartin that a child could not have climbed into the Pack 'n Play at the day care and that Maria could not have been pounded in the head with a heavy object. Neither would have caused an accelerated/decelerated head injury with blunt force trauma.

Thogmartin says there was not enough movement *in* the Pack 'n Play but there certainly was *outside* of it. He also states that it is major league stuff for a child to stand outside of the Pack 'n Play and reach in. "He's not going to be able to do it."

This ends Thogmartin's testimony, and in fact, the defense does not even call Brian Daniels to question him on how often Thogmartin discussed whether "a child could have done it" with him. There are no other witnesses, and both sides get to pose closing arguments at this hearing.

Kurpiers, unsure of himself, having not questioned Brian Daniels for reasons unknown, stands and says, "I think what we heard is basically this—he [Thogmartin] felt that, without any prompting, it was prominent enough to him to bring it up on multiple occasions. He suggested it was prominent because he raised it immediately after the trial with no outside prompting. [In a class], this could have occurred...Maybe Your Honor needs to review his trial testimony...He never references this, but yet two weeks after the verdict he brought it up. Years earlier [?] he made it a prominent part of his discussion with Brian Daniels."

(I put the question mark by "years earlier" because I didn't know what Kurpiers meant by this. How many years ago? Right after the injuries to Maria took place? Kurpiers was not the attorney on the case then and would not be for around two more years. So did he mean after he became one of the attorneys for Spurgeon? If so, he could not have meant more than two years earlier. This statement was never clarified because Daniels was not questioned).

Kurpiers talks about the state's obligation to disclose information under Brady and reviews the *Brady v. the State of Maryland* case from which it was created. He says this favorable information was brought up to the prosecution but not the defense. He then explains that the defense must show that under reasonable circumstances, if this information had been disclosed to them, the results of the case "would have been different."

He references another case, and then says, "It is not required for the defense to prove that this was an intentional withholding. It clearly states it can be inadvert. We feel it was inadvertent, but it is still a violation."

Kurpiers repeats that this issue was prominent for Thogmartin because he brought it up to Brian Daniels years ago, then to a class, then to "me and Brunvand. But he never mentions it at trail, but mentions it again after the trial."

Then he makes a very critical statement: "If the defense would have known this, we would have used a different strategy to the case."

In other words, Dr. James Ipser would not have been a witness for the defense, since he would have contradicted the very notion that a child could have caused these injuries. However, if the defense would have used this possibility, by its very nature, this method of introducing another detractor could have caused the state to say, "What child? Let's look at each child." And then a whole can of worms would have been opened. For one thing, as mentioned before, if a child injured Maria, it would have been Spurgeon's responsibility to report it, and she certainly would have, because why would she want to be in court by hiding something she knew a child did? At worst, she would be negligent in her care, not on trial for murder one. As Thogmartin repeatedly stated and would have stated if questioned under oath at trial, *"It does not fit the circumstances of this case."*

Kurpiers pleas to Judge Newton, "As soon as we became aware of this issue, we raised it to the court. He [Thogmartin] said it is something that we should have had in our arsenal regarding the defense of Ms. Spurgeon. There is no obligation for us to depose him."

He says that the defense should have been given the information that was only relayed to the state by Thogmartin.

When Holly Grissinger steps forward to summarize the state's side of this hearing, she starts by explaining that just because Thogmartin told the state that it is anatomically possible that a child could have done it, that this in itself is not exculpatory information. She says that other accidents were anatomically possible. It was not the state's responsibility to go to the defense and say, "Did you know that it is anatomically possible?"

Grissinger relates to the judge that the defense has the burden in this hearing to show that this information was exculpatory or impeaching. Striking back at Kurpiers for his criticism of the state withholding evidence, she says, "We shouldn't have to do the discovery work for the defense."

"The evidence must be present in light of all the circumstances of the trial." She explains that this information is not favorable based on medical fact and that the testimony would not have changed.

She delves into Thogmartin's statements at the hearing, reminding the court that he admitted that "had they [the defense] gone down that path and not the medical path, he would have brought up the medical path. Nothing would have changed his testimony."

Grissinger highlights that Thogmartin, as the medical examiner, gives the cause and manner of death, that he doesn't come out and say that Stephanie Spurgeon killed this child.

"They knew there was a three-and-a-half-year-old in the house. They knew she was put in the Pack'n Play and didn't want to take a nap. He [Thogmartin] discusses anything you ask him. Lots of things are not included in the autopsy report that the state asks him in order to prepare their case. It's not the state's job..."

She goes on to reiterate that because Thogmartin brought it up in a law class, it is Monday morning quarterbacking. And then, "They brought it up in a meeting because they wanted to know how they screwed up." *Ouch.*

Again, she says that nothing would have changed, and that statutory provisions state that any and all information must be provided that go to cause and manner of death. The three-and-a-half-year-old child could not have done it based on facts and circumstances. "That three-and-a-half-year-old child could not have killed Maria Harris. The motion should be denied."

On this note, the hearing comes to a close, and Judge Newton states that she would set a written order for the motion for Tuesday, July 24. The actual motion would be filed that morning or before. So it appeared that an entire month would go by before we would return to court and know whether a new trial would be possible for Stephanie Spurgeon.

CHAPTER 33

AS WITH ANY number of factors in this bizarre and tragic case, what occurred in the month prior to the next hearing was anything but normal. Fabrications and rumors were spread on blog sites and Facebook about the Harris family. It is an absolute waste of time to even mention the specifics here, as the people who spread them know who they are, and have to live with the lies that they told. Spreading such false accusations certainly didn't help Stephanie Spurgeon in any way, so it made no sense to me. The Tampa Bay Times newspaper inaccurately reported that another judge had made the ruling when it was actually the same judge who did

On the twentieth, the Friday prior to the hearing, Curtis Krueger, the *Tampa Bay Times* reporter who has been closely following this case from the beginning, reported in the evening on the *Times* website that "a judge has denied a motion to order a new trial or dismiss charges against Stephanie Spurgeon."

Judge Newton wrote the following ruling in her motion for denial:

> [Although] Jon Thogmartin said that it was anatomically possible for a child to cause such injuries, he also concluded that "such a theory did not fit the circumstances of this case" and has never been his opinion about this case.[1]

As a result, Judge Newton surmised that there were no exculpatory statements made by Jon Thogmartin that would have proved the innocence of Stephanie Spurgeon.

July 24, 2012

Today is my son's and my niece's birthday. But for most of the people in the courtroom attending this hearing, it is not a day of joy. A quiet pall has descended upon the room. It does seem though that some people present are unaware that a ruling has already been made.

This was supposed to be the day that the motion for dismissal or for a new trial based on the Brady Disclosure was to be made. However, since that actual motion was already denied last Friday, the proceedings that take place today are just for the court to have the attorneys present and state the denial for the record. Spurgeon has also been brought into Judge Newton's fourth floor courtroom from downstairs.

Holly Grissinger arrives just before 8:30 a.m., and several pre-trial hearings are brought before Judge Newton. It is a rather harried morning as public defenders crisscross the courtroom and bring their defendants to the stand to set dates for various proceedings. Notably absent are both Bjorn Brunvand and Ronald Kurpiers. I overhear someone ask where Brunvand is. He does show up at five minutes to nine o'clock, while pretrial hearings are still continuing.

But Ron Kurpiers is not going to be present. He may be under suspension for the charges against him of forgery and false acknowledgement in another case (not relevant to this one), apparently for only ninety days. Any sentencing date that was scheduled for Spurgeon would need to fit into the schedule of Mr. Brunvand alone, unless it was set beyond the ninety days of Kurpier's suspension. Usually, judges like to get sentencing accomplished within a reasonable time window, and in this case it had been scheduled once before, prior to the introduction of the Brady Disclosure argument by the defense, which had temporarily brought everything to a screeching halt.

Now things are back on schedule. Spurgeon's conviction of manslaughter was upheld. Judge Newton wants sentencing to be over and done with. She mentions that she could schedule it this same week. But Mr. Brunvand's own schedule prevents that, so in the convoluted manner of court bureaucracy, a status hearing is scheduled on Friday to see if sentencing can take place the next Monday, on July 30. Brunvand mentions that he has a major trial pending that could last three weeks. If that trial begins on Monday, he will not be able to be present for sentencing until the last week of August.

Not only is it strange how the lives of both defendants and victims are trapped within these court schedules—a delay would keep Spurgeon in the county jail for another month not knowing her sentence—but also that the very strict nature of what types of hearings can be held on which days and times also seems so archaic. Since I am not knowledgeable in matters of the court, in my rational thought processes, I wonder why the sentencing simply could not just take place on Friday at 8:30 a.m. instead of a status hearing. But most of these rules have been in place longer than I have been alive, and I'm sure there are good reasons for them.

At any rate, the courtroom will be packed for the sentencing date, whenever that may be. This is the date that both the supporters for the Harrises and for Stephanie Spurgeon will be allowed to speak. Spurgeon's two children could even speak and make an emotional plea for her to be released early and be located near them so they can visit often. The placing of a prisoner though often does not take into account family members, as much as it does the nature of the crime and the security measures necessary to protect both the criminal and the other inmates.

Stephanie Spurgeon, the person who is the reason for this hearing and the previous ones and the trial and the crime, stands forlorn next to Brunvand who gallantly towers above her at the podium in his trademark wide pinstriped suit. The cliché "jailhouse pallor" is evident in her pasty white skin and unhealthy puffiness. She has put on a noticeable amount of weight during her time in jail. Since she is only allowed out of her cell for one hour a day (according to posts on one of the blog sites), that doesn't give her much time to move around. There is no doubt she is in a state of depression as well, which would discourage exercise. Any hope she had of a new trial or a dismissal altogether had been shot down when that motion had been denied the previous Friday. I cannot begin to imagine the despair she must have felt upon receiving that news. In spite of my closeness to the Harris family, I feel a deep sense of sadness for Stephanie, a woman who would likely be sent away to a state prison labeled as a child murderer, far from her friends and family, and who would have no hope of parole since there is none for manslaughter in the state of Florida. She could only work toward seeking an appeal, and with a marginal hope of retaining a private attorney. She will always have the option of a public defender though.

After today's hearing, the Harrises are graciously escorted from the courtroom again by a bailiff, all the way downstairs and to an alternate exit. Bjorn Brunvand has gone down the hall from the courtroom and is now surrounded by Spurgeon's friends and family, answering questions and probably explaining the circumstances surrounding the sentencing dates. Like Spurgeon herself, the gravity of the pending sentencing has yet to really sink in for the defense. Although they had kept her from a life sentence, they had lost this case. If she gets the maximum sentence, fifteen years is a long time. Spurgeon's young granddaughter will be in middle or high school. Her two children will possibly be married. There will probably be more grandchildren whose births and formative years she will miss. Spurgeon's friends will need to be a loving network for her young family, encouraging them and being there for them for many years. Who will be up to the task? Which ones would prove themselves to be true friends and not disappear a couple years from now or just say, "Hey, how are you holding up?" on Facebook?

The impending sentence could encompass a wide scope. Spurgeon could actually get a very lenient fifteen years of probation and not even go to prison if the judge deems that to be the most suitable punishment. That doesn't seem likely, since a manslaughter conviction carries a prison term of up to fifteen years, and there is also aggravated child abuse associated with this charge. With a prison sentence, her best result would likely be eight and a half years based on a ten-year sentence and 15 percent time off for good behavior. Since she turned forty-one years old in April, she would be nearly fifty years old upon release. And that is the best scenario. She could end up with the maximum sentence of fifteen years with no early release time for good behavior. A judge also has the right to override the maximum sentence under a conviction and make it longer, but doing so would create stronger grounds for appeal. It is not probable, but Judge Newton could sentence Stephanie to life in prison if she was so inclined. Of course, for the Harris family, no sentence is long enough to punish her for what happened to little Maria. They would trade any length of time just to have their sweet baby girl back again.

Justice on earth never is truly balanced for either side, and closure is never truly complete.

Fortunately, the Harrises are not vengeful, and they choose daily to leave everything in God's hands. "That is what gets us through," Pat has told me on more than one occasion. Such faith is rare in any crime against a person, let alone a murder. Faith brought this family closer together and has seen them through one of the most devastating events anyone can experience in a lifetime—the taking of the life of their child and grandchild. Even though this whole process would soon be over after nearly four long years, it will never be over in this lifetime for Esther, Patricia, and Clyde. They will always have unexpected reminders of Maria and feel the emotional scars almost as deeply as physical pain.

August 20, 2012

This day has been a long, long time coming. In fact, tomorrow will be four years to the day when little Maria Harris went to Stephanie Spurgeon's day care to be dropped off for the first and only time. What goes through the mind of someone who has been sitting in jail for a long time, waiting for a sentence, only to hear of numerous delays; attending hopeful hearings that might involve dismissal of the case; and spending agonizing weeks filled with nothing but time? She has had little else to do but wait for the time to pass, not wanting to face the inevitable: a judge's decision on how long she will spend in prison. She has never seen the inside of a prison, only the county jail. It looms ahead in her future—another great and formidable unknown.

As I park my car in a shady spot and grab my notebook off the passenger seat, I spot a couple from church walking up to the courthouse. I flag them down, grateful to not have to walk in alone, not knowing how many of Spurgeon's supporters might be there already. As it turns out, we are one of the first ones there outside the courtroom, waiting on uncomfortable wooden benches. The sentencing hearing is scheduled for 1:30 p.m., but it is only about 12:45 so we have plenty of time. We just want to be sure to get in the courtroom and get a seat. This was a good decision, because once the doors opened to the room, the gallery seating area fills up rapidly. A bailiff points out that one side is for the state and the other side for the defense. Although Spurgeon has a full showing of support, the Harrises do as well, and we quickly take up all the seating area on our side. The defense's side lost a row of seating as no one is allowed to sit directly behind the defendant. Only Yolanda Fernandez, the reporter from News Channel 8, and Curtis Krueger, the courtroom journalist from the *Tampa Bay Times*, are allowed in that row. I remember at the last hearing that a request had been made for a larger courtroom to allow for more people to observe the sentencing, but we are in the same room as before.

Our pastor, Jason Wiley, and our associate and youth pastor, David Brown, both came all the way down to the courthouse from Palm Harbor to show support for the Harrises. There are several other members of the church present, especially those who had been so fond of Maria, and there are friends of Esther Harris here as well. As always, Bobbie Hodson, the devoted child advocate for the Harrises, is there, exuding her perpetual optimism and warmth.

One couple from church, the Campbells, came prepared to speak on behalf of the Harrises regarding Maria. None of us realized that only the Harrises would speak as per the instructions of their attorneys. It is a little disheartening because Diane Campbell had taken time to write down her heartfelt feelings on paper, and now she is not able to speak and put them on record. The Campbells also recognize someone who is supporting Spurgeon.

It is Julia Galpin. Since they are both in the real estate business, a small world in North Pinellas County, the agents tend to know each other. After she was released on bail and had to wear the GPS monitor, Julia had given Spurgeon a job in her real estate office. When I did some research, I could only find one property listing under Stephanie's name. I assume that this meant she was a licensed real estate agent. This was during the time that the real estate market had dried up, so it was nice of Julia to take Spurgeon on, but I don't know if she was paid beyond potential commissions for selling real estate. However, it is a surprise for the Campbells to discover that their fellow agent was supporting the defendant, even after the jury had convicted her.

Much earlier in this case, at a hearing being overseen by another judge, Spurgeon's attorneys were asked by that judge why, if she was in real estate, her house was not on the market. "You put that house up for sale!" He told Spurgeon. She needed money to pay for her attorneys and court costs, as well as her GPS ankle bracelet. Her mother was helping with much of the costs, but she couldn't help with all of them.

Bjorn Brunvand arrives at about 1:20 p.m., again in his signature pinstriped suit, although I note the stripes on this one are more subdued. His powerful personality can radiate through a courtroom, and people always seem to be interested in what he is doing or saying. As with the last hearing, Kurpiers is not present because he is still under suspension. It is likely he is relieved that he does not have to be here for the sentencing of his client. Soon after, Holly Grissinger comes in, looking relaxed but prepared in a light tan suit. She doesn't know what the outcome will be any more than Brunvand does, but they have been in this type of situation many times before.

Just before 1:30 p.m., the Harris family enters the courtroom. Some people from church leave the row where I am seated to make room for the Harrises since it is the front row. Esther looks very apprehensive, and I can tell she is on the brink of her emotions. Patricia and Clyde are visibly somber. Their son, Esther's brother, Christopher, is not with them. It has been very hard on him to experience the loss of his niece, and he has chosen not to attend any of the proceedings.

After the Harrises are seated, I lean across a young attorney for the state who is there to observe the sentencing, and tap Esther on the shoulder. I tell her that it's okay to cry when she goes before the judge and just be herself. Don't hold back. And I tell her to remember that God will be with her to get her through. Esther nods, unable to speak. We all have trials to go through in life, and knowing that God is with us can make them much more bearable. We can lean on him and give him our problems. He doesn't promise to take them away, but he allows us to get through each situation with his help and mercy if only we call upon him. Although we all have our own trials to face and surmount, few of us ever have had to deal with the homicide of a family member, especially an innocent child. The Harris family, unlike other families in similar circumstances, has never become angry with God for what has happened. They have had to keep turning their anger and sorrow over to him, time and again, and because of their faith, he has granted them the grace to remain calm, all the while seeking his justice.

As one would expect, there is a television camera in the courtroom. It will be shared by all stations covering this case as it is the only camera here. However, in the parking lot outside the building, there are three or four vans from the press all set up for interviews and news coverage as soon as the sentencing is over. The stations want the emotional stuff. They also want to talk to the attorneys. I'm not sure if the state will talk to them, because most of the time, state attorneys do not go on camera.

We all rise as Judge Newton enters the courtroom, looking regal with her light blond hair pulled back tightly and dark framed reading glasses accenting her high cheekbones. She is striking today, and I can't help but wonder if it could be an omen of things to come.

At 1:40 p.m., Judge Newton asks for Stephanie Spurgeon to be brought into the courtroom. She is escorted by a bailiff and walks briskly to the defendant's table. She looks even heavier than a few weeks ago, and the roots of her hair have grown in darkly, in contrast to the cinnamon color of the rest of it. Her curly waves are pulled back in a loose twist. It appears as if she is wearing a black band across the front of her head because of the color contrast. Spurgeon actually seems to be in a pleasant mood. She holds her head high and looks about the gallery for people that she knows. I recognize quite a few of the faces from the trial and hearings.

Before the actual proceedings begin, the judge admonishes the courtroom gallery as before that we are to be quiet and make no comments out loud. She tells us to please step out of the courtroom if emotions become upsetting or if we are showing displeasure. This request applies if anyone wants to react to any sentence applied in this case. She could be referring to our side becoming upset with a very light sentence, or Spurgeon's side reacting to a stiff sentence. I feel in my heart that the latter will be the case. Again, Judge Newton states that no opinions or displeasure shall take place in the courtroom.

Bjorn Brunvand rises and approaches the podium. He makes a standard request for a new motion for trial because of the Brady Disclosure rule. Judge Newton says, "All motions are denied."

The defense is now permitted to allow people to speak, including Stephanie Spurgeon herself. But Brunvand calls no witnesses. He says that there have been many letters received by the court, and a large majority are on behalf of his client. He notes that what the family and friends would say is already reflected in these letters. Because of the tone of some of the statements made on the Internet on Spurgeon's "behalf," I wonder if Brunvand has decided not to allow her supporters to speak for fear of someone saying something insulting about the jury, legal system, or the Harris family. Judge Newton asks if Stephanie Spurgeon has anything to say at this time.

To the dismay of many of the people present, she chooses not to speak. She has a right at this point to make a statement, even to declare her innocence, even to express sadness to the Harris family for the death of their child and grandchild in spite of what she proclaims to be her innocence, yet she chooses not to speak. I feel it is a huge mistake on her part since it cannot possibly harm her sentencing if she says something and expresses sorrow for the family. But she holds her peace, with no remorse evident in the least.

Since there is nothing else for the defense to present, the state calls Esther Harris to speak to the court, and she comes forward with Bobbie Hodson close at her side. Her testimony is sworn in, and she responds weakly, overcome with emotion. Bobbie takes over and begins reading Esther's statement on her behalf.

Esther's heartrending testimony lasts but for a few minutes, but the most difficult part of it contains emotions that she has kept buried while in public for four long years. "You killed my baby...All I wanted was for you to hold my baby..." She talks about the children and grandchildren that Maria would never have. She is saddened at seeing the children of her friends getting bigger and going to school. "On February 16, I watched you get handcuffed...You did this monstrous thing to Maria." (It is here that this whole case strikes home with me as I think back to when my sons were toddlers and how helpless, angry, and torn apart I would have been if this horrible thing had happened to either one of them. But it didn't. And I could not begin to even know what suffering the Harrises had endured).

Bobbie continues to read Esther's statement, mentioning that another innocent baby had been hurt in Stephanie's care—a wonderful, innocent child. This was the child, Gabrielle Anderson, who was the focus of the Williams Rule hearing where no jury was present, and the state had decided to exclude this information from the trial, although they were allowed to use it. Mentioning it here brings it out in the open so that Spurgeon's purported innocence might be questioned in the minds of those who had doubts. But the main reason that Esther mentions it in her address to the court and to Spurgeon is to show that there is a history to her abusive behavior. Apparently, Spurgeon's supporters did not want to hear about or believe this account, but the hearing had taken place and is memorialized in court documents for future reference.

Esther's statement continues to be read by Bobbie. "This is the first time I've been able to speak outside of testifying. Thank God. I made my baby a promise at her graveside...[And then talking directly to Spurgeon] You can see your children. I have to go to a graveside and stare at blades of grass."

Her testimony goes on to talk about the lives saved by Maria's organs that were donated. During the entire reading of this statement by Bobbie Hodson, Esther cries quietly. And Spurgeon sits stone-faced, aloof, with all emotion gone as if she has none left within her. I notice that even a couple of people on the defense side of the gallery were wiping away tears. How Spurgeon could not show any feelings is amazing to me. It's almost as if she is not in her own body. Esther's comments end and are left hanging in the air. The reason for the case, the loss of a one-year-old's life, the dying ember of too brief a candle, becomes real and personal as it has finally been put into words by her own mother.

Clyde Harris steps up next to speak. His testimony reveals that he still doesn't understand how something like this could happen to his granddaughter. She was supposed to be safe. "Four years ago, our granddaughter was murdered. Why did it happen? What did she do? Stephanie will always have her kids and grandkids. Why? Why did she do it? It's been a long, hard life without her. Why did this thing have to happen to a small child? She couldn't defend herself. She couldn't protect herself."

Of course, Spurgeon will not ever answer these questions because her attorney says she insists on her innocence. But what about it? Why won't she proclaim it herself? I would be so angry for being punished for a crime that I didn't commit, that the bailiffs would have to hold me back from yelling out that I didn't do anything! But Spurgeon just sits quietly, peacefully, like she is watching an old movie. Maybe she doesn't understand that she really could serve the entirety of a long sentence, that an appeal may never happen. Maybe she plans on getting her college degree in prison. What will the other inmates think of a child abuser that was convicted of killing that child? This thought does not seem to concern her, although it's probably entered her mind. For the first time, I'm beginning to see the possible marks of a sociopath in her behavior—the lack of emotion, the detachment from her surroundings. It's very surreal.

Sociopaths are very good at convincing those closest to them that they are innocent and "good" people. I am reminded of the bond hearing back in 2008, when one of Spurgeon's supporters stated that she had never seen Stephanie get angry in her whole life. This is an impossible accomplishment for any human being. We want to believe the best of those we care about, and often people will deny obvious truths in order to protect their loved ones, but sometimes the ability to hide behaviors becomes a highly developed skill. Did she pull the wool over the eyes of all these supporters, or are they just protecting her out of love? What about her ex-husband? What would he have to say about her ability to remain calm in a high stress situation or her detached attitude at sentencing? Also, I recall the words of the elderly gentleman that was not a friend of the Harrises sitting next to me at jury selection: *"Maybe she did do it."*

Last, and likely because she was the most involved in the events of the day of August 21, 2008, Patricia Harris comes forward to speak. Her voice is shaky at first, but her confidence builds as she continues speaking. "My life was forever changed. I took a precious little baby girl...[and found her] in a condition I wouldn't want anyone to find their child in...We wanted to fix this, but it was all out of control. We prayed and prayed more...

I loved that baby so much," Pat says, breaking down, "I would have gladly died in her place, but I couldn't…Stephanie made the choice herself to not stop what she did!" Pat tells the judge that she had told Stephanie she would have come any time to pick up Maria instead.

"We will have no opportunity to see Maria as a baby girl. We had one more chance to hold her lifeless body." She also talks about the body parts that Maria donated and her living testimony in the lives of other children and adults. "Stephanie can see her children when she is in jail. My baby girl got nothing." Pat asks for the maximum sentence possible from the judge. "Children are hurt every day. It is about children. Adults should not be able to hurt children and get away with it."

The judge is then given a couple of photographs of Maria around the time of her death, which she looks at somberly.

There are no other speakers. If Diane Campbell would have had the chance to speak, she had a prepared statement. This is what she would have said:

> I knew little Maria from the day she was born. One thing I noticed was the great love the Harris family had for Maria. I saw Maria at church the night before she went to the Day Care Center. I thought then, how *precious* that little child was as she played in the church lobby. Everyone at church loved that happy little girl.
>
> Her mother and grandparents will never see her go to school, graduate, have a career, get married, and have her own children. All of their dreams for Maria were ended when you, Stephanie, neglected your responsibilities for taking care of this darling child. If only you had thought twice before you hurt Maria. If only you had called 911 to get help for her. If only you had taken responsibility for her life and death, the outcome might have been different. May you ask the Lord for forgiveness for your actions upon this lovely child.

Brunvand then stands and states quite unconvincingly that Stephanie Spurgeon is not making a statement because she is continuing to maintain her innocence. He says that throughout this case and the bond hearings, there has been support in the community of those who believe in her, including those who have had their children be "raised" by her. Their support has been in person or in court letters.

He says that the court needs to consider these circumstances where children were not harmed. Brunvand then makes a very interesting statement to the court. He relates that two of the jury members indicated that the deliberations were between either not guilty or manslaughter. I know for a fact that these jurors, if this is in fact what they said, were not truthful, because I also spoke with two jury members on separate occasions after the trial, and both indicated to me that there were members of the jury who stood solidly on a murder conviction. Some believed it was murder. Others said manslaughter, only because there were no witnesses, and some said not guilty. But deliberating together, they reasoned that manslaughter made the most sense. So Brunvand saying that murder did not come into play during deliberations simply is not true, and I will stand by that statement with all my heart because I know what I was told. I cannot, for obvious reasons, reveal the names of the jurors that I spoke with, but suffice it to say, each did not know what the other one told me, and they both told me the exact same thing. Also, it is important to note that neither one, at my request, told me which jurors believed which verdict should apply. I did not want to know who was on which side, and I think that it is inappropriate that anyone should know this information. It was just general information that murder was strongly believed by some of the jurors.

Next, Brunvand requests of the court that Spurgeon be placed in part of the "facility" where she can use her sleep apnea machine at night. When she is transferred by the Department of

Corrections, he wants them made aware of the fact that she has a health ailment—sleep apnea.

Sleep apnea is a serious condition where a person stops breathing in his or her sleep for several seconds. It is not a normal breathing pattern and has been suspected of causing more serious heart conditions and even death. It is usually seen in men, and seldom in a woman as young as Spurgeon, who is only forty-one years old at the time of this sentencing. If she continues to stay at her current weight, this condition is a danger to her health, even with the machine.

Brunvand then asks, as he should, for the low end of the sentence to be applied: 9.3 years.

Holly Grissinger stands to briefly summarize the state's position on the sentencing.

"She tore her brain and made her eyes bleed! The state never claimed premeditation. (In this type of case, premeditation is not necessary for a murder conviction.) "She was killed at the defendant's home. The jury made their ruling. The state feels that fifteen years is the only time [that should be considered]. That maximum sentence makes sense in this case on behalf of the victims and on behalf of Maria Harris."

Then Judge Newton asks if DNA has to be ordered in this case, and she is told that it does have to be ordered. The prosecution agrees to waiving fines and court costs, and the DNA would be ordered.

Judge Newton now addresses the courtroom with the culmination of the sentencing proceeding. "I have given a lot of consideration to this case," she says. "There was a lot to learn...a lot that the jury had to take into consideration. [There were] support letters for Ms. Spurgeon—support in the community greater than what is represented in the courtroom. It is important that the supporters understand that it is entirely up to the jury to make the decision." The judge relates that if the jury would have decided upon first-degree-murder, and that was an option, then she would have had no choice but to sentence her that day to life in prison.

Recall that the manslaughter verdict option was allowed by the judge so that the jury would not have to decide between first-degree murder and acquittal. In spite of the fact that Spurgeon, in all likelihood, committed this crime, Judge Newton was very wise in adding this option. There would probably have been jurors holding out on both sides, and the case could have ended in a hung jury. Or, if Spurgeon would have been convicted of murder, the chance of a successful appeal would have been heightened because of the severity of the sentence and because her new attorney would have focused on the fact that no one saw her commit the actual crime.

Manslaughter may not have provided a sentence long enough for the Harrises to see justice done, but it will probably keep an appeal from fruition for several reasons. First, there has to be a reason to justify an appeal. Any conviction just can't be appealed because the defendant claims innocence, or every case would go back to court on appeal. An attorney needs to run with a justifiable reason, and the knowledge that he or she has a good chance of getting the appellate court to overturn the case so that there is a new trial. If so, that involves money. There are few pro bono appeals cases for manslaughter convictions, since the sentences aren't extremely lengthy. It helps if the defendant has a source of funds to pay for an appeal. Otherwise, a public defender is appointed and will often be replaced because he or she is fired by the defendant or decides that the case does not have merit for appeal. Then the clock is set back to zero with a new PD.

Second, it takes time and effort to get an appeal rolling, and the backup of appeals cases on the court dockets must be considered. Before the actual appeal even gets on the docket, the attorneys on both sides must review the files of all the transcripts of the hearings and the trial. This is done by the defense attorney first. There is frequently an extension of time (EOT) granted by the court to review the case. Then the appeal is submitted to the state, and it must be answered by the state attorney, who also often requests an EOT. Sometimes several EOTs are requested. How many months would drag on before an appeal would get in front of a judge in this type of case?

Judge Newton explains that it is not the role at sentencing to consider that Spurgeon is not guilty of the crime for which she has been found guilty, as opposed to the life sentence of first-degree murder. The judge explains these things so that supporters can understand the different functions of the court and jury. But of course, they are well aware that Judge Newton holds the length of sentencing in her hands.

She relates that this verdict is something that the jury has already decided. She has thought about that a lot and considered the evidence. The family situation has its "own set of unique circumstances." Judge Newton summarizes that there is a young, single mom without much in income and resources who moved in with her parents. (Actually, Esther had never left home.) The family all worked together to care for this child.

"[There is a] challenge to raising this child in their home. They did a very good job. They stayed at home with her. Then changes had to be made due to her [Esther's] financial situation. [She needed to] pursue her education and [her mother had to work]. [Maria] saw the pediatrician regularly. She was a healthy baby, well taken care of. They did their research and their homework. They had a one-year-old child that had to be placed in a day care facility. They interviewed Miss Spurgeon. They did everything a parent and grandparent could do to find a place that they could trust in a day care setting. Sadly, that child did not survive the very first day. [She was] unconscious, listless, and never regains consciousness, and shortly after is deceased. [They will have nothing], except old photographs and nightmares about this case for the rest of their lives. It's an incredible tragedy. The guideline range is 9.3 to 15 years."

Then Judge Newton addresses Spurgeon directly. "Having found you guilty of manslaughter, I sentence you to fifteen years in the DOC with credit for time served. [I will request] placement in the Lowell Facility, but that is up to the Department of Corrections."

The Lowell Facility is in Marion County, and it is the most convenient one for Spurgeon's family to visit. She first will need to go to Orlando, as all convicted felons do, for processing. The inmates are usually spread out throughout the state, so that no one facility has too many violent offenders. An exception could be made for Spurgeon to go to Lowell, where she can maintain treatment for the sleep apnea. However, there are other prisons in the state of Florida that could also do that.

"You have thirty days to appeal," the judge states. "Can you afford counsel?"

Spurgeon indicates that she cannot, and Brunvand has prepared a Notice of Appeal. He tells the judge that he has done all the work on this case pro bono and that he has also filed a motion to withdraw as counsel, requesting that a public defender be appointed. The judge says that she will appoint a public defender.

This news does not seem to bode well for Spurgeon, as public defenders will not fight as hard as a private, and highly paid, attorney. Spurgeon has lost her home to foreclosure because she had to take out all the equity to pay legal fees and bonds. Bjorn Brunvand had handled this case pro bono. I don't even know if Spurgeon was able to pay anything to her first legal team or how much she paid Ron Kurpiers. There was some information from a previous hearing that her first legal team agreed to $100,000, but I am not aware if it received all of those funds. Other family members no doubt have spent thousands on her defense. Will her supporters follow through as they had stated on their now defunct Stephanie Foundation donation website and gather enough donation money to help with the appeal? Not likely. Will they provide her with money for the commissary in prison? Probably at first, but that will dwindle down to a few loyal people as they get on with their own lives and have their own bills to pay. After all, they did not put their money where their mouths were and raise $35,000 for her bond when she was arrested on murder charges. She had to remain in jail over Christmas in 2008. If they were so convinced of her innocence, credit card advances could have been pooled to bring their friend home for the holidays.

As Stephanie Spurgeon is led out of the courtroom at the end of her sentencing, I am overcome with an eerie sensation. She glances around at the gallery and catches the eyes of some of us on the Harrises' side. She looks smug, not upset in the least. As she is being fingerprinted, she holds the gaze of one of the male bailiffs and blows an "air kiss" at him. He remains soldier-faced. Is she actually in denial about what will be going on during the next fourteen or so years of her life? Does she think that prison will be a cakewalk compared to jail? Does she want her friends and family to see her content and not distraught? It could be any or all of these things. I hear lots of sniffles coming from her supporters, but as she takes her final steps out of the courtroom, Stephanie Spurgeon is actually smiling. A voice is heard amidst much murmuring and sniffling. "Bye, Mom, I love you!" And then, a woman yells out, "It's not over!" Well, yes it is, for all practical purposes.

The defense side of the court leaves first, and then there is a delay. Then we get to leave. Holly Grissinger hugs each of the Harrises in turn, and she is teary-eyed, the emotions of the case overwhelming her.

There was such a void in this sentencing today, and it was because of Stephanie Spurgeon. She showed no remorse—no emotion, as the News Channel 8 anchor stated later on the lead story of the six o'clock news. She would not speak. What was she afraid of? The truth? Perhaps, but she will have many, many days to dwell on what happened at the day care that day while she sits in her small rectangular cell. She won't get to go to the beach. She won't get to snuggle with her beloved cat who is now adopted out. As the days go by, prisoners often go through the same grief steps as a person does when someone dies: denial, anger, bargaining, depression, and finally, acceptance. But many never own up to their guilt. It remains buried, deep inside, where God cannot even reach it if they don't let him.

When I arrive at home, I wait for the six o'clock news. I know that Yolanda Fernandez will be reporting since she was the only television reporter present in the courtroom. I think that the station has been giving the story a somewhat liberal slant. Yolanda had originally interviewed Ron Kurpiers about the "new evidence" that was revealed back in May on a local radio show, hosted by a friend of Kurpiers at the time. Little did Ron know, but his defense of Spurgeon would later be severely criticized by his former friend on that same radio show. He shouldn't have been surprised by this. This same radio host would play a parody song about dead babies during the time he would rant and rave about Spurgeon's innocence on the air, calling the Harris family "white trash." This was typical of the tactics the Harrises had to deal with on top of their grief due to losing Maria.

Yolanda Fernandez could not very well come out on the news and say she was wrong to initially cover the side of the story that failed to materialize, the Brady Disclosure, while ignoring the side that won in court. So instead she mentioned all the supporters in the courtroom at the sentencing for Stephanie Spurgeon, but neglected to say that the Harrises side was full too. There was no other media outlet that I found that mentioned anything about the radio talk show that found "new evidence" in this case. I was surprised that Channel 8 did so because the "new evidence" that a child could have injured Maria turned out to be nonexistent, and it was a risk on the station's part to present the story indicating that Spurgeon would likely get a new trial. In fact, if the defense had wanted to, they could have easily made the leap, and possibly did, to consider that a child could have injured Maria if it would have made any sense to present it during the trial. They knew that other children were present. It doesn't take a rocket scientist to say, "Let's consider every single person present and what could have happened." But then they would not have been able to present Dr. Ipser as a witness with his fantastical testimony about physics and motion and that it would have been impossible for a person weighing less than two hundred pounds to have caused these injuries. He was one of their key witnesses, and his testimony would have been in direct contradiction to the consideration of a child causing injuries to Maria.

After the sentencing, Fernandez only interviewed Spurgeon's friends and family and no one on the Harris's side. This seemed like blatant media bias to me, but that is nothing new. She mentioned that Spurgeon's attorney had already filed an appeal. Fernandez did not mention that Brunvand had withdrawn from the case and asked for a public defender to be appointed in his stead. Spurgeon's mother said on camera that Esther had anger issues. Considering what had just been ruled on in court, it was a rather ironic statement.

The aftereffects of the final stage of this entire ordeal will find their way onto various blogs, websites, articles, and opinion columns. But my purpose is to put the entire tragedy on the table, out there for everyone to see and challenge, because I have covered all my bases as well and as in-depth as I possibly could.

Bloggers commented after articles that had been released about the trial. They posted their own theories as to what happened that had no documentation or evidence, as if they could have been better attorneys than Brunvand and Kurpiers in the courtroom. Wild and fantastical theories were floated, many by even the same person who would contradict him or herself. None of these were documented by the witnesses introduced by the defense so these blogs were often entertaining to read. One blogger suggested that she had somehow, as a nurse, reviewed the actual medical records of the case, and that Maria had pneumonia when she had arrived at Spurgeon's house, that she had a rare condition called pansynocytosis[2] (which, when one researches it, will note that the outward manifestation is a misshapen appearance of the child's head, but Maria obviously did not have this condition), and that Esther had somewhere and somehow admitted that she had killed her own beloved daughter. This "nurse" had concluded that all three of these issues were present on her own and that the defense totally missed all of them.

Other online "experts" said that the vaccinations killed Maria, or as mentioned earlier, her own *absent* father did it or it was diabetes. The red flag that negates both vaccines and diabetes are the torn bridging veins in Maria's head. Assuming that a very rare possibility even existed a week later that a vaccination caused her to suddenly become comatose and have a subdural hematoma and retinal hemorrhaging her first day ever away from home, it does not explain the torn bridging veins. They are only explained by blunt trauma to the head—by something external that caused Maria's brain to tear away from the dural protective layer and bleed from those veins that tore. This tearing cannot be explained by vaccines or diabetes, try as her proponents might. It does not fly. And Maria's father had not seen her in months.

Some said that Patricia Harris caused the injuries on the way to Spurgeon's or on the way home from there. These were just angry commenters as there was no logic at all to this statement. Spurgeon saw the unresponsive child. Many people bashed this family with strange accusations, saying they were covered in tattoos and piercings, which somehow led to Maria's injuries. Admittedly, Esther and her mother have pierced ears, but no tattoos and no other piercings. But what does that have to do with anything? What odd things to say in the defense of their friend, Stephanie Spurgeon. How does that help her, besides making themselves look bad? I have not looked into other murder investigations, but no doubt, since the advent of social media and the instant ability to post one's thoughts and feelings about situations on public Internet sites, this case is not alone in its amateur legal commentary. These rants are from frustrated people who want to see their friend set free; who, like any of us, cannot believe that someone we know and possibly love is capable of harming a child. But if someone really and truly feels that a person he or she cares about is innocent of a crime she is convicted of in a court of law, then money should be no object when it comes to trying to obtain her release. These people should be pooling their assets and taking out loans to get Spurgeon a good appellate attorney and not just spewing opinions on blogs that do the woman no good whatsoever; possibly even harming her case further when what they are putting into print about the Harris family is not true.

As of this writing, there are approximately 315 people who have clicked the Like button on the Stephanie Foundation Facebook site. Some are just curious; some are probably teens or young adults with no money at all. But many are more than just people who know Spurgeon by name only. Assuming that half of them are in this camp, if they each chipped in $1,000 it would amount to $150,000—not a bad start for an appeal. It is a small sacrifice to pay for someone if they believe with all their hearts that she is innocent of what she is accused of and can win on appeal. Spurgeon needs money if she wants to retain a private attorney for her appeal. Why aren't her supporters really trying the things they have probably considered, such as fund-raisers? No one seems to want to step up to the plate and really put money on the table for his or her friend.

But the site seems to be struggling to get people to even send the woman stamps to write letters. If the true measure of a friend is one who sticks with you in all ways and will sacrifice time, money, and effort to do for you what should be done to seek justice, who can Stephanie Spurgeon count on to be her friend? I have seen other cases where appeal money is raised in a matter of weeks. Friends and family get home equity loans, liquidate IRAs, cash in vacation funds, and do whatever they can to get someone they feel was wrongfully imprisoned a new day in court. What are these friends really willing to do for their friend, in their hearts of hearts? I don't know the answer to that, but if I were Stephanie Spurgeon, I would surely be posing the question.

CHAPTER 34

AFTER THE SENTENCING is over, I am finally free to inter-view a few people. First on my list is Curtis Krueger. Krueger is the only reporter for the courtroom beat at the *Tampa Bay Times*. He has covered courtrooms full-time for three years, and before that he was a reporter for twenty-five years. His goal is to be impartial in writing about any courtroom trial.

We decide to meet for the interview at the *Tampa Bay Times* headquarters. The building is quite old, but nicely decorated inside in an art deco style. The open lobby is surrounded by an atrium of windows going up four or five stories. We walk down a hall and across a walkway to what used to be the cafeteria for the employees of the newspaper. It is now closed due to budget cuts, but what remains is a beautifully appointed open area with a few tables left—something right out of the thirties or forties. We sit down at a table near a window, and I ask Curtis about his career.

Curtis works on about sixty to eighty cases at a time. Some never get written about in the paper. He decides together with his editor which ones are newsworthy. Occasionally, he is on assignment for other news stories in the community. This summer, Tampa hosted the Republican National Convention, and Curtis had that assignment along with most of the other journalists at the paper. Most of the time, he remains right here in Pinellas County, but sometimes his investigative reporting takes him out of this county. And once in a while, a story will even take him out of the country.

I ask him about whether he notices any media bias in courtroom reporting. "Most reporters are trying to get it right," he says. But he does tell me that it is very difficult to come into a case on the last day and have an accurate viewpoint. There is a much greater chance to get something wrong. He says that, "It is not easy to sum up a case if you are only there for the end of it." Bad journalism, he notes, is different from bias.

We had agreed not to talk in specifics about his own feelings regarding the *State v. Spurgeon* case, so in general, I wanted to know why a reporter would only interview the victim's side or the defendant's side in a case and ignore the other side, assuming both sides were able to be interviewed.

Curtis thinks about this for a moment. "I don't know. The story may be more on one side than the other."

This makes sense to me, since a journalist is always going after the story. Specifically, when I think about the Spurgeon case, I recall News Channel 8 reporter Yolanda Fernandez surrounded by Spurgeon's supporters, who were all clamoring to be heard after the sentencing. She interviewed several people, including Stephanie's mother. But no one from the Harrises' side was sought out. It is doubtful that there was a story there for Fernandez since, unlike Curtis Krueger who always wrote from a neutral standpoint, she seemed to be biased for the defense since the verdict. Apparently, she had even been in contact with someone who knew Spurgeon to discuss the case prior to the Brady Disclosure hearing. This contact made by Fernandez was posted on the Stephanie Foundation site on Facebook by the administrator of the site. Fernandez also interviewed defense attorney Ron Kurpiers, which was shown on the Channel 8 evening news, regarding the "new evidence" discovered due to Medical Examiner Jon Thogmartin's lecture to law students. This was that statement about "a child could have done it [caused Maria's fatal injuries]." Fernandez had interviewed Kurpiers based on information discussed on a radio talk show, the same show that later maligned Kurpiers for what they called his horrible defense of Stephanie Spurgeon.

I ask Curtis how he keeps from showing personal bias in his stories, even when he feels in his heart that the defendant is not guilty or is obviously guilty of the crime. "I try to call it straight. I stick to the facts and what was actually said in court." Interestingly, he says he also likes to bring in facts outside of what is said in court—information that the jury and sometimes the gallery is not privy to. He relates that it is fine to say that there is a mountain of evidence against a defendant, if there is, or that there is more evidence than had been previously disclosed. He presents these types of details in his articles and lets the facts speak for themselves. "If you look at people on trial for felonies, the majority are truly guilty. When you plead, there are only two choices: guilty or not guilty. To have leverage, you have to plead not guilty."

Curtis has written about many child abuse cases, including sexual abuse. These must be very difficult for him to sit through. Most recently, he wrote about the Tenesia Brown child abuse case in St. Petersburg that was mentioned earlier in this book. Ron Kurpiers won that case against Holly Grissinger, who represented the state of Florida. Brown was the foster mom who was acquitted from being sentenced to first-degree murder. She came close to receiving life in prison, and the jury decided that there was not enough evidence to show that she did what no one saw her do to the child.

J. M. BARLOWgment>

The term *shaken baby syndrome* was mentioned in that case just as the defense used it in the *State v. Spurgeon* case. Curtis agrees with me that the term *SBS* is being used less and less by the prosecution and being replaced with *abusive head trauma*. He says, "The American Pediatric Society no longer prefers SBS. Grissinger studiously avoided that term." Curtis believes that they want to contend that SBS does not really exist on its own. The state's case wasn't based on SBS. (This begs the question of whether SBS does exist at all, and we will examine that contention later).

I ask Curtis about the Williams Rule. "Have you seen cases showing evidence that a person committed a similar crime in the past where the person was not ever convicted, but where that prior circumstance was admissible and then used as testimony in the trial?"

"Yes," he responds. "In fact, I can think of one. Todd Pierce.[1]" Curtis's recollection was that Pierce was accused of lewd and lascivious behavior while employed as a school resource officer. Another student had testified prior to the trial, but Pierce was never charged. The student's testimony was then allowed at the trial itself. This was a direct example of use of the Williams Rule. The case was appealed, as nearly all cases that admit use of the Williams Rule are, but this one was not successful upon appeal.

"Have you ever interviewed a juror posttrial?" I ask Curtis.

He tells me that he has done so, and he has also discussed the deliberations with jurors. Sometimes jurors are ready and willing to talk, and other times they are very tight-lipped. I had asked him this question because I wanted confirmation that it was no problem for me to write about having talked to two jurors after the trial who had deliberated with the other ten for just over twenty one hours. Curtis did not talk to any of the jurors in this particular trial, so we could not compare notes.

We discussed cameras in the courtroom, and he verified that there was only one filming camera in the courtroom, a pool cam-

386

era, which was used by all the local affiliates. They traded off which station would be running the pool camera each day. There was also a still camera in the courtroom. This I did not see, so the photographer did a good job of concealing it. Curtis feels that the use of cameras by the press in the courtroom is good so that the public can see what is going on inside. It takes the mystery away. I agree, because the less conjecture and speculation, the better. There are enough rumors that go flying around as it is, and if a camera can quell some doubt as to what the truth is about a witness's behavior or attitude, it is a good thing.

Curtis does not spend much time reading the blog posts after his articles. Sometimes he will do so, but often he doesn't agree with them. He wants to tell them to "read the article! The answer to your question is in the article!" The comments allow the readers a venue to get involved in the story. He tells me, "Sometimes you see a good debate about the issues."

Bobbie Hodson is the victim's advocate who works at the Pinellas County Sheriff's office. She was crucial in assisting the Harris family emotionally as well as keeping them informed with the ongoing progress of the case relayed to her through the state attorneys. I spoke with her a couple of weeks postsentencing to find out how she helps families who are going through tragedies and are attempting make sense of the court system.

A victim's advocate, Bobbie tells me, varies in job description depending on the county or state one is in. Some states locate the position directly out of the state's attorney's office. Others connect it with social services. In the case of Pinellas County, it is connected with law enforcement. "*Victim* is a fluid term," she says. Some people have called her and said that they are victims of law enforcement, of circumstance, of identity theft, or of burglary.

But for Bobbie's understaffed department of two people, they can only handle reactions to violent crimes against persons. These are typically crimes of homicide, sexual assault and/or battery, child abuse, and other very violent crimes. A victim's advocate offers outreach to those who have to deal with the emotional pain and suffering that goes along with what has been done to them or to their family members. There is not nearly enough manpower to focus on less personal crimes. The victim's advocate department only deals with the worst of the worst. It doesn't get much worse than the death of a baby.

"These families need somebody with them to walk them through an environment that they never would have been exposed to otherwise," Bobbie says. She explains that the families often have questions about the court system and the hearings, such as why a bond was lowered and why a hearing was delayed again. They are in need of a little information that they would be unable to get otherwise. To have someone like Bobbie help them understand what is going on in the months, and in this case years, leading up to a trial is invaluable.

Bobbie has been a victim's advocate for twelve years. She says that you would have to be robotic not to become emotionally involved with some of the people that you are working with. "You learn to walk a very thin line." She compartmentalizes; at five o'clock, she goes home to her family. "It's a scale that you practice." She goes on to tell me that, sadly, there are exceptional cases that remind her of things in her personal life. "It is like when you go into a grocery store one day and see a baby and you smile, and the next day you don't even notice. You have your guard down on some days, and it just hits you." She pauses, and then says that she used to get embarrassed when it hit her. "Really, how could you not?" But she goes on to tell me that it is impossible not to be human, but she has learned to not get involved so much that she gets burned out.

"It's hard not to get involved if you get too deep. I don't have a magic wand. I can't get too involved." But she needs to walk with the victims through their tragedy because a lot of times, people have friends who either leave them or say the wrong things or do the wrong things because they don't know what to say or do. Bobbie is a good listener. It is imperative to her job. The victims need someone to hear them because of how the system works. It's all about the defendant. It always is. That's the way it works.

I ask her if she stays in touch with any of her families after the cases are closed. "You have to be careful, but you can't help but have connections." Some do stay in touch. One of her very first cases involved a young teen who stayed in touch over the last nine years and still calls. Some send pictures, which she keeps on her desk to remind her of what they went through and how she helped them. But others dread the sound of her voice. They don't want to take her call because it could mean something bad. Maybe she is calling to tell them about a new hearing or an appeal or information that is not good for their case. She has to be careful; she is not their friend. Regardless of her connection to the victims, she needs to maintain an arms-length relationship for her personal well-being. She cannot change that. She can love the people she has helped forever, but she can't go out to lunch with them. They need to go on with their lives.

I ask Bobbie about how she helps the families deal with all the repercussions and backlashes that occur against them from the defendant's family and friends after the defendant is sent to prison. Her answer is enlightening and demonstrates how she is able to help victims rise above the attempts to hurt them in a public venue. "Nothing happens in a bubble," she says, frankly. "In a neighborhood, people always choose sides. I'm biased. They bang on desks, say ugly things on Facebook. That's not the forum that counts. Who cares what they say on Facebook? That doesn't count." Bobbie tells me that we are judged by our peers in a very weighted system that is designed to be fair. It is our system of justice. It may not be perfect, but it usually works. It's the only one that counts here and now.

We discuss revenge, and what it does to people. All the rude lashing out and verbal slandering of the victim's family will not reverse the crime and free the person from jail any more than a victim's family slandering a defendant will bring back a murdered child. People should seek answers from a spiritual realm, not a vengeful one here on earth. What does that solve? Anger only eats away and destroys a person from within.

I reflect back on our interview and this well-known Scripture verse comes to mind: "Vengeance is mine, sayeth the Lord."[2] The Harris's have handled themselves with grace and humility throughout this ordeal. Of course, Patricia showed some emotion over the loss of her granddaughter at sentencing. It only demonstrated that there was no doubt about how much she loved Maria and grieved that she had lost her forever on earth. The fact that Esther could not even speak on her own behalf showed the same thing in a different way. Clyde revealed it too, in his lack of understanding of how anyone could hurt a baby. He could never even imagine it, so it made no sense to him that anyone had the capacity to do this to a child.

My conversation with Bobbie had helped me see the case through a bigger lens. I realized that Spurgeon received fifteen years behind bars. It may end up being less, and it could have been more had the verdict been murder. But none of it truly matters for no sentence is long enough to bring Maria back. She is gone from earth forever. And until her family, one by one, reach the end of their own lives and join her in heaven with Christ, they must live here without her, missing her each and every day. Does it make it right? Does it balance the scale? It is the best we can do, as humans, with the system we have. As Bobbie said to me, "It is hard not to be jaded. There is some negative in everyone, but there is good too."

There is a special feeling that comes with vindication, when one knows the truth has been sought out and found. It has been patiently waiting to be discovered, hidden under rocks and stones, swept away under carpets, and buried in the shadows of forgotten corners. Restlessly, I kept trying to overturn every rock, stone, and rug, and shed light on every shadow that I could in this case. I wanted to know scraps of details that were never revealed at the trial, or were perhaps mentioned briefly at long-ago hearings but were whisked away by those who wanted to hide the truth. As I gradually uncovered the information, I was rewarded with a sense of relief that all my searching, praying, and sleepless nights had not been in vain. What I had set out to discover did exist and needed to be put into words. Bringing the scattered pieces together allowed me to see the total picture, albeit with a piece missing here and there; and the tragic story of Maria Harris's death now lies open with crystal clarity. The innocence of a child rises above all efforts to hide the truth.

Maria's candle was snuffed out all too early here on earth. But now it shines brightly from heaven for all eternity. Rest in the arms of your Savior, little one. Rest.

Maria Ruth Harris
August 10, 2007
August 28, 2008

APPENDIX A

SHAKEN BABY SYNDROME DEBATE AND OTHER FORMS OF CHILD ABUSE

IN RECENT YEARS, shaken baby syndrome has become a hotly debated topic. Every year, children die or are admitted to hospitals with severe head trauma where SBS is suspected. The real dilemma is not whether a baby can be shaken back and forth to the point of severe injury and even death, because the results of such cruelty have been documented by many confessors. No, it is not whether a baby can be harmed in this way, but rather, whether it is used to point the blame at parents, guardians, or caretakers of the child. Without a doubt, people have been accused of shaking a baby when in fact, the infant was involved in an accident or even had an illness that manifested itself with severe head trauma.

When a child is brought into the ER in a lethargic or unconscious condition, and a CT scan reveals a subdural hematoma, there will usually be suspicion of abuse if there is no other explanation or witnesses. If the child has the classic red irregularities in the back of the eyes, suggesting retinal hemorrhaging, and/ or has seizures, the cause usually points even more toward child abuse. But there is a fine yet distinct line between SBS and other forms of abuse that will also have manifestation of these symptoms. Defense attorneys will try, as in the case of Maria Harris, to turn this line into a gray and blurred area. But by the admission of their own expert witnesses, a shaken baby's injuries will be accompanied by neck trauma, perhaps broken ribs, and bruising. These injuries would not, however, be a prerequisite to picking up a child and slamming it, headfirst, into a malleable yet unforgiving surface. And illnesses or vaccinations cannot explain torn bridging veins, which were present in Maria's case.

In Dr. Plunkett's own playground study, which was not discussed in this trial, some children developed subdural hematomas and later on died when their heads hit a grass-covered ground with soil underneath, which would constitute a malleable but unforgiving surface. None of the children who died in his study had a lucid interval of more than three hours, which safely encapsulated Maria's time spent at the Spurgeon home. And almost all of these children were much older than Maria, with thicker and less pliable bone forming their skulls.

An angry parent or caretaker doesn't think in that moment where she simply snaps and grabs the child who won't stop crying and screaming, that she needs to prevent a subdural hematoma or make an injury look like an accident. Some may shake the child, causing whiplash symptoms that can actually go unnoticed for years. They are invisible on X-rays and even on scans. Do people with severe headache issues as adults recall being shaken in anger by someone when they were little? That would be a very interesting study.

Perhaps an angry person is more prone to picking up the child and throwing her down onto a couch or a bed maybe multiple times. The momentum generated in the action and the amount of times the action is repeated could certainly play a significant role in the severity of injuries. Many times, the person will be "off the hook," as no injuries will occur, but in any case, this is not a form of punishment that should ever be condoned in our society.

Attempting to calm and comfort the child should come first. If the child is crying for attention and is used to getting a response because he or she is spoiled as was the case with Maria, and the caretaker is angry, the caretaker needs to put the child in a safe place, shut the door if possible, and walk away, not ever letting her temper take over. One snap only takes a few seconds. One snap can take a life.

Unfortunately, because there is so much child abuse in our society, the medical professionals and police often have doubts about the honesty of the parent or caretaker and the credibility of her story when she truly was not at fault. Too often, we hear on the news that a boyfriend was babysitting, the child wouldn't stop crying, and he ended up slamming the baby into something or shaking it violently to stop the noise. Sometimes, there is no issue with guilt because it is admitted. But other times, the boyfriend or babysitter will insist that he or she did not harm the child, and the ensuing injuries were the result of a fall or something unexplainable.

So the debate really should be narrowed down to whether a child's injury is the result of an accident, an illness, or child abuse which could involve shaking. And most important to this debate: the link of SBS to what happens next. No one shakes a child in extreme anger then simply and gently lays it down. It is what happens next that is the coup de grâce. The child is pushed, slammed, thrown, or tossed down hard enough to cause the final damage to his head. The bridging veins, already damaged, break away. The retinae, already bulging, begin to bleed. The subdural hematoma, on the brink of bursting through, does so and the oozing of blood continues. Maybe only one accelerated/decelerated movement has happened. One simple shake back and forth and then *slam*! It is child abuse, blunt trauma to the head, nonetheless. There is no disguising it, no hiding behind a rant that SBS does not exist. The term itself needs to disappear and be replaced. To deny that a condition such as SBS exists just because it is misnamed is foolish. It begs the question of whether the situation warrants further investigation of the parent/caretaker, which could result in serious charges.

The pediatricians and medical examiners are wise to dismiss the term *shaken baby syndrome* because what they really see presented in these abusive cases is head trauma resulting from impact, or a combination of shaking and impact. For example, if someone is angry enough to shake a baby or a young child enough to cause the classic triad of injuries—subdural hematoma, retinal hemorrhaging, and brain swelling—does the person just stop the shaking when he is done and just walk away or, more likely does he throw the child, with momentum, away from him into a hard surface, such as a carpeted floor? When the hospital staff looks at the injuries in a living child in a case like this, what do they see? The obvious injuries. Do the neck injuries show up? Oftentimes, they may not, just like whiplash. Whiplash is one of those undetectable injuries like muscular injuries in the back that must be taken at the word of the person, hence the huge amount of lawsuits due to auto accidents from whiplash. Children still alive after abuse from shaking cannot speak about neck injuries and these may be overlooked or not noticeable on X-ray or CT-scans.

What about broken ribs? They don't necessarily have to be part of the symptoms presented from shaking plus impact, and definitely not from impact alone. A child larger in size or over a year old could be shaken by grabbing him or her on the shoulders while he or she is standing up, shaking, and then throwing the child backward. This avoids contact with the ribs and even lessens strain on the neck to some extent, but does not change the momentum placed on the head when the child is thrown backward into an immovable surface.

It is no wonder that there are two schools of thought on this issue: that SBS is real or it is a condition that is going away as we become more educated. As Dr. Plunkett said in his interview for CBC, it is possible to shake a baby to death, but whether or not the triad of symptoms will accompany that situation is not known. There are known cases of children who have severe brain injuries who are now alive or lived a number of months or years and then died, where the perpetrator admitted guilt to abuse by shaking. Obviously, they weren't lying about their guilt. The triad of injuries was present after the incident in these cases. (One was even a local case in Tampa that became well known at least state-wide, baby Kaleb Schwade who was shaken by a babysitter, who pled guilty even though she claimed she was innocent, which was rather strange.[1] It is not clearly known which cases are accompanied by impact. It is quite possible that the abuser does not even remember throwing or slamming or dropping the child at the end of the incident. Likely most of the time, it happens.

Also, it is a good thing that the medical community is being educated about conditions that are not the result of abuse so that they are not suspect of every case presented in the ER or even in the doctor's office. There are numerous situations where children have congenital conditions that have nothing to do with abuse where the parents are unjustly accused or when there is even phantom abuse where one parent wrongly accuses the other.

My sons are adopted from an Asian country. Asian children are often born with birthmarks known as Mongolian spots, which appear on their trunks. They can be numerous and large or small, or there could just be a couple of them. They look just like bruises—brown, greenish tinged, and yellow. They fade over time so that by the time the child is around three years old, they are no longer visible. But in the United States, many health practitioners, social workers, and caretakers are not familiar with these marks and they call the authorities on the parents. A friend of mine was accused of abusing her adopted Asian son and had to prove to the police that these spots are normal and harmless, and that she didn't hit her child and cause them to appear. She actually kept an article on hand from the adoption agency that explained Mongolian spots so she could give it to any accuser.

A common but nefarious global tactic often happens when a couple separates, and one parent is trying to obtain custody of the children. This parent, often the mother, will call social services or the even the police and file a report that the estranged spouse/partner is abusing their child or children. SBS has been suggested in some of these situations, but more often than not, there is no abuse at all. This is a disgusting ploy, wasting the time of the state and local authorities and courts. It is my feeling that if a parent is shown to be falsely accused of abuse for the purpose of the other parent gaining custody, that the accusing parent should be fined and even lose custody or have it limited. Child abuse is not something to toss around as a blackmailing tool between parents. It needs to actually be happening in order for it to tie up the courts, not to mention to subject the child to hours of stressful physical examinations, tests, and questioning. These procedures can be devastating to the psyche of a child, and he or she may never get over them.

One of the very worst forms of child abuse is sexual abuse. One of the parents or often a boyfriend will take advantage of being alone with the child to do despicable things. Even worse is when the spouse or partner knows this is happening but slides into a state of denial for fear of losing their partner. Thus, the relationship becomes more important than the protection of the child. I have no sympathy for either party in this situation and find that the silent person is just as guilty as the one doing the harm. If the abuse is discovered and had not been reported by the partner, then both people involved need to be charged and imprisoned. The child would need to be immediately removed from the situation and placed in a place of safety. Even foster homes often have abusers, so the protection and well-being of the child is of utmost importance and careful vetting before placement is a priority.

I, like many others, believe that there is no cure for pedophilia. These people, when released from prison, have a higher recidivism rate than other criminals in general. I support chemical castration and confining these people to live in areas far from schools and parks. I have no problem with the abuser's file being available to the public even after the person has served time. There is a tremendous amount of justifiable risk that pedophiles will again sexually abuse a child.

I would, however, separate pedophiles from people who are involved in a relationship with a minor. For example, if a minor girl is sixteen and is seeing a nineteen year old and having consensual intercourse, then this is a much different situation than pedophilia. Of course, the parents should be involved enough to not allow this sort of behavior, but alas, many are not. As a Christian, I am a strong proponent of abstinence, since marriage is sacred and intimacy should be reserved for a husband and wife, but in a legal sense, a consenting sixteen-year-old with a nineteen-year-old is not the same thing as forced sexual abuse on a child, and a line should be drawn when it comes to punishment. These adult perpetrators who commit crimes of sexual abuse on children, just like rapists commit violent crimes, need to go away for a long, long time. Sure, many social workers and psychologists who counsel these offenders try to get them to become "normal" citizens of society, and often indicate that the condition which causes their pedophilia is a treatable sickness. Even if this is the case, and I do not for a minute believe that it is, it doesn't mean that they should be cut any slack at all. Children never get over these horrific experiences.

If analyzed enough, any habitual violent offender can be deemed not normal. Serial killers, for instance, are usually diagnosed as psychopaths and do not exhibit normal behavior in society, having no emotion or compassion. But just because a sexually abused child may still be living and not shot in a mass murder or a string of them doesn't make the adult abuser less of a criminal. What frightens me is how many pedophiles are still out there, committing crimes perhaps under their own roofs with their own children and they are not caught. It is the responsibility in these cases that the other parent or partner gets the child physically away from the abuser as soon as possible and report the crime. Protection of a spouse or boyfriend is aiding and abetting and should be punishable even if the spouse fears retribution from the abuser. There are many places of safety. There is no excuse for this demented behavior to continue.

Also, cases of teachers, both men and women, who are sleeping with students, are in the news every month. This is wrong. It is tragic that a teen can be persuaded by an adult who is supposed to be the student's trusted teacher to have sexual relations with him or her. And the adult teacher needs to have enough self-control to turn away a student who is making advances. It is more than his or her teaching career that is in jeopardy. A teen may seem to be culpable and blame may be wrongly placed on the teen, but it is the adult who has no excuse for his or her actions in this case. Even if they become involved enough to say that they are "in love" and possibly hoping to marry at some point, it is still wrong and sends the wrong message to other students. Professionals who work with teens need to recognize that they are being entrusted with their care and must never get involved in any intimate relationship with them. It has often been suggested that teachers not share their Facebook page with their students. They should not! They need to maintain an arms-length relationship. Also, as responsible adults, teachers and other professionals need to report any suspicious activity noted among their peers.

This may be easier said than done because it is whistle-blowing, and no one likes to be accused of it. But again, first and foremost we need to protect our children. Many parents are fearful that their children are not even protected in a school environment from adults who wish to prey on them. More often than not, the adult teacher is also married.

All this discussion circles back to the question of "What is child abuse?" How do we recognize it and separate it from accidental injuries and illnesses? How do we punish it? We cannot just state that certain forms of abuse, such as SBS, are not real, when in fact many cases point to the contrary. It would be more appropriate to say that verbal abuse doesn't exist because of how difficult it is to define. Where is the effect of the consequences of verbal abuse? Where do we draw the line? It is so much more unclear than abusive head trauma and frequent death. Children are people. They are fragile, especially when they are very young. To argue against something so obvious, shaking a baby with extreme force and anger is ridiculous. One only needs to spend a few days online as this writer has done and peruse the countless cases where SBS was the cause and the culprit admitted to it.

Who makes the decision that it was not abusive head trauma that caused the death of a baby who was possibly also severely shaken? It is denial of the evidence, the facts. If we are to conclude that SBS with impact does exist for the sake of argument, and I believe there is enough documentation out there to show that it does, then how do we make the leap to what injuries are really a result of this abuse as opposed to what is not abuse at all if the accused insists that he or she is innocent? It all boils down to reasonable doubt.

Earlier, we looked at each of the alternative possibilities for Maria's injuries outside of Stephanie Spurgeon causing them. Consider all her problems now as an entirety. A child presents with an acute subdural hematoma, bilateral retinal hemorrhaging, torn bridging veins, superior sagittal sinus thrombosis (discovered at autopsy), brain edema, and is in an unresponsive state. She has difficulty breathing, she vomits in the car, and she needs to go on a ventilator that evening. Her blood glucose level is high but is brought under control at the hospital, which would have been much harder to do in a child in a diabetic coma. She cries—according to the defense, it is her and not her grandmother—sporadically on the 911 tape. She cries in the ER when touched with pain-producing stimuli, which is not uncommon shortly after injury resulting in an acute subdural hematoma. Her condition worsens as her brain swelling continues and displaces matter into her spinal cord juncture, and cell death occurs. She becomes brain-dead and needs to be disconnected from life support eight days later without any lucid interval after being picked up from the day care. Remember that a lucid interval would involve normal behavior for her age, not just a gurgling noise and vomiting on her shirt.

What are the alternatives that are viable in this situation? According to every doctor that testified, it is not possible that Maria could have sustained the injuries that she did and still have walked, talked, and eaten afterward. It would have been necessary for her to have a remarkable and lengthy lucid interval after sustaining these severe and traumatic injuries but before arriving at Spurgeon's. Maria would have needed to exhibit perfectly normal behavior right up to when Pat left her there. She would have had to have been injured or been ill enough to cause devastating brain bleeding in previous days, slept peacefully in previous nights, ate, played, walked, talked, went swimming, ran around laughing in the church lobby the night before, got up early the day she went to Spurgeon's house, ate breakfast, played in the car on the way there, wanted to play with the cat when she arrived, etc. She also would have had to have "played hard" and "got tuckered out" according to what Spurgeon told Pat. This would have been quite a massive and sudden decline in an otherwise healthy and normal behaving child for nothing to have happened in the hours that ensued after Patricia Harris left the premises.

The only other possibility that was not argued at the trial was that Maria had an accident of some sort at the Spurgeon home. If she did of course, she was under Spurgeon's care, and first and foremost this would have been immediately evident, and emergency measures would have been taken and/or Patricia Harris would have been notified. Second, it would have been brought to the forefront at the trial so that Spurgeon would have had an obvious defense that made sense. But it never was, so it could not have been considered by the jury. Also, Dr. Thogmartin testified that it could not have been an accident, so the evidence that it was an accident would have needed to be pretty compelling. Ultimately, it appears that the prosecution has put forth the only logical and reasonable explanation for Maria's fatal injuries.

All the way through the *State v. Spurgeon* case, Spurgeon had publically insisted on her innocence through her attorneys. Her friends, family, and supporters did too. Not surprisingly, even people who never met her or even spoke to her deemed her to be innocent just because they read the online blogs and or talked to friends and acquaintances that they had in common. People often want to jump on the bandwagon of the defense of someone that they feel has been wrongly accused or convicted. They may know someone in a similar situation, or they may just be relying on information provided by friends and family of the defendant. Maybe they read an article on a natural health site about how vaccines cause death in children. (Name the children –not newborns- for me please, their ages, the proof, the types of vaccines they received, and how they ended up with an acute subdural hematoma, retinal hemorrhaging, and torn bridging veins a week after the vaccines. You won't find any.)

Perhaps we should be more discriminating in how we justify our conclusions. It is one thing to sit through an entire trial, hear both sides of testimony, and still come away from it believing that there was not enough evidence to convict. But it is another issue altogether to strongly believe in someone's innocence just because she doesn't look guilty, or because someone knew her in high school twenty-five years ago, or because she is a nice person who loves children.

When I take a step back and weigh what both sides said in the case, having been privy to the information in the hearing about former abuse by Spurgeon; when I know the sort of child Maria was and how she certainly could scream and cry relentlessly if she had no immediate access to her family; when I recall how Judge Newton fairly adjudicated each bit of information brought to the bench, favoring neither the state nor the defense; when I watched with fascination how the defense changed courses post-trial and tried to say the state did not provide them with exculpatory information under the Brady Disclosure (a scenario that they themselves, without much effort, could have conjured up—that another child at the day care could have done this); when I look at all of these situations and more—the guilt of the defendant is very transparent. The defense kept trying to detract from it, but the weak arguments and uninvolved and often contradictory expert witnesses only took away from their case. Their goal was to keep Spurgeon out of prison. It worked for Kurpiers in his last child abuse case defending foster mom Tenesia Brown. The facts were different. It did not work this time. In fact, they did not even reference other similar cases of abuse where the defendant was acquitted.

No other person who could have caused Maria's death was suggested at all by the defense. They only needed to protect their defendant. They did not, under the law, need to show how Maria could have become injured in another manner. But they chose to introduce so many other possibilities that it looked to the average observer, that they were just grasping at straws. It was diabetes. No, it was the vaccinations. She could have been hurt before coming to the day care in spite of arriving content and alert and then walking, talking, and eating. She could have been hurt on the way home by Patricia. (Why would Pat hurt her semiconscious granddaughter?) None of these possibilities were more than touched on in the trial, probably as we have seen, because they were so implausible under the circumstances.

Or Maria could not possibly have been shaken because, according to Dr. Ipser, the physicist, it would have taken someone with superhuman strength to cause those injuries...no wait! A child could have done it! Whatever claims the defense was intent on making, they stuck with none of them. They chose not to depose Dr. Thogmartin prior to the trial. Perhaps there was bad blood between the defense and the medical examiner. Thogmartin had said he was willing to talk with them, but they never contacted him. He was rather surprised since he said he usually talks to both sides prior to a trial. The defense had its own reasons for not calling him.

In reflecting back on this tumultuous year of events, I feel at peace with the jury's decision. Juries are rarely wrong. We can point to some cases where we may feel that they were, such as in the O.J. Simpson trial. Did the jury know that O.J. murdered Nicole and Ron? Probably. But their decision was based on what they agreed was a botched police investigation which led to reasonable doubt, not on the innocence or guilt of the defendant. They are allowed to do this under the law, much to the dismay of our Monday morning quarterbacking.

The same holds true in the Casey Anthony trial. Did the jury believe she was guilty? Most likely they did. But there was not enough evidence in their minds to convict beyond a reasonable doubt. These cases stick out like sore thumbs when we consider justice gone awry. But we were not in the windowless locked rooms deliberating with those juries. We really cannot say what we would have decided upon walking out of those courtrooms. It is foolish to believe otherwise. What would any of us have done in the Spurgeon jury room? What if it was a stranger whose trial Stephanie's supporters were watching and not that of their friend? Would they have viewed the case any differently?

In the Spurgeon trial, the jury deliberated for over twenty-one hours. They had been provided with an out by Judge Newton with the manslaughter conviction. They had hold-outs among the jury members for murder one. Somebody also thought that the evidence wasn't strong enough to convict at all. But was it strong enough to prevent reasonable doubt? They knew that if they deliberated much longer, however, that the result would be a hung jury. Nobody wanted that.

I have been on a jury, and that is what it boiled down to in the case that I observed. There was some doubt. Usually there is. But the doubt the defense tried to insert was not reasonable. It was, in fact, far-fetched. We deliberated far longer than necessary, over four hours on traffic-violation-turned- felony where the accused evaded the police by fleeing, resulting in a vehicle chase. The reason for the delay was that one juror did not like law enforcement and thought that the defendant had been bullied by being chased and the police officer just could have waited and caught up to him later, charging him with a misdemeanor instead. Then he wouldn't have sped and endangered others. This was a poor argument to suggest for someone who was guilty and admitted that he fled the scene of the violation at the trial, but these are the details that cause gray hair for attorneys and judges.

Fortunately, there were no permanent hold-outs in the Spurgeon case, and twelve people finally agreed that she must have done something to Maria, and they convicted her of manslaughter. There was no one else suggested by the defense that could have done it during the trial phase. They chose to blame it instead on other unrelated situations and conditions, and it was these suggested causes that were in themselves unreasonable.

Yes, Stephanie Spurgeon has friends and family who insist on her innocence. Most convicted felons do. This is even more so in this case because she had never been convicted before. Maybe while in prison, the truth will come out. But that is up to Spurgeon. If and until that happens, I will continue to trust that she is guilty and caused the death of Maria, unintentional though it may have been. We have heard nothing to the contrary from her, and I am more than curious about what she might reveal about what happened that day. We will just have to wait and see if she will ever tell her story publically.

Appendix B

Regarding a blog on a shaken baby syndrome site that the moderator would not post

Throughout this ordeal, the Harrises silently stood up for their little girl who died unjustly. I became rattled by the media on many levels as people stated and posted outright lies about the family and about what happened that day. Blog sites that had been set up in the past for people accused of child abuse started showing posts from Spurgeon supporters about this case. One in particular allowed me to respond to some outright lies that were posted, but when I attempted to post a follow-up response to some additional misinformation, I received an apologetic response from the moderator that my post would not be permissible on the site. Since it would not be permitted there, I will put the stream of posts here, including the one that was denied so that it gets visibility. I am not one to walk away from the truth when it is shot down; I tend to pick up the torch and continue. My response was only to a couple of the many lies within the body of what was posted. It amazed me that someone would go through the trouble to contradict sworn testimony in a courtroom. Maria, once in the hospital, the afternoon of August 21, 2008, never came home again.

The reader will note that the person I responded to was not being vindictive in any way and in fact asks me to keep an open mind, which is something we all should do. But of course that works both ways and to say that a person is not allowed to address her own innocence in a court of law is simply not true. That is what our legal system is all about. I will let these posts speak for themselves. I have removed the names out of respect for the privacy of the posters; however, the site is a public domain and these posts are also visible online for as long as the moderator chooses to leave them there. (The first case highlighted under the name "Stephanie" is *not* this case, but it is just ironic that the caretaker has the same name.) If you go to the site (onsbs.com/cases), scroll down to find the posts below.

POSTER # 1
March 6, 2012, at 4:36 p.m.

Stephanie Finley-Spurgeon is a dear friend of mine who has been wrongly accused, prosecuted, and convicted a crime that she did not commit. Our goal is to raise funds to help pay for her costly appeal process and to bring this horrible injustice to light so that it will not happen to someone else.

For nearly 18 years, Stephanie ran a state licensed in-home daycare center in the state of Florida. She was very well respected in her field and was looked upon by the state to act as a mentor to other people starting an in-home daycare. In all of her years, Stephanie only had one minor complaint that was investigated and determined to be an unfounded complaint. All parents loved her. All the children that she watched (most of which were developmentally and physically challenged) loved her.

In 2008, Stephanie took in a new child – a one year old little girl. Just days prior to coming to Stephanie's house for her first day, this little girl had received several vaccinations. As always, Stephanie carefully documented this child's first day in her house. The child was fussy, wouldn't eat, did not want to lay down to rest, did not want to play, and did not want Stephanie to leave her sight. According to Stephanie, for children this young this is typical of their first day in a strange environment. She even called the grandmother to let her know the baby was a bit fussy, but she would try to put her down again for a nap. Finally, the little girl decided to rest. Stephanie figured she had to be tired. She left her to sleep, but continued to check on her.

That afternoon, the grandmother returned to pick up the child. The baby did not want to get up, but again, as fussy as she had been the earlier part of the day, Stephanie did not find this unusual. Later that evening, the little girl's grandmother called Stephanie and said that she was going to call 911 because the baby was unusually fussy and unconsolable. [sic] She asked if there was anything that happened at Stephanie's that she should tell the paramedics. Stephanie pulled out her daily logging notes and did not see anything out of the ordinary. The baby was taken to the hospital. The grandmother called later that evening and said that everything was fine and that they were back home. She said they would just keep the baby home for the next day or two because she might have some sort of "bug."

Several days later, the police showed up at Stephanie's house and arrested her for aggravated child abuse. One week later the baby died and Stephanie was charged with first degree murder. They said that the baby died of shaken baby syndrome – a brain bleed. There were no bruises, no bumps, no neck injury, no broken bones, no scratches, just a brain bleed that really could not be explained. It was simply a "theory" that it "could" be shaken baby syndrome despite the fact that scientists have proven that the amount of force that it would take to shake a child hard enough to cause the brain enough injury to bleed in the manner that this child's did cannot physically be done without causing severe bruising, neck injury, and likely crushed ribs.

The science did not add up, but that did not stop prosecutors from finding their paid experts to say that it was "in fact" shaken baby syndrome. In fact, one of their experts, just months before taking his place on the stand and telling the jury about shaken baby syndrome, was on a PBS Frontline special talking about how shaken baby syndrome is usually a disease or undiagnosed underlying disorder and that MANY innocent people go to prison. Here is a link to the show: ttp://www.pbs.org/wgbh/pages/frontline/the-child-cases/ There is other scientific research that shows a more than casual link between these brain bleeds and vaccinations (check out the videos posted).

Stephanie was the only person who was investigated. Stephanie did not hurt this child. She spent all of her money – her and her husband's life savings – to pay for her defense. Unfortunately, it was not enough. She was found guilty of manslaughter and is scheduled to be sentenced soon. Her sentence will likely be 15 years in a maximum security prison. She has lost her life. Her children have lost their mother. Her husband has lost his wife. Her mother has lost her daughter. We have lost our friend.

Please help us prove Stephanie's innocence. Just think of how easily this could have been you. All that it takes is for a sick child to have been in your care. It could even be your own child. Research how many innocent parents, grandparents, nannies, and baby sitters have been wrongfully accused and convicted of this. It is sickening.

Me:
August 9, 2012, at 7:39 p.m.

Half of what you state about what happened that day is not true. Spurgeon did not call the grandmother that day. The grandmother never called her back after picking up her comatose granddaughter later that evening. By 3:30, within an hour after she was picked up at the daycare, she was in the local ER, unresponsive and with severe internal head injuries that would later show that she had been abused within hours before arrival. SS is also now divorced. You ask to help prove her innocence. She refuses to proclaim it herself. Her first lawyer even resigned the case.

POSTER # 2
September 12, 2012, at 12:50 p.m.

Anytime Shaken Baby Syndrome is suspected, there are certain assumptions. One of those is that the triad is always related to shaking, and the the [sic] last person with the baby is guilty. That means that the situation is not well researched. And the police and prosecutors have a vested interest in encouraging people to believe their version. Keep an open mind: Stephanie is not allowed to proclaim her innocence by our court system. And there are all sorts of reasons for a lawyer to resign.

Regarding my post that was denied, the Moderator said this: "I do apologize, but I am not going to approve your comment for posting." Here is what I submitted that did not get posted:

(Name omitted), anyone is allowed to speak with respect to his or her innocence at a sentencing for a prison term. This is part of the judicial system in the U. S. Spurgeon chose not to. This is a mystery to me. Why would a person stay silent if she is wrongly accused and given a chance to tell the world? Her silence speaks volumes. Also, this was not a case of SBS, but of blunt force trauma to the head–impact.

The moderator then provides this generic statement to me in her email:

September 12, 2012, at 9:52 p.m.

> This blog site is in support of people who have been accused of abuse by shaking based on the classic model, which I believe is flawed. While I acknowledge that abuse CAN cause the triad, I have also seen many cases in which the triad resulted from other causes.
>
> I do not want this site to be a dangerous place for innocent people who face abuse charges. Therefore, I have not approved all comments submitted on this thread.
>
> I apologize to those who must feel unheard. If you're mourning the loss of a child, please accept my condolences. Nothing any of us can say or do will fill the hole in your lives.

The whole issue with not posting my comment is that people only see one side of the story because what is allowed to be shown is only that which supports the cause of the site. As one media outlet states, whether or not it actually provides the news this way, information provided should be "fair and balanced." The site has the right not to be, but if it chooses not to be, a disclosure should be made that it is not responsible for information posted that may not be honest or truthful. At least here, in this forum, I can post the entirety of what was left out. What is fascinating is that in my omitted post I comment in the last sentence that the case was really about a blunt force trauma to the head, not SBS. And accordingly, the moderator also states that "*I have also seen many cases in which the triad resulted from other causes.*" The Spurgeon case was an instance where this triad of classic SBS symptoms that is referred to *was* a result of other causes, as in the sudden impact of a child's head into an immovable object.

One other interesting point I noted but did not comment on in my first post, because I didn't want to get refused by posting too much at once, was that the first poster said that Stephanie was the only one investigated. The police certainly would have considered anyone else who was a person of interest. They had no vested interest in putting this on Spurgeon alone. Did they have information not released to the press or available at trial that pinned this on Spurgeon? When the poster says that she was the only one investigated, we already know that she was the only one who could claim that she was the sole person at home all day the day of the incident. If anyone else had been in the home that day, no one would have known unless Stephanie Spurgeon told her attorneys or the police this information. So this would automatically rule out any friend, neighbor, or family member based on the word and the word only of the defendant. Only she could have opened that window to the investigation of those other parties.

If one were to take a step further in the direction most likely implied by this first poster, why were the Harrises not investigated? Well, actually, they were. They were questioned extensively by police detectives with respect to every minute of that entire day and even days prior. By extensively, I mean in detail and more than once. There was absolutely no indication that they had any involvement in this horrendous incident.

Patricia drops her happy and healthy granddaughter off at a day care, and there is no way she has any clue what goes on in the Spurgeon home during the time between approximately 7:30 a.m. and 2:45 p.m. when she arrives to pick up Maria. Maria is limp and unresponsive. Spurgeon is acting completely normal, conversing with Pat about how hard Maria played that day, about what foods Pat should bring the next day, and whether she should leave a bottle for Maria at the day care. There is absolutely no mention of any accident having occurred at the day care at this point. There is no suggestion by the defense of an accident at the day care brought up at the trial. Apparently, an accident had been ruled out.

On the prosecution side, the medical witnesses, including the medical examiner, were in tandem on the death being nonaccidental and not a result of an illness or metabolic condition, which left an intentional act as the only viable choice—homicide.

The original post is loaded with inconsistencies. Maria obviously ate at Spurgeon's house or she could not have vomited solid substance on the ride home in her grandmother's car. There was never any call from Patricia Harris to Spurgeon saying she was going to call paramedics or that she was "home" from the hospital and had a "bug." This is outrageous, to publically post lies that were contradicted in a court of law and were never disputed. Of course, we shouldn't be surprised. The Internet is not the pinnacle of truth. And the mention of Spurgeon's "daily logging notes" is very interesting because they were never mentioned at all in the trial or in any hearing. With all the time she spent on the phone while at the same time caring for children and Maria, who needed constant attention, when would she have had time for "daily logging notes"?

It caused me to consider whether this was the person who was on the phone with Spurgeon all the time because she states that Spurgeon herself told her much of the information in her post. I think I'll vouch for the sworn testimony in the courtrooms and not such nonsense as this. But it is a warning to not trust what you see online, even if it is on a site about a topic that you are very interested in. Know the validity of your sources.

Appendix C

Choosing a Day Care for Your Child

A DAY CARE setting can be in a home, licensed or not, or in a public building with licensed caretakers. The Harrises had decided on a home day care setting for Maria. I personally do not recommend this for a number of reasons, but they had their own reasons for doing so. Among them was that they preferred a home setting for Maria because it was supposed to give her more one-on-one care similar to the one she had received at the YWCA program while Esther attended high school in the same building. However, no one can tell by a visit what truly happens at a home day care when no parent is there. This same truth can be applied to a nursing home or even a public day care setting. But there are many differences between a home day care and a structured public day care that a parent should consider.

The safest place for a child is with a caring parent. However, if a parent needs to work, that parent needs to research many avenues. Much of the time, especially in a single parent household, a parent has no choice but to look for a day care while he or she works to earn money to provide for a child. Grandparents or other family members are often unavailable or not healthy enough to help, or cannot be trusted. The parent wants what is best for the child. Several steps really need to be taken in order to try to ensure the maximum safety of the child. There is no way to guarantee this 100 percent but there are certainly ways to minimize risks.

Here are some guidelines.

If the child is fortunate enough to have both parents available, then the parents should try to arrange flexible work schedules so that one parent can always be with the child. If this is not possible, perhaps one can start work early and pick up the child from a day care setting at 3:00 p.m. while the other parent starts later and drops off the child at 8:30 a.m. That way, the child or children are not left in the care of others for long hours. Also, with the ability to work some days from home now, it may even be possible to only have the child in a day care setting three or four days a week instead of all five. It helps to have an understanding employer.

A home day care may have the feeling of "home" to a child, but it should always have more than one caretaker if there are more than three small children present. The person whose home it is may be distracted with phone calls, or be tempted to do things not involving caretaking, such as laundry. Also, there is much meal planning and serving involved, as well as clean up, diaper changing, assisting with potty training, possibly sick children, and of course inevitable accidental injuries. One caretaker cannot be in more than one place at the same time. Who is the backup in these situations? There was no backup in the Spurgeon home. It was revealed in a hearing that Stephanie often cared for children with handicaps. These special needs children require an even higher level of care and I would think, special training and licensing, and I don't believe Ms. Spurgeon had either from the state of Florida. She was alone in the home. Parents certainly do not want their child with other young children in this situation.

A home day care caretaker needs to be all three of the following: licensed, bonded, and insured. As far as I could tell from the Spurgeon case, she was licensed, but that is all. She had homeowner's insurance, but it is not known if that covered operating a business out of her home, which would have made it much more costly because of the liability. There was some question as to what she actually told the Harrises, but that doesn't matter. The documents themselves matter. A parent or grandparent needs to ask the caretaker for documentation of the license, bond certificate, and insurance policy. They need to have dates that are current and not expired. The license can be researched on the Internet. In the state of Florida, this information can be found on the website of the Department of Children and Families. I also recommend a phone call to the licensing agency to make sure the license is current. Do not just rely on the website information, as it may not be up to date.

An uninsured home day care can be a major problem. If a situation occurs, such as was the case with Maria, there is no recourse to recover damages without insurance. For instance, if Maria would have lived, but as a severely handicapped child for many years requiring a high level of skilled care, that would have drained the Harrises' resources. Spurgeon, if she did not have insurance, would have had little that the Harrises could have sued for in a civil trial. It goes without saying that any day care must be adequately insured for the purpose of being a day care. These are separate policies. It is probable that many home day cares are not properly insured. Be careful.

Is the home day care childproof? Other people probably live in that home. Do they have medicines in the bathroom within a child's reach? Are there cleaning items accessible to the children that contain poisons? Is there a pet that could scratch or bite a child if it is unintentionally intimidated? What about allergies? What about insect stings? Is the caretaker fully trained in these areas to know what to do on the spot? Is there a fully stocked first aid kit? Who will watch the other children while she is handling an emergency situation? What if the caretaker herself becomes ill?

In a home day care, what are the age differences among the children? Do they all play together, or is there someone overseeing the older children while someone watches the toddlers and yet another takes care of the babies? Even churches separate the children by ages, usually in different rooms, so little hands don't get trampled on, and nine-month-olds don't try to eat something that they could choke on.

I would hope that the caretakers in a home day care aren't glued at any time to the television, watching silly court TV shows for instance. Or, perhaps more relevant to today's lifestyle, I hope that they aren't sitting in front of a computer or with iPads on their laps or with smartphones, looking at Facebook, or texting their known universe of friends. These items should be prohibited in all day care settings from being used by day care providers and workers except for emergency phone calls. It is work after all. It is what they are getting paid to do.

Most home day cares do not provide the parent with a weekly menu. Some ask that you bring the child's food for the day. Some may not stick to an exact feeding/nap structure. There may be some very good home day cares in your neighborhood, however, that meet all the requirements that I have noted. Check each one out with extreme caution and care because they do not have the oversight that a public day care has. Some home day cares keep a daily logbook of things that happen at the day care, but many don't use it. Spurgeon was supposed to have one. I don't know if she actually used it the day Maria was there. It was not mentioned during the trial.

In summary, the most important components to be certain of at a home day care are: licensing, bonding, and insurance, and making sure there is more than one caretaker present, especially if more than three children are being cared for.

With public day cares, it is also important to check licensing, bonding, and insurance, although if you walk into one, they are so accustomed to being asked for this information that the director usually has these documents in a binder right on the desk for you to examine. The atmosphere is usually louder because there are more children. These day cares are more like schools with lots of activities going on all day. The children learn games, do crafts, solve puzzles, paint, have story-time, etc. Of course, these things are often done in home day cares too, depending upon the involvement of the provider. There is a schedule of activities sent home weekly with the parents. There is a mandatory logbook documenting all behaviors, incidences, and routines at public day cares. This is because this logbook is often asked for during unannounced inspections by a state or county inspector. Unfortunately, these inspectors rarely, if ever, are known to inspect a home day care. I wish they would do so.

Any injury, no matter how small, must be reported to the parent according to public day care guidelines. It is at the discretion of the day care provider to either call the parent immediately or let them know upon pickup time if it is a minor injury, like a finger cut or a knee scrape. But something like a fall where a child hits his or her head requires an immediate phone call. I remember my older son falling off of a piece of gym equipment outside and bumping his head after school in what is known as aftercare when he was about six years old. I raced over to the school from work. He was fine and back playing, with a raised blue bruise above his eyebrow. I was relieved but grateful that the caretaker had called me. This is what is supposed to happen. Patricia Harris had never received a phone call at all from the Spurgeon day care on August 21, 2008.

A sick child is sent home from a public day care and not allowed back until there has been no fever for twenty-four hours. This may not be a hard and fast rule at a home day care, so a child who is sick may be there for the whole day with your healthy child, especially if the sick child is the son or daughter of the caretaker.

A prospective client of a day care, whether public or in home, should check and see if there is a website for the facility, but that is not enough in itself. Also, check the licensing board for day cares in the state or county. Look at recommendation comments. Look for complaints. Look especially to see if any formal complaint was ever filed and why. Even if no action was ever followed up on, this alone should send a signal to that parent to look elsewhere. It is important to do your homework when seeking care for your most precious commodity, your children.

There are numerous websites that have supplemental material to what I have discussed here as to what to look for when choosing a day care. Some favor public day cares; others favor home day cares. The choice must be made by you, but just be sure it is an informed choice. Go online. Google "choosing a day care." Plug in your city or county if you want to narrow your search.

BIBLIOGRAPHY

Prelude
1. "Statutory Rape," Serving South Florida | The Hoffman Firm, http://www.thehoffmanfirm.net/service/statutory-rape (accessed January 18, 2013).

Chapter 2
1. "Tampa & Clearwater Criminal (Fraud, Drug, DUI, Murder) Defense Lawyer / Attorney | Acquitter.com," Acquittercom, http://acquitter.com (accessed March 15, 2012).
2. "Mr. Ronald J. Kurpiers II," ZoomInfo, http://www.zoominfo.com/people/Kurpiers_Ronald_733306683.aspx (accessed March 15, 2012).
3. Curtis Krueger, "Former St. Petersburg foster mother not guilty of murdering baby," *Tampa Bay Times*, http://www.tampabay.com/news/courts/criminal/former-st-petersburg-foster-mother-not-guilty-of-murdering-baby/1117902 (accessed February 18, 2012).

Chapter 3
1. L. J. Richaud, F. P. Rivara, W. T. Longstreth Jr., and M. S. Grady, "Elevated initial blood glucose levels and poor outcome," U.S. National Library of Medicine, http://www.ncbi.nlm.nih.gov/pubmed/1942143 (accessed January 27, 2012).

Chapter 4
1. 2011–2012 Bill 487: Kendra Gaddie–South Carolina Legislature Online, 2011–2012 Bill 487: Kendra Gaddie–South Carolina Legislature Online, http://www.scstatehouse.gov/sess119_2011–2012/bills/487.htm (accessed February 7, 2013).
2. Elizabeth Owens, "12 On Your Side: Investigation shows many home child care providers not in compliance with law," WRDW RSS, http://www.wrdw.com/news/onyourside/headlines/News_12_On_Your_Side_Investigation_Shows_Many_Home_Child_Care_Providers_Not_in_Compliance_with_the_Law_135058498.html (accessed February 9, 2012).

Chapter 5
1. Kelley King Heyworth, "Vaccines: The Reality Behind the Debate," Parents.com, http://www.parents.com/health/vaccines/controversy/vaccines-the-reality-behind-the-debate (accessed April 12, 2013).

Chapter 8
1. George Rush, Kelly Burke, and Corky Siemaszko, "Natasha Richardson's family, friends gather as spokesperson announces she has died," NY Daily News, http://www.nydailynews.com/entertainment/gossip/natasha-richardson-family-friends-gather-spokesperson-announces-died-article-1.368097 (accessed August 12, 2012).

Chapter 10
1. WebMD, "Subdural Hematoma: Symptoms, Causes, and Treatments," WebMD, http://www.webmd.com/brain/subdural-hematoma-symptoms-causes-treatments (accessed February 13, 2012).
2. "Subdural Hematoma Guide: Causes, Symptoms and Treatment Options," drugs.com, http://www.drugs.com/health-guide/subdural-hematoma.html (accessed February 13, 2012).

Chapter 11
1. Jean-Louis Dufier, V. Pierre-Kahn, O. Roche, P. Dureau, Y. Uteza, and A. Pierre-Kahn, "Ophthalmologic findings in suspected child abuse victims with subdural hematomas," *Ophthalmology* 110 (9): 1718–1723. 2003–09.

Chapter 12
1. William R. Maples and Michael Browning, *Dead Men Do Tell Tales*, New York: Crown Publishing Group, 2010.

Chapter 13
1. David Frim and Nalin Gupta, *Pediatric Neurosurgery*, Georgetown, Texas: Landes Bioscience, 2006.

Chapter 16
1. Dennis Nicewander, "Williams Rule, Evidence," Locatethelaw.org, http://locatethelaw.org (accessed February 21, 2012).
2. *Ibid.*

Chapter 18
1. Jorge Castillo, "Seemingly Ordinary Game, Then a Player Dies," *New York Times*, October 20, 2011.
2. M. Vinchon, O. Noizet, S. Dhellemmes-Defoort, Ares G. Soto, and P. Dhellemmes, "Infantile subdural hema-

tomas due to traffic accidents," National Center for Biotechnology Information, http://www.ncbi.nlm.nih.gov/pubmed/12411716 (accessed August 11, 2012).
3. U.S. National Library of Medicine, "Subdural hematoma: MedlinePlus Medical Encyclopedia," http://www.nlm.nih.gov/medlineplus/ency/article/000713.htm (accessed February 11, 2012).
4. J. Alex Becker and Keith A. Johnson, "Neuroimaging of Brain Hemorrhage," In *The Whole Brain Atlas* (Harvard Medical School, 1995).

Chapter 19
1. Melissa Fletcher Stoeltje, "San Antonio Express-News–News, Sports, Business & Events," Does Shaken Baby Syndrome Exist? http://www.mysanantonio.com (accessed February 15, 2012).

Chapter 21
1. http://www.cbc.ca/player/Shows/Shows/the+fifth+estate/Web+Exclusives/ID/2186568691/?page=2 (accessed December 3, 2011).
2. Allen G. Breed, "Studies split on shaken baby syndrome," USATODAY.com, http://usatoday30.usatoday.com/news/health/2007-04-28-shakenbaby_N.htm (accessed August 26, 2012).
3. *Ibid.*
4. *Ibid.*
5. John Plunkett, "Fatal Pediatric Head Injuries Caused by Short-Distance Falls," *The American Journal of Forensic Medicine and Pathology* (1): 1–12., 2001-04-22.
6. Brian Harding, Anthony Risdon, and Henry F. Krous, "Shaken Baby Syndrome," British Medical Journal, http://www.britishmedicaljournal.com (accessed March 3, 2012).

Chapter 22
1. Balasubramanian Venkatesh and Hayden White. "Clinical review: Ketones and brain injury," *Critical Care* (2004), 219.

Chapter 30
1. Curtis Krueger, "Palm Harbor day care provider guilty of manslaughter in death of infant," *Tampa Bay Times*, http://www.tampabay.com/news/courts/criminal/palm-harbor-day-care-provider-guilty-of-manslaughter-in-death-of-infant/1215752 (accessed February 16, 2012).

Chapter 32
1. Curtis Krueger, "Law class discussion raises questions about day care operator's manslaughter conviction," *Tampa Bay Times*, http://www.tampabay.com/news/courts/criminal/law-class-discussion-raises-questions-about-day-care-operators/1228484 (accessed May 5, 2012).
2. Yolanda Fernandez, "Attorney: Evidence would have cleared Pinellas child-care provider," TBO.com, http://tbo.com/news/attorney-evidence-would-have-cleared-pinellas-child-care-provider-399204 (accessed March 22, 2013).
3. Martha Neil, "Medical Examiner's Visit to Law School Class Sparks New Defense Claims in Local Manslaughter Case," ABA Journal, http://www.abajournal.com/news/article/medical_examiners_visit_to_law_school_class_sparks_new_defense_claims_in_lo (accessed May 9, 2012).

Chapter 33
1. Curtis Krueger, "No new trial for Palm Harbor woman convicted of manslaughter in day care," *Tampa Bay Times*, http://www.tampabay.com/news/courts/criminal/no-new-trial-for-palm-harbor-woman-convicted-of-manslaughter-in-day-care/1241430 (accessed July 22, 2012).

2. "Surgery for Craniosynostosis," http://emedicine.medscape.com/article/248568-overview (accessed August 14, 2012).

Chapter 34
1. Curtis Krueger, "Ex-school resource officer gets 10 years for sex with teen," *Tampa Bay Times*, http://www.tampabay.com/news/courts/criminal/ex-school-resource-officer-gets-10-years-for-sex-with-teen/996036 (accessed January 9, 2013).
2. Deuteronomy 32:35, KJV

Appendix A
1. Ileana Morales and Vander Velde, "Shaken baby who captured hearts on MySpace dies in Tampa," *Tampa Bay Times*, http://www.tampabay.com/news/publicsafety/crime/shaken-baby-who-captured-hearts-on-myspace-dies-in-tampa/1148056 (accessed March 10, 2013).